A VOICE IN THE WILDERNESS

Gerald Prager

TerraPro Press

For information concerning special discounts for bulk purchases or to book a live event with the author, please email TerraPro Press at

ISBN: 978-1-63821-435-9

A Voice in the Wilderness

Howls From Vox Deplorables

Gerald Prager

Contents

INTRODUCTORY NOTE

The chapters that follow are slightly modified articles from a soon-to-be extinct weblog called *Vox Deplorables: Notes from Flyover Country*. *Vox Deplorables* lived through the last two-thirds of Donald J. Trump's presidency and a few months beyond, a turbulent period of American history that provided ample subject matter for a blog that was dedicated to thoughtful analysis (with a touch of humor). This book contains those articles that are primarily concerned with government, politics and certain other matters related thereto. A second book that concerns itself with such other subjects as science, philosophy, the arts and so on will follow.

The articles of this book are sorted as chapters by general subject matter into seven parts. The "general" in that sentence is operative; without doubt many of the chapters cover varied issues that could fit into more than one part. Despite the overlap, the titles of the sections provide a reasonably accurate idea of the information in the chapters therein. The nature of blog posts is such that there is some repetition of information and observations from chapter to chapter. The articles are not arranged in the chronological order in which they were written, so there are adjacent chapters that were penned as much as two years apart and some items inevitably recur. Perhaps that is not a bad thing; much of our lives seems to consist of repetition of what went before.

In some respects, this book is a historical archive, or perhaps an archive of an alternative history. When reading the various articles, please keep in mind that by far most of them were written before the pivotal election of 2020, and more than half even before the invasion of the coronavirus. The last part, *2020 Hindsight*, specifically includes those articles that predicted a future that might have happened had the coronavirus not invaded when it did. The reader may judge how insightful the various articles were -- or might have been had that black swan of history not intervened. It is, in part, with that in mind that this book is offered.

Regardless of their predictive value, the articles render a picture of a not-so-distant past that is almost difficult to remember after one has lived through the strange year 2020 and the dark weeks that followed. All the certainties of the first three and a half years of the reign of the recently departed presidential administration have vanished like dew in the sunlight. It now seems an idyllic time, despite the bumptiousness of the president and the savage unrest of the Left that tainted it: a booming economy that was certain to bloom forever, America returning to the world's center stage, prosperity available for everyone. These pages recapture a piece of that lost, and all too brief, era. There is a haunting quality about them when viewed from the viewpoint of our current state.

We live in history. Every day we experience will be thought of as history for a future generation. During some periods of time, events occur so rapidly and of such consequence that even yesterday is already history now. The last few years, the brief Trump era, have been of that nature. We look back on the days we lived just months ago and see a different world from that of today. The pages you hold are infused with history, and they speak of a time that shapes today and tomorrow.

The *Vox Deplorables* blog had three contributors besides the author of these articles, and the reader is encouraged to read the others if that opportunity appears. There is much material of value therein, and possibly the other authors will present their work elsewhere. Meanwhile, I trust you will find some entertainment – and possibly instruction – in what follows. It constitutes a view of a world that could have been, and perhaps a prediction of what yet may be.

PART I

Governance and Tyranny

There is an old saying that the people of a nation get the government they deserve. As with any adage, there is wisdom in it and there are exceptions to it, but in a democracy, at least, it is largely true. The United States may not be quite the republic it started out to be (our apologies, Mr. Franklin), but it is indisputably a democracy. At times, one may be excused for thinking it is too much a democracy: we have indeed gotten the government we deserve and are not especially justified in complaining about it. Where we are and how we arrived there are the primary subjects of the chapters of this section. It's not altogether a pretty picture – but it is what we deserve.

Among the gems of wisdom given us by Ronald Reagan is the statement that freedom is always just one generation away from extinction. One generation from tyranny – that is a frightening thought, all the more frightening now that the shadow of tyranny stretches over our free land. As this is written, just two weeks have passed since Joseph Biden's inauguration as president of a nation that has already approached too closely for comfort to the edge of the abyss, and he has done nothing to allay the fears of free men for the future. One could hardly imagine a work of fiction stranger than the reality of the past year, during the course of which we passed from the assurance of success of a populist movement into the depths of continued dominion of the Deep State. That could not have come to pass, even with powerful institutional forces working against freedom, but for the strange intervention of a virus. Even so, neither could the success of the Democrats come about without a substantial number of ordinary people who voted for them. Therein lies the mystery.

Who would vote for tyranny over freedom when it was blatantly obvious that freedom was working for prosperity and tyranny for decline? A year ago, it could hardly have been predicted that what happened would happen, but even then it was evident that a substantial percentage of the populace was vulnerable to the call of the progressive cause. That phenomenon is examined in several of the articles below, notably *Little People* and *Depraved New World: Beauty and the Beast. Deep State Rising* treats the origins of that aspect of our current government, and the *Praetorians* articles, with *Noblesse Oublie* and *Depraved New World: New World Disorder* describe certain tyrannical aspects of the government itself.

So governance and tyranny – what we have and how we got it. Please read on ....

Chapter One

Noblesse Oublie

Throughout the ages there have been elites. These have included priesthoods, merchant leagues, political machines and noble classes. They have set themselves apart from – above, actually – the common classes of people in their societies and have lived better. If they didn't necessarily live better than ordinary Americans live now, it was at least better than the rest of their fellow citizens of the time. Besides better food, fancier clothes and room service, they had whatever additional perquisites went with their stations in life. Perhaps most important, at their best they had the respect, however willing or grudging, of their fellow men.

All this, desirable though it may have been, came with certain implied or delineated responsibilities. The expectations people had for their elites may have been spiritual comfort, alms and charity, prudent governance or protection from enemies foreign and domestic, depending on the office. In the case of the nobles, obligations were summarized in a wonderful old phrase: *noblesse oblige*. The literal translation from French is "nobility obliges." That is, the status obliges its holder to behave in certain ways toward his less well-favored compatriots. The individual noble might not have been a paragon of virtue but he was expected to do his duty in military service, to look to the well-being of his servants and the people of his holdings, to keep his word and maintain his sacred honor, and generally to bear himself up to certain standards. In practice, it meant that he might be a drunken woman-chaser and carouser, but he must be a gentlemanly and reasonably generous drunk and sinner all the while.

And no – the title of this article is not a typo. The following will explain why.

The United States was founded, in large measure, as a refuge from elitism. Formation of a noble class was scrupulously avoided and even the highest leaders of American society went to great lengths to separate themselves from the taint of formal elitism. Even the plantation owners of the Old South, as close to a *de facto* nobility as Americans ever came, rejected any association with the name of such a class. And although they declined the name, and despite such dramatizations as Stowe's *Uncle Tom's Cabin*, plantation owners felt themselves bound by *noblesse oblige* in their treatment of employees and, for the most part, slaves. This does nothing to excuse the evil of slavery, but neither did it excuse serfdom in the Old World. The point is that privilege, whatever its nature or source, was accompanied by obligations that were enshrined by custom if not by law.

After 1865, industrialization enhanced by the spoils of war and Reconstruction produced another class based on wealth alone. The so-called Robber Barons were a new breed, not just wealthy but super-rich to a degree theretofore unknown in the young nation. They had gained their status in a manner which was, as the nickname implies, not entirely scrupulous, but they nevertheless tended to take on the burden of *noblesse oblige* to an impressive extent. As their wealth exceeded previous fortunes, so their giving of alms went beyond the usual practices.

Andrew Carnegie, among other charities, founded libraries in towns large and small throughout the country in an effort to provide to common people a means to gain an education he himself never had. Leland Stanford, whose rise through questionable political influence put him atop the railroad world, founded a great university in the new West. John Rockefeller, through a notorious oil trust, funded a major foundation that continues to function today. And so on. The rough-and-tumble of an unfettered and gameable market wasn't enough to knock the *oblige* out of the new class of not-so-*noblesse*.

More recently, the computer age has given rise to a new class of elites of the wealth-based sort, this time involving wealth at a level almost unimagined in all of human history. This new elite includes financial as well as technological tycoons, who add themselves to those who gained wealth through more traditional routes. It is not the purpose of this article to argue whether a hedge fund manager produces more for society than an oil baron; the question here strictly concerns the observance of *noblesse oblige*. The answer is that, for the most part, the designs of the current ultra-wealthy have not entailed much sense of obligation. Even those who donate heavily tend to give with a sharp eye out to favored political agendas and to possible political advantage.

There has emerged over the last few decades another entirely different route to riches – a shortcut called political careerism. There have been career politicians as long as there has been politics, but only in the last thirty years or so have political careers been quite so potentially lucrative. True, there is elitism in power independent of wealth, and from the earliest years of the nation those in power were able to dispense favors to supporters and friends. Now that it is a routine matter for powerful politicians to become rich as well, it might be expected that they use some of that wealth for the general good of the people from whence it came. That is to say, we might look for a touch of *noblesse oblige* on the part of our new class of political multi-millionaires. We would mostly look in vain.

In the old days, presidents who entered office with modest means also left that way, and generally lived in a state of moderate affluence the rest of their lives. This was true of Truman, Eisenhower, Nixon and most others. Some came into office with a degree of wealth and lived out the remainder of their lives on about the same level of wealth. Former presidents had influence and respect but were not expected to be wealthy unless they started that way. That changed radically with the Clintons, who came from Arkansas with much ambition but little money (despite Hillary's amazing luck with cattle futures) and now have a fortune of well over $100 million. President Obama came in with a rather anemic fortune and is now buying mansions in D.C. and Martha's Vineyard. The Presidents Bush, of course, don't count, since they started their political careers with mansions and ranches in hand, as did Presidents Reagan and Trump. As far as *noblesse oblige* is concerned, we've seen little from the newly enriched among the former presidents. It must be admitted that among the already rich ones it has been different. The much-maligned Trump, for example, gave his entire presidential salary to veterans' causes.

We have also come to expect a sharp increase in wealth from other elected officials at the highest levels of federal government. Senators and long-serving representatives seem to do very well indeed. Few are notable for alms-giving or other charitable efforts. There are even many unelected employees of the government and political hangers-on who do well financially. Some are top-level bureaucrats whose life-long careers were made possible by the Pendleton Civil Service Reform Act of 1883; some are merely lobbyists and denizens of government-related think tanks. The latter classes are in many cases extensions of the political careers of former elected officials. Few members of such classes show much tendency toward *noblesse oblige* in any form.

But what of it? Americans as a whole aren't angered by people making money, and making it through politics in whatever manner is slightly more respectable than scamming old people out of their hard-earned savings. Political fortune seekers are surely preferable to rich suburban drug dealers who have built their wealth on the wrecked lives of their clients. And while charity and other means of "giving back" are noble, they are only worthy if done willingly and, ideally, even anonymously. Besides, one might think that in a society that has rejected the whole notion of a noble class, *noblesse oblige* as a concept is outlandish.

One would be wrong. First, we do indeed have the functional equivalent of a noble class in this country. It is even, to a significant extent, hereditary. It is not strictly money-based, although certainly affluence comes with it. Neither is it education-based, although where one goes to school makes a difference. Basically, if one's parents graduated from one of a few elite universities and went from there into one of the elite professions and from there to a career in a prestigious organization, one's chances of following in those footsteps are extraordinarily high. If one is the third or fourth generation (or more) to follow that path, the chances are all but certain, unless one makes a personal choice to become a starving artist or country parson or the equivalent. Note that one doesn't have to be superbly intelligent or gifted in any way. One doesn't have to be especially good at the chosen (usually by the parents) profession or successful in one's position. Not to worry: most nobles weren't particularly good at anything either, back in the day.

It is no more difficult, in fact, to get through Harvard than through most decent state universities. Nor will you necessarily be better educated if you graduate from Yale than from Appalachian State. The difficulty isn't in graduating from the elite university, it's in getting admitted to it. And for that, having parents that are alumni is an overwhelming advantage. In addition to direct preferences, you will have special tutoring for the entrance hurdles, including standardized exams. Only those competitors for a slot in the freshman class who are very gifted indeed will have a chance against you, and even then a special slot may be added in your favor. Once you are in, what you come to know through your studies is as nothing compared to whom you will come to know among your fellow students. Once out in the world, you will continue to associate with those people in your professional and social lives, and with those from other elite universities. You have a reservation to a place in America's new nobility.

The new *noblesse* is found in the upper tiers of Goldman Sachs and other financial powerhouses, in the top law firms, especially in Washington, D.C., and New York, and of course in government, again at the higher levels. It combines with the most influential people in journalism, industry and elsewhere to form what is loosely known as the Establishment. The arm of the Establishment that inhabits the federal government includes career elected officials and the most useful among career bureaucrats, including certain members of the Intelligence Community. We may add certain peripheral operatives of government such as lobbyists and think tankers. Individuals may move among these various groups at different stages of their careers. The amorphous amalgam of people who constitute what has emerged into the light of day under the name of the Deep State are a part of the Establishment with a keen political bent and an obsession to dominate the political processes of the country from behind the scenes. It should be no surprise to anyone that the people of the Deep State tend to be progressive in their views.

There is a natural inclination among Americans to reject manipulation by a nobility and its servants and allies, especially those within government. Establishments are viewed with suspicion and something like the Deep State with outright revulsion. Perhaps that was always the case among common people who retained a glimmer of free will, throughout history and around the world. Certainly it was the case in 18th century France, even though the French had an entrenched nobility and priestly class that had lasted many centuries. But something had happened in France during those centuries: the elites had lost their original functions and with them the sense of *noblesse oblige*. The upshot was the storming of the Bastille, the symbol of the ancient regime in Paris, on July 14, 1789.

Libraries are filled with scholarly explications of the causes of the French Revolution. Perhaps the best explanation, however, comes from art rather than scholarship. A scene from Charles Dickens' celebrated novel *A Tale of Two Cities* encapsulates the spirit of the times. The Marquis St. Evremonde orders his carriage driven at reckless speed through a town and a child is hit and killed. Bored and irritated by the delay, he tosses the grieving father a coin for compensation and rides on. There's more to the scene, of course, but the upshot is that the father later stabs the nobleman to death in the latter's chateau, with a note pinned to the corpse by the dagger – "Drive him fast to the cemetery." People may accept bad behavior and even corruption by elites; they will not accept contempt or disrespect.

Correction: people will not accept openly demonstrated contempt or disrespect. There can be little doubt that elites have held common people in low esteem throughout the ages, but they have saved themselves by either doing something for the people to make up for it in the way of gracious acts or competent service (both forms of *noblesse oblige*), or by managing to conceal their contempt. In our current society the elites have failed on all counts. Nearly all the needs and desires of the people are being either ignored or actively contravened. The best current example is the immigration issue: by large margins, the people of the country want legal immigration limited and reformed and illegal immigration stopped altogether. The elites, who are happy with unrestrained immigration for their own short-sighted economic and political reasons, casually ignore the needs of the people. Another example is costs of health care, a problem that has been so bungled by incompetence on the part of the elites as to boggle the mind. Let us not even go into the public education fiasco – that requires a volume of its own.

Which brings us to the subject of public disrespect of the commoners. If the French lower orders, beaten down for centuries, could be goaded to rebel by both the uselessness and contemptuousness of the *ancien regime,* how can we wonder that Americans, with a long tradition of dignity and freedom, refuse to swallow such treatment from our own elites? President Obama's comments about American losers clinging to their guns and religion, Hillary Clinton's remarks about the "basket of deplorables," numerous snide references by coastal elites to "flyover country"—all of these and more have generated a wave of counter-contempt among large swathes of the populace for these self-appointed elites.

One result was the election of Donald J. Trump. Americans are basically law-abiding souls. Instead of storming a Bastille equivalent they went the route of orderly process. Their reward was the outright refusal of the elites and their leftist followers to recognize the election – in effect, the rejection of democracy. In their arrogance and utter lack of self-awareness, the elites have determined to go their own way, and if the country doesn't follow, they will watch it sink into violence. The Deep State contrives one effort after another to engineer impeachment of the president. Perhaps the efforts would have a bit more credibility if the calls for impeachment had not begun before Trump was inaugurated.

In any case, so much for *noblesse oblige*. Our elites no longer feel the need to perform competently or give back in any way, even so small a way as treating the deplorables with courtesy or even basic respect. Like the old French nobility before them, they have exchanged *noblesse oblige* for *noblesse oublie*. That is also French – for "nobility forgets."

1/27/20

Chapter Two

Deep State Rising

What is the Deep State? A great deal has been written about it lately, but a good definition is hard to come by. Some pundits, mostly those on the Left, even deny there is such a thing. Even Hugh Hewitt, an avowed conservative and generally honest commentator, recently claimed that no Deep State exists. It should be remembered, however, that Hewitt is an old hand at politics within the Beltway and a quintessentially American Establishment figure. He is perhaps too close to the phenomenon to recognize it. And he is, in a technical sense, quite correct. There is no house in Washington, D.C., the door of which bears a tasteful brass plaque that reads "The Deep State Club." There is no secret handshake with which members greet one another, no passwords to identify them, no initiation rituals or dues collector, no official membership rolls. It is the very indefinability of the Deep State, its amorphous nature and invisibility, that lends it such power and makes it invulnerable to outside authority or control. Perhaps the best way to describe it is to recount the history of its development and growth through the course of American history.

First, the Deep State stands today upon three legs: a professional bureaucracy, an intelligence community (actually a discrete part of that bureaucracy) and a mass media establishment that has morphed over the years from a diverse group of journalistic organizations into a more-or-less unified propaganda machine. It is tempting to include the Democrat Party in this picture, but in fact politics are only ancillary to the Deep State, and since many Republicans dwell in the Deep State along with Democrats, partisan politics are secondary indeed. If the Deep State could be said to have a home, that home is the nation's permanent federal bureaucracy, and the story of how that institution was founded and its long evolution into what it is now is a good starting point for this narrative.

For the first century of our republic, there was no professional bureaucracy. There was a bureaucracy, of course, but it could hardly be called professional, at least not in the sense we now think of it. The bureaucrats of the early decades were for the most part temporary office holders, their positions dependent on the results of the last election. Each incoming administration had a free hand in assigning personnel, from Cabinet members down to messenger boys. The power of appointment in this politics-driven bureaucracy was, in general, applied with a degree of restraint until 1829, the year Andrew Jackson was inaugurated. Jackson's administration was anything but restrained; in fact it was notoriously rambunctious in every respect, and especially in its use of political patronage. It was then that the term "spoils system" first entered the American vocabulary. That broke the ice, so to speak; all administrations following Jackson's used the power of patronage to fullest extent to award political loyalty and hard work in the successful campaign. All administrations, that is, until 1883 and the passage of the Pendleton Act.

The Pendleton Act was the culmination of a governmental reform movement that had been active at least since the end of the Civil War. That movement was a response to the very real abuses that the spoils system permitted at every level of government from federal down to municipal, although the act itself applied only to the federal bureaucracy. Prominent among the ill effects of the spoils system was simple incompetence among many federal employees, whose qualifications were based on party affiliation rather than education and experience to fit job requirements. It might be noted that, although the spoils system began with Andrew Jackson's Democrats, Republicans may have been the worst offenders in the years prior to the Pendleton Act. Reconstruction in the South was a toxic version of the spoils system on a grand scale. The role of "carpetbaggers" and "scalawags" has been whitewashed by revisionist historians of a leftist bent in recent times, but by the mid-1870s the scandals of Reconstruction had soured even Northerners on the whole idea of political spoils.

That said, it must be admitted that the professional Civil Service, initiated by the Pendleton Act and refined in following decades, was not free from a downside. One advantage of the spoils system (among all the serious disadvantages) was that the tenure of its beneficiaries was limited to the period of ascendancy of their political party. While this may have been detrimental to professionalism, it prevented the establishment of a permanent cadre of bureaucrats who had little accountability to anyone outside their own agencies, including, for better or worse, their own political parties. Actually, steps were taken to further distance federal employees from outside political pressures or incentives. The Hatch Act of 1939 severely limited the partisan political activities permitted to those employed in the federal Civil Service. States were slower in adopting these practices, with the result that political "machines," such as Tammany Hall in New York, continued in places well into the 20th century. By mid-century, however, state civil service rules throughout the country largely mirrored those of the federal government.

Despite the Hatch Act, which is by and large still closely observed, there can be no question that government bureaucracies in general, and the federal bureaucracy in particular, are politicized to an alarming extent. This situation does not appear to be the result of a deliberate takeover by the Progressive Movement, as has been the case of other American institutions, but is rather a systemic phenomenon. That is, the marriage of bureaucracy and progressivism is inherent in the nature of both. Progressivism from its earliest days demanded a government of experts, the united efforts of whom could bring society to a state of earthly utopia. The Pendleton Act, which was enacted at the very birth of the Progressive Movement, was conceived not just to rid the bureaucracy of politics but to ensure the expertise of the professionals who occupy its offices. The two were designed for each other, although it is doubtful that their marriage was intentional at the time. As the federal bureaucracy grew, its bond with progressivism became ever stronger, whether or not it was so planned.

And grow it did. By the mid-1970s the number of federal bureaucrats had grown to over two million, spread over hundreds of agencies. Efforts to reign in the size of the bureaucracy stopped the numerical growth almost completely, so that the number is about the same today. But this fact is deceiving: in reality, the number of federal employees in bureaucrat-equivalent roles is a multiple of that. No one has any clear idea of what the actual number is, but the best estimate is between 7 and 9 million in the "blended workforce" at present. The difference in numbers is made up by mostly by contractors (about 3.7 million), who represent an outsourcing of bureaucratic work, and non-profit workers (about 1.6 million) in sundry nonprofits funded by federal tax money. As to the number of agencies within the bureaucracy, it is a stunning fact that literally no one knows how many there are. The best guess I've seen is 456, but this is no more than an estimate. Part of the problem is defining what an agency is, since many organizations employ both Civil Service people and contractors or others. Are they regular agencies, NGOs, private companies or what? Can anyone know? Does anyone care?

Presumably, all these people and agencies are doing something, so the scope of the federal bureaucracy's work has expanded greatly over the last few decades, and apparently continues to do so. And no wonder, when one looks at what it has to do. It is now the primary law-making organization of the country, having gradually assumed that job from the legislative branch over time. The obvious problem with that is the anonymity of the federal bureaucrat and his organization. The permanent, or professional, bureaucracy, unlike the higher level political appointees, is by design insulated from most political pressures. Its members are also unelected, in addition to being effectively tenured.

The latter privilege has been criticized for promoting incompetence by making it excessively difficult to terminate non-performers, but that isn't its worst effect. Effectively, federal bureaucrats are unaccountable to anyone except each other in carrying out their functions. Not only are they not accountable to politicians, but their permanent and tenured status means they are unaccountable to their ultimate employers, the people of the United States. This is not all bad; as the foregoing history shows, that is precisely what those who designed the Civil Service intended. The objective was to insulate the bureaucracy from political pressures, including those induced by elections. What the designers did not foresee was the expanded functions of the bureaucracy. They did not anticipate that an unaccountable body would be making most of the nation's laws.

That, in a nutshell, is an account of the genesis of the Deep State. Almost by chance, the best intentions of the civil service reform movement and its positive role in eliminating the spoils system were perverted into something even worse. The confluence of that reform movement with the Progressive Movement seems, in retrospect, inevitable. That confluence combined with mission drift caused by the laxity of the legislative branch of the federal government, which devolved its main duties to the bureaucracy, fulfilled all the conditions for the rising of the Deep State. Agencies that exist under the aegis of the executive branch, but are effectively independent of everyone and accountable to no one, now make the nation's laws, and to a great extent enforce them. Thus the core of the Deep State, its first leg, was formed.

The second leg was, in a sense, cloned from the first. It is an integral part of the Deep State, also a part of government bureaucracy but even more secretive and anonymous by its very nature and as a result even less accountable to the people of the Republic. The history of the Intelligence Community (IC) is as long as that of the professional bureaucracy, since the first of its agencies, the Office of Naval Intelligence, was founded just one year prior to the Pendleton Act, in 1882. This can be misleading, however, since during the next 65 years only one other agency, that of the Coast Guard, followed. The turning point was World War II, which saw the spawning of a number of *ad hoc* intelligence outfits that were put together and subsequently made over into permanent agencies after the war. Most prominent among these was the Central Intelligence Agency in 1947. The Federal Bureau of Investigation, which has been around since 1908, was brought into the IC in 2005 in response to the Twin Towers disaster.

The IC is now a huge and unwieldy amalgam of 16 separate agencies, plus the Office of the Director of National Intelligence at its head. More than 30 other intelligence organizations (about 40% of them government, 60% private) work for the main agencies. No one has much of an idea of the total manpower involved, but nearly 860,000 people hold top secret clearances. The budget of the combined IC is over $50 billion, but with all the "dark" money it's hard to be more exact. More detail on the IC in general and the FBI in particular is provided in an article herein titled *Praetorians of the Republic* that was published nearly two years before this one, and the interested reader may go there for additional information. It suffices here to observe that the spectacular growth of the IC coincides with the full flowering of the Deep State, and the latter is highly dependent upon the intelligence establishment. The IC is, after all, part of the permanent bureaucracy, and it is by its very nature even less accountable to elected authority than the rest of the bureaucracy. It is also evident that the secretive and unaccountable nature of IC agencies has within the last few years been used by certain political elements (including some of the "spooks") to undertake sinister and illegal activities against other political entities. The Deep State couldn't function as we know it *is* functioning without its second leg.

In contrast to the IC, the third leg of the Deep State is the most obviously exposed. The tragic deterioration of most of the country's mass media into a propaganda machine for the political Left is covered in another article of this book entitled *Pravda West* and can be examined there. Again, its history coincides with the expansion of progressivism and further illustrates the marriage of the Deep State with that movement. In a sense, the seduction of journalism by the Left is "the unkindest cut of all," since the primary duty of the journalist is to reveal truth about government to the people, not to disseminate the tendentious concoctions of a political party and its dogma. This third leg differs in important ways from the other two, not the least of which is that it is not part of the bureaucracy. Although the support of the media has been vital to the prosperity of the Deep State, its independent (and exposed) status has made it more vulnerable than the others to public reaction. Over the last half century its credibility as a provider of disinterested information has eroded substantially, and for good reason. Pravda West is still important to the Deep State but is a declining asset.

The history of the genesis of the Deep State, even in a brief summary, therefore provides a better sense of its nature than is possible with mere description. It began with the good intention of ridding government of its spoils system and replacing that unsatisfactory institution with a competent and nonpartisan permanent bureaucratic workforce. Over time, much of the lawmaking work of the legislative branch devolved upon the agencies of the executive branch, which expanded in response. The foundation for the Deep State was thus laid almost unintentionally. To this foundation was added a large and largely unaccountable bureaucracy of intelligence agencies that were shrouded in secrecy by their very purpose. The Progressive Movement, meanwhile, being ideologically compatible with the idea of a government of experts, largely coopted it for its own ends. Finally, the "fourth estate" that was supposed to shed light on government instead became politicized to the leftist cause and served to help hide and protect the growing power of the Deep State.

The Establishment and the Deep State certainly overlap, but they are by no means the same. Not all federal bureaucrats, by far, would think of themselves as part of the Deep State, and only a minority of employees of the IC. Even some members of the mass media, although they may be of a leftist political persuasion, are not really Deep State loyalists. Establishment politicians who are sympathetic to the Deep State are at least visible as such to the voters and therefore not actually part of it. But when one visualizes the nature of the Deep State, as revealed by the history of its growth, it becomes obvious that its power rests more on its opacity and amorphous nature than on the numbers of those who fill its ranks. And even of the latter, many are only part-time supporters of Deep State activities and perhaps unaware themselves of their affiliation with it. But no matter: the Deep State exists and moves within the bowels of the national government.

The nature of the Deep State is such that "draining the swamp" is no simple task. It is not a question of simply pulling a plug. How does one even know where to start? Whom does one seek to remove from a responsible position, given the fact that most of our laws are even now being made by bureaucrats and the system is dependent on lawmaking by executive agencies? Wholesale termination of bureaucrats, even if it were possible under current administrative law, would result in governmental chaos, besides inevitably removing many capable and honest people along with the chaff. How can we eliminate the Deep State from our Intelligence Community without inviting disaster to our national security apparatus? Yet, the Deep State shenanigans of the past few years tell us that we must do something about the situation or we will have permanent chaos in Washington, D.C., and danger emanating from it. We have, over the decades, placed ourselves as a nation in a very deep slough, and if we become serious about extricating ourselves, it will be an arduous, painstaking and time-consuming project. This is a lesson that the story of Deep State genesis teaches us clearly.

1/13/20

Chapter Three

Praetorians of the Republic

In the Year of our Lord 312, the great Emperor Constantine issued an edict that ended a three century old institution of the Roman Empire. To wit, he disbanded the celebrated – and infamous – Praetorian Guard. The Guard was instituted in the form we recognize by the first emperor, Augustus, during his struggles that culminated in the naval Battle of Actium. Its primary duty was to provide security for the government of Rome, and picked veterans from the Roman legions were recruited for the purpose. Whatever else may be said of the Praetorians, they were an elite fighting force throughout the many generations of their existence.

Actually, the name of the Praetorian Guard is much older than the reign of Augustus; it goes back to the Roman Republic. In those days it existed as a small escort guard for generals and other high officials, and it seems to have been more of an *ad hoc* sort of arrangement than a permanent standing force. Octavian (Augustus' name before he became emperor) and his rivals put together more cohesive units during the civil war that ended the Republic (as well as the lives of his rivals and their ally, Cleopatra). With the cessation of hostilities, Augustus combined these various units into the Praetorian Guard as the primary official security force of the new Empire.

The Guard was much more than a crew of personal bodyguards for the emperor. Actually, for much of the history of the Roman Empire, that duty was more specifically assigned to the Imperial German Bodyguard, commonly referred to as the Batavi, who were recruited (for reasons you may imagine) from parts of the empire distant from Rome itself. As the name implies, the members of that personal bodyguard were mostly

Germans, whose loyalties to the emperor as an individual were undiluted by local political considerations.

For the Praetorians, specific bodyguard duties were only a small part of a broader calling. Cohorts of the Guard often took an active part in campaigns around the Empire's borders, especially those involving the putting down of revolts. They were commonly used as a final reserve in battle, to make a victorious charge or last stand. Throughout its mixed history, no one ever doubted the fighting qualities of the Praetorian Guard.

As far as internal duties, the role of the Praetorians is best illustrated by their physical disposition at the imperial palace in Rome. There, the Guard was assigned to positions outside the palace building, while the Batavi provided security inside. The Guard is thus more accurately viewed as guardians of the Roman imperium rather than the Roman emperor. They were at times bodyguards of the emperor's person, but only as part of their larger obligations to the government and to the Roman state as a whole.

The distinction mentioned above is subtle but vital, and not restricted to Roman history. Many rulers have tried to blur the distinction or wipe it out altogether, most overtly Louis XIV of France with his famous quote, "L'etat c'est moi." The guillotine cut that sentiment short, along with his successor, but to this day some tyrannically-minded types seem to believe their countries can't exist without them. The Praetorians rarely thought that way about the Roman emperor of the moment, which had a profound effect on Roman history.

Let us digress from this train of thought for a moment to examine the makeup of the Praetorian Guard itself. It is a common misconception that the Guard was a band of bullies, perhaps a few dozen or so, who hung around the palace in Rome, ate grapes, drank wine and bothered pretty girls. This was far from the reality; the Guard was a formidable fighting force of variable but substantial numbers. It was formed of cohorts, which originally consisted of 500 men but later of one thousand. Octavian brought five cohorts with him to Actium; his enemy Marc Antony had three in a campaign in the east and probably had at least that many at Actium. Later, as Emperor Augustus, Octavian raised the number of cohorts to nine. The number varied from nine to as many as sixteen under later emperors. In addition, there was the Praetorian cavalry, organized into thirty-man *tumae*. In all, from 9,000 to as many as 16,000 seasoned warriors were Praetorians at any one time.

Service in the Guard was rewarding in a number of ways. The pay varied over time, but it was always notably higher than that of a common legionary, from half again to several times as much. On top of regular pay, a guardsman could expect a share of the occasional *donatium*, paid upon the succession of each new emperor and at other odd times such as special celebrations or after an act of fidelity in helping to put down a plot. Another perk was the shorter term of duty for a guardsman as compared to that of a legionary, and yet another (after Vespasian) was suspension of taxes on land given them after their service.

The downsides of Praetorian service were less material. They had a reputation of arrogance and callous indifference to civilians. That rep was enhanced by their status as the only people who could bear arms within the city proper, but was probably well-justified in any case. Even Roman nobles, including senators, feared them since they answered mainly to the emperor (and, of course, bore arms and knew how to use them). The result was that they were roundly hated by most of the population, of station both high and low. That didn't seem to bother them a great deal, but it could make them more vulnerable to rioters in unsettled times.

In command of this substantial force was a prefect. The earlier prefects were themselves mostly veterans with an extensive background of military command, but later in the Guard's history, as their political involvement became more open, many prefects were drawn from the ranks of jurists. The first prefect to be caught with his hand in the political cookie jar was Sejanus, who served during the reign of Tiberius. He was executed in 31 AD (by other Praetorians loyal to the regime) when his plot to gain the throne was discovered. Later prefects were perhaps less personally involved and certainly far more successful with their seditious activities.

The first imperial assassination carried out by the Praetorian Guard was that of Caligula, just ten years after Sejanus' sad end. The Guard elevated Claudius in Caligula's place, which may have done Rome a favor but set a very bad precedent. It became evident to both the power players of the empire and the Guard itself that the latter held the ultimate key to emperorship. It was a key that would be used with wearisome regularity over the following centuries.

To attempt a complete account of the non-military activities of the Praetorian Guard from the time of its politicization in the first century would be both futile and tiresome. A typical episode from the heyday of the Guard should suffice. In 192 AD, Emperor Commodus was assassinated in a conspiracy led by the prefect Quintus Aemilius. The new emperor, Pertinax, was elevated to the purple after bribing the Praetorians with three thousand denarii each. This might be considered a rather trivial sum for a position that conferred upon its possessor not only power and luxury but the potential for even more wealth. It was not such a bargain for Pertinax, however. He was assassinated by the Guard in his own turn just three months later. The Praetorian Guard then put the empire up for auction. It was sold to Didius Julianus in 193. History does not disclose the exact payment, but rumor has it that it was the substantial sum of 25,000 sestertii (8,250 denarii) to each guardsman. Considering the impressive size of the initial bribe and the requirement of continually rendering a *donatium* to the "protectors," it may not have been much of a bargain for Didius either. And this is but one example of many possible ones.

From time to time a half-hearted attempt to disband the Praetorians was made, but no emperor was strong enough to accomplish the deed. Most were afraid to do anything except bribe and placate them, and for good reason. Finally, in 306, Galerius made a serious attempt, giving strict orders to have the Guard disbanded. The attempt failed and the Praetorians turned to a man named Maxentius and proclaimed him emperor. By this time, the Roman Empire had been divided into eastern and western divisions, so the Guard's actions applied only to the western half. The east had (unfortunately for the Guard) a strong emperor of its own, Constantine the Great. In 312, Constantine marched to Rome with his legions and defeated Maxentius and his followers at the Battle of Milvian Bridge. The empire was reunited (for a while) and the Praetorian Guard finally definitively disbanded, its sordid history ended and its soldiers scattered among the legions. Constantine could no longer tolerate the supposed protectors of the Roman imperium meddling in politics to the detriment of the empire's people.

Does this sound familiar?

The Federal Bureau of Investigation (FBI) is the United States' top law enforcement agency. Its Intelligence Branch is one of sixteen agencies that make up the Intelligence Community (IC) (the Office of the Director of National Intelligence, to which they all report, is sometimes considered a seventeenth agency). Eight of these agencies are military, under the Department of Defense. More detail on the IC is furnished in the preceding chapter; it may be said here that it is huge, unwieldy and expensive besides being politicized to an uncomfortable degree.

It wasn't always that way. The first government intelligence agency was the U.S. Navy's, the Office of Naval Intelligence, which was formed in 1882 and existed alone for fully 33 years. Then it shared the intelligence stage with Coast Guard Intelligence, and the two stood alone for another 30 years. Somehow the nation survived with this paltry spy force. The expansion of the IC from WWII onward is also detailed in Chapter 2, in particular the formation of the CIA and inclusion of the FBI. Recently, new intelligence agencies have sprung up like daisies, including separate agencies for such unlikely entities as the Departments of the Treasury, Homeland Defense and even Energy. Apparently, you haven't made it in Washington without your own set of spies. I expect to see one for Education before long, and perhaps the EPA as well.

The FBI's official entrance into the IC late in 2005, with the formation of its Intelligence Branch, helped to formalize a relationship with the CIA (and the others, of course). The intelligence breakdown that allowed 9/11 to happen was, at least in part, quite correctly attributed to a failure of communication among the agencies. In fact, the division of duties between the FBI and the CIA was both deliberate and logical: the FBI was to focus on internal matters within the U.S. and the CIA on issues involving other nations. This is still the case in a general way, although things can get blurry, as one would expect.

Actually, the FBI already had something of a toe in the water of the sea of international intelligence. Since It was established in 1908 its purview always included protection of the nation from foreign terrorists and counterespionage against foreign spies. The agency has, in terms of its mission, much in common with the old Praetorian Guard of ancient Rome. There are differences, of course: a major focus of the FBI is domestic detective work in support of local police and against interstate crime, which the Guard didn't do. Specific bodyguard work in protection of government officials is the job of the Secret Service, not the FBI. Of course, as was described above, in Rome the protection of the emperor was mostly a job for the Batavi, and the Guard's work was protection of the imperium. In a similar fashion, the FBI's larger mission is protection of government and nation. FBI agents are, in a realistic sense, Praetorians of the Republic.

It might be argued that the responsibility of being modern Praetorians is shared with other agencies as well, the CIA among them. I am picking selectively on the FBI because of its prominence in recent headlines, not at all because it is the only transgressor. In fact, the Long March of progressivism through American institutions during the last century leaves more targets than time to shoot at them. The educational system, the journalism profession, labor unions, even religious establishments and chambers of commerce, all are now guilty to some extent. But intelligence, which is protected by a shield of secrecy as the Praetorians were by their swords, is an especially painful contributor to the rot. These are the people who are supposed to be protecting us.

The modern FBI, of course, is not new to the game of politicization. J. Edgar Hoover was director (should I say "prefect"?) from 1924 to 1972, and only departed feet first. He definitely was involved in politics for most of that long period, notoriously so. His main targets were the communists who had secretly infiltrated much of the government, and other radical groups whose activities were much less secretive. As with the Praetorians who disposed of Caligula, his intentions and results may have been for the benefit of the country, but the precedent was dangerous. After him, the directorship was limited to ten years, with appointment by the President and approval of the Senate. The director's tenure is subject to resignation or removal by POTUS, which helps to limit the damage a political appointment can do, but senior officers tend to hang on regardless.

The generalized politicization of the American bureaucracy during the Obama administration affected the entire IC, the FBI included. Certain agencies, notably the IRS, were spectacularly affected, but no department more than the Department of Justice.

The FBI had the misfortune of falling under that department. It didn't take long for the highest echelons of the agency to become thoroughly politicized in the Establishment pattern. As of 2010, there were almost 34,000 FBI employees, including 13,412 special agents. Most of the rest are specialists of various stripes, including analysts, language experts, IT people, scientists and lawyers. A substantial majority of them are thorough professionals, dedicated to their nation and their jobs, able to put their politics in their back pockets as they handle their work with real distinction. They are, as the rank-and-file soldiers of the Praetorian Guard were, competent and dedicated. As those soldiers were led astray and betrayed by their prefects and ranking officers, so are the good people betrayed by the top leadership of their agency. The majority are humiliated.

So it is that when I look at a TV screen (a rarer event these days than formerly) and watch the antics of high-level FBI officials who have been in the recent past assigned duties of great import, I'm profoundly depressed. I watch their buffoonery and their open contempt toward representatives of the American people they were supposed to protect and defend and am disgusted. I watch them defended slavishly by representatives of the other party for wholly partisan reasons and am sickened. This is the way of Rome, the way of degeneration and defeat. It is the way of the Praetorians.

Where are we going now? Will we be redeemed by a strong leader from the grotesque politicization of the last decade, at least for a while? Or will we inevitably be drawn into the Swamp – the malignant pit of corruption into which mighty Rome sank? The future is in our hands, we the Americans of this generation. Let us hope that we can still shape the Praetorians of our Republic into the force they were meant to be.

1/6/20

Chapter Four

Praetorians of the Deep State

There was always something bewildering about the firing of Trish Regan from Fox Business Network. If it were only the result of something as mundane as low ratings or getting crossways with the executive suite there wouldn't be much to it. The network's official excuse, however, that they needed to make more airtime for coronavirus news, was a bit weak and, more significantly, ran up against a more compelling story. It happened just after the popular conservative commentator came under intense fire from the Left for her "rant" in the introduction to her March 10 show. I did not watch the incident at the time (no knock on Ms. Regan; I rarely watch any TV), but read about it in several leftist articles (yes, I do read material from the dark side). From everything I read, her diatribe was indeed nasty. The titles of those articles indicate the content; it would take excessive space to list them all *in toto*, but selected phrases from them will suffice: "anchor's bonkers coronavirus rant;" "off-the-rails coronavirus rant;" "on air meltdown;" "rant on coronavirus is something else." That's just a sampling of written material; the spoken comments on the Pravda West channels were worse.

What was bewildering was that this didn't sound like Ms. Regan at all. She has always been level-headed, calm, thorough and factually accurate. "Bonkers" and "off the rails" ranting seems far out of character for her. The articles were typical of leftist journalism in that they all said the same thing and used many of the same phrases, but they did seem firm on one important point: she called the whole coronavirus epidemic a hoax that was devised by Democrats as a means to get rid of President Trump. To prove it, they all showed a screen shot of Ms. Regan over a broadcast banner that stated: Coronavirus

Impeachment Hoax. According to the articles, her claim was that there was no reality behind the virus hysteria; it was manufactured by the Democrat Party to demonize Trump before the November election. The "rant," according to the writers, was so foul, nasty and generally over-the-top that Fox had no choice but to terminate the show and fire the commentator.

Puzzled, I managed to find a transcript of the actual speech. It bore little relation to the unhinged rant described in the articles. In fact, it was about the politicization of a real public health crisis by Democrats in an effort to get Trump. For the most part, the language was temperate rather than ranting, given the subject -- far more temperate than that routinely used by leftist pundits against Trump. As to the notorious banner, it appears that those pundits have trouble reading three words in a row. It was as though the word Hoax applied to the first word of the phrase -- Coronavirus -- rather than the second. In fact, the context of Ms. Regan's monologue clearly indicates that the banner referred to an impeachment hoax based on the virus, not a hoax about the virus itself. In short, the articles (really, one article with myriad tongues) were a standard product of our modern media: an amalgam of distortion and deceit that attempts to skate around outright mendacity. Which raises a question, not so much about why Fox caved to the same old pressure and fired Trish Regan -- Fox is no longer the "fair and balanced" source of old -- as about why the Left should become so hysterical about what was really a pretty ordinary monologue.

What part of Regan's short monologue triggered the Left so violently? Surely it wasn't the main point, which is that Democrats have used the coronavirus crisis to demonize the president; they have used everything in the kitchen to demonize him since before his inauguration and it has become boringly routine. Nor, in all probability, was it the suggestion that leftists may have hyped the situation to promote hysteria, thereby harming the economy and removing the president's best argument for his re-election in the fall. Frankly, they have been working toward that end all along and it's an old story that the Left never lets a good crisis go to waste. A close study of the entire monologue makes it evident to the reader that nothing specifically stated in it could be considered sufficiently novel or acute as to give the Left collective vapors. But there are "emanations and penumbrae" (excuse me, Justice Douglas) in monologues as well as Supreme Court decisions, and I suspect that Regan triggered just such a shadow. That penumbra hinted at a conspiracy theory that the Left would prefer the public not think about. It concerns the origins of the coronavirus and who knew what and when.

At this point, the reader is referred to several previously written articles that are found elsewhere in this tome. The first is entitled *Conspiracy Theory*, the gist of which is that although the term is freely used as a weapon, not all conspiracy theories are crackpot, any more than all conspiracies are fictional. A related article is *Debunked*, which debunks one of the Left's favorite words that is commonly used against its critics. Primarily, an article originally published two years before this was written is *Praetorians of the Republic*. It contains a brief history of the Praetorian Guard of imperial Rome and shows its relevance to the role of politics in the Intelligence Community (IC) of our own day. A quick glance at *The Third Bite*, a review of the unsavory antics of the Left against the current administration, might also be useful.

But on to the nervousness of the Left in reaction to the Trish Regan "rant." First, a knowledge of the origins of the coronavirus is both important for the sake of combating it and highly sensitive for a number of entities. The communist Chinese government is the most obvious of the sensitive entities, but it is hardly alone. Although it is hotly opposed by quite a few interested parties, the notion that the virus was accidentally released by a research institute in Wuhan, China, is increasingly supported by circumstantial evidence. It just so happens that said institute was supported in part by American money given through the Obama administration. That being the case, it is hard to believe that no one in this country knew anything about what was going on there. In particular, not only the NIH but certain agencies of the IC, and specifically the CIA, should have had a spoon in that stew. It is significant that a message from the American embassy warned of security problems at the Wuhan facility two years ago. Trust me on this: a high percentage of American embassy personnel in Beijing have IC, mostly CIA, connections, and everyone, including the Chinese, knows it.

To date, U.S. intelligence agencies have been uncharacteristically diffident about expressing opinions about the virus' origin. So far, not much has been heard from them except weak suggestions that the virus just happened as a result of a natural human-bat interaction, without totally eliminating the possibility that the Wuhan Virology Institute was involved. To those who have followed the brash involvement of the FBI and CIA in the Russian collusion and Ukrainian telephone call fiascos, this backwardness must be viewed with a grain of skepticism. In fact, the IC has been so quiet during the current crisis as to raise suspicions even within the breasts of the most gullible among us. Have its agents learned something from the tarnishing their services have suffered over the past few years? If so, I must presume what was learned has less to do with making trouble than with getting caught. After all, even within the last week there have been revelations that the FBI has all along --even under a different director -- been hiding documentary evidence of its past misdeeds regarding the persecution of General Flynn and others. Are we to believe that they are taking no part in political activity surrounding the coronavirus problem? Or indeed, in any political shenanigans at all? Has the IC reformed itself and shrugged off the Obama-induced politicization of recent years? As noted above, there is abundant evidence to support the thesis that that is highly unlikely. It is no crackpot conspiracy theory to suggest that the FBI and CIA are still the Praetorians of the Deep State.

And why, indeed, should they not act as did the Praetorian Guard of ancient history? There is certainly every incentive for it. As a powerful element within the federal bureaucracy of the country, the most prominent IC agencies, namely the FBI and CIA, are themselves part of the Deep State. They are the Deep State's sword and shield and have proven themselves as willing as their Roman forebears to wield their weapons in their own interests. Those interests are clear enough: every national election is important, but the presidential election of 2020 is more pivotal for the future of the nation than any since that of 1860. With our populace so evenly divided over fundamental Constitutional questions (the main one being whether we should still have an effective Constitution), the decision of this November will shape the fundamental nature of our country for the foreseeable future. The issue of the composition of the Supreme Court alone is critical, and that of immigration perhaps even more so. From the narrower view of the Deep State's denizens and dependencies, its very survival in its current form is at stake.

Are we to believe the intelligence power structure of the country will sit idly by and simply allow its entire future to be left to chance and the voting power of the nation's deplorables? That wasn't the case in 2016, neither was it the case during the first three-plus years of the Trump administration, and we may be confident it isn't the case now. The options for our latter-day Praetorians narrow. There is little time left to develop another major intelligence-driven coup attempt on the order of the last two, as is explained in *The Third Bite*. The current coronavirus situation had its origins, in all probability, in an accidental incident of some sort (to assert that it, too, was manufactured by the IC would indeed be a conspiracy theory), but one can hardly expect that the Praetorians will let it pass without taking some advantage from it. Thus the worrisome question about the apparent passivity of the IC operatives during this period. Perhaps what the secret services have learned from their recent embarrassing failures is .... how to be secret.

One way or another, there will be no going back after November. If the current president is re-elected, and particularly if control of the House of Representatives changes at the same time, his agenda will soon be completed. Even under constant obstruction and harassment by the opposing party, he has accomplished a great deal; there will be no way Democrats can continue to deter him for four more years. The advance of socialism in this country, probably worldwide, will be set back a generation. On the other hand, if the Democrat candidate prevails and the party holds the House and possibly takes the Senate, the Right will be drastically diminished as a political force. It is possible that there will not be another truly free election in this country within the lifespan of any citizen now alive, absent an outright armed rebellion. The Left will not allow the chance of another miss if it is successful this time. There will be elections, of course, but we have seen how that went in Soviet Russia and every other socialist state. The old adage, "One man, one vote, one time" holds more than a bit of truth in a socialist regime.

Which brings us back to the Praetorians of the Deep State. Will they supinely await the outcome of the critical events of this moment in history? Have they nothing to do with the coronavirus crisis except be passive spectators and perhaps sift through some data for the benefit of the administration? The histories of both the old Praetorian Guard and its modern analog persuade us to believe otherwise. Time will tell.

5/3/20

Chapter Five

Little People

There is a scene in one of the James Bond movies where 007, played by Sean Connery, has penetrated some lab facility by impersonating an employee who checks personal radiation meters (or something). He is verbally abused by a scientist who doesn't want to be bothered and admonishes the self-important fellow by reminding him that the "little people" have their place in the organization as well as the big shots. The rest of the movie is forgettable (or at least forgotten), but that line remains in my memory. There's something poignant about 007 himself, and the Connery 007 at that, standing up for us commoners. But when one thinks about it, who are the little people?

On reflection, it's obvious that the term is relative. In a small business in a middling Midwestern city, the owner is big and the lower tier employees are little people. At city hall of the same town, the mayor, police chief and council members are big and that same business owner is a little person. In Washington, D.C. or New York City, the leading political, legal and financial industry figures are big and the whole midwestern city is just little people. While recognizing this reality, for present purposes let us look at the national picture. Those who are generally recognized as belonging to the elites will be perceived as big and members of the working class at all levels will be our little people. Those who have never worked much are, no doubt, in a classification of their own, but are certainly among the little people for all practical purposes.

Much has been written of late about elites, the Establishment and the Deep State, including a recent article herein (*Noblesse Oublie*). All these cannot exist, however, without minions from those classes called little people by the less discreet elitists. That term is not often seen in its unvarnished form; more common are references to desperate souls clinging to guns and religion, or "working stiffs," or "losers" of some sort, or, of course, deplorables. But who are those among the various categories of little people who support the elites? What kind of little people are those without whom the elites couldn't exist?

Certainly the little people who form the base upon which the elites proudly stand do not include the deplorables. Hillary Clinton used that word to describe those who most ardently opposed elites in general (and her in particular). In fact, the meaning of the word has morphed from people who are "racist, sexist, homophobic, xenophobic, Islamophobic – you name it" (in Hillary's immortal prose) to ordinary citizens who oppose the excesses of an arrogant and incompetent elite class that they find offensive. Deplorables are the truly "woke" among the little people. So who are the others?

Some of the little people who support the elites, by their votes and otherwise, do so for reasons that may be unsound but are perfectly understandable. Foremost among these is a huge proportion of the black community, with motivations that are deeply rooted in a history unique among Americans. This subject has been covered by a number of articles herein, including *From the Back of the Bus (to Under It)* and several definitive articles by my blogger colleague Janus. Other groups that include a high percentage of little people who favor our elites are single women, college graduates, certain religious minorities, people who prefer to think of themselves as intellectuals, young people with more ambition than judgment and holdover Democrats from times past.

Explanations for all of these groups are necessarily generalizations, but they are largely both true and logical. Single women have their individual reasons, of course, but there is certainly a tendency to view government as something of a surrogate husband. This may sound condescending (and in many cases is), but in fact it makes a degree of sense. If nothing else, it helps explain the striking statistical difference between them and married women. College graduates have been exposed to years of brainwashing in an educational system dominated by the Left. Among religious minorities, the leftist tendency of Jews has been examined in the article *The Moth and the Flame*; other minorities have other motives. Many young people grow out of leftism and elite-worship; the more ambitious among them may aspire to elitism themselves. Intellectuals (not to be confused with people who are intelligent) are, in many cases, simply intellectually lazy. It's easier to go along and get along than to develop logical arguments against dominance of the elite. Even some non-intellectuals may go along with supporting elites for similar reasons: it's easy, trendy, faux-rebellious. Holdover Democrats are different altogether – they still think of the party as for the little guy. George Soros and his fellow billionaires doubtless agree with them.

The littlest of the little people who uphold the elites are those captured by socialism in the form of the welfare state. These unfortunates are truly captives of the Left. All the others mentioned above have, one way or another, made a choice to be minions of the elites; long-term welfare recipients have, in many cases, lost that power of choice. It might be noted in this regard that, stymied by a growing economy at home, the Establishment has been assiduously importing large numbers of potential supporters, many of them illegally, and attaching them to welfare dependency. This is in the face of strong opposition of a majority of little people across the political spectrum. Which brings us to a strange conclusion: we seem to be entering, under the aegis of our elites, into a entirely new form of slave state here in the Land of the Free.

It would appear that those who consider themselves members of the modern American elite class have been working to divide the little people into two major divisions: those who labor for a living and those who do not. Many of the latter spend time on a job and draw a salary, but the "work" they perform is hardly productive. These people constitute a large percentage of bureaucracies at all levels of government and are essentially welfare recipients. Those bureaucrats who actually perform productive duties combined with the majority of private sector workers, both blue and white collar, sustain both the economy and the substantial and growing non-productive division of little people (as well as the elites, of course). The primary duty of the non-productive group is to provide the votes that keep the elites in charge of society.

The theory is that enough additional votes can be siphoned from the productive group, through various manipulations that include brainwashing by an elite-controlled educational system and browbeating by the propaganda of a mendacious mass media, to put enough elite-supporting politicians over the top to keep things under control. A bit of election fraud can be applied here and there as necessary, but when the system is going well that should be needed but rarely. In practice, elitists are not quite where they want to be as to control of the electoral process – the 2016 election was a nasty shock – and are rapidly losing patience with the whole idea of democracy. The sort of democracy enjoyed by Soviet Russia in its prime, with 99% or so of the votes going to Communist Party-designated candidates, seems far more orderly to our elites. In lieu of that socialist perfection, the elites are working hard to sabotage politicians who were elected without their approval while continuing to perfect their new slave state.

Perhaps it is a relief to know that the current elites aren't entirely incompetent after all. They have, over the decades, accomplished a great deal to establish the slave state of their dreams. They now control all the American institutions to an impressive degree; some, like the educational system and the mass media, are virtually completely mastered by them. They control our very speech to an amazing extent, and through it our individual thought processes. The elites may be shiftless bunglers when it involves running a city, state or country, but when it comes to something they care about, like preserving their own preeminence, given enough time and the inattention of little people who are busy making a living they sometimes get the job done.

To repeat, the slave state into which we are on the precipice of falling is composed of two divisions of little people. Those are welfare slaves and tax slaves. Both will be under the heel of a system controlled by the elites, the former voluntarily and the latter through a combination of intimidation, coercion and shaming. Welfare slaves, on the surface, will be beneficiaries of this earthly paradise, along with the elites themselves, of course. The tax slaves will be tolerated, as pointed out above, as necessary to keep the country running. Presumably, everyone will be happy under this regime. Ecstatic, even.

The problem is that there is a refractory streak running through the little people of the American populace, one that has existed since early colonial days and remains right to the present. As Alexis de Tocqueville noted nearly two centuries ago, the little people in America are not so little after all. For better or worse, there is an ingrained contempt for elitism that remains in American culture and that has made the lust of our modern elites to dominate far more difficult to satisfy. It might be said that much of the effort of the progressives over the past century has been focused on overcoming that unfortunate resistance of the little people to elitism. It wasn't for nothing that they worked so hard to control education and the media in this country – both have been used to good effect to wear down the little peoples' refractoriness. To put it another way, they have labored to make the little people (who weren't so little) smaller.

To a substantial extent, they have succeeded. Not all the tax slaves are as resistant to their serfdom as one might expect. A good many vote for the elites and their causes. Some support elitism for reasons that are understandable, if fallacious, as discussed above. Others aren't so easy to understand; they seem to think elitism is kind of cool, even when they are kowtowing to it. These are the saddest serfs of all: little people who become even smaller by choice. If enough little people choose to further diminish themselves, even to the point of assenting to the elites' recent attempts at suspension of democracy in the world's greatest democracy, we shall see the end of freedom in America in our own lifetimes.

Chapter Six

Depraved New World I: Beauty and the Beast

Fairy tales are misnamed. For the most part they have little or nothing to do with fairies, and it is somewhat misleading even to call them tales. They are more properly named fables, because unlike the general run of tales they are, like Aesop's fables, built around specific moral lessons. Also, the most typical of them have no known author in their original versions, but have been written down by collectors who hear them from natives, who in turn heard them from those of a previous generation. The traditional ones are, like myths, products of an oral tradition, and the origins of many are lost in the mists of the centuries. Such is the case with the celebrated *Beauty and the Beast*, which has been traced back in its various forms well over two millennia. Its first written precedent appeared in the Indian collection *Panchatantra* in about 200 BC, and another version was authored by the Roman writer Apuleius in the 2nd century AD. The first "modern" written version was by a French noblewoman in 1740, but the more familiar (and much shorter) form was that of Jeanne-Marie Leprince de Beaumont in 1756. It is this latter work that is the basis of the various more recent iterations of the fable.

The moral of *Beauty and the Beast* from the beginning and in all its many forms is simple: don't rely on outward appearances but seek the inner truth. In summary, a young, handsome (of course) and good-hearted prince is changed into a foul-looking beast by an evil witch. To be redeemed and returned to his original form, he must win the love of a young woman, no mean feat for a beast. A young beauty named Belle becomes a captive in the beast's enchanted castle in order to save her father. At first, she regards the creature with fear and loathing, but as he treats her with gentle kindness she begins to lose her terror of him. She still cannot bring herself to love him or agree to marry him until much later, when he is close to death from missing her. She then discovers that she cannot bear to lose him, and that in fact she does love him for his inner virtues and despite his ugliness. At her declaration of love, the spell is broken, he regains his old form, and happily ever after, etc.

The most recent iterations of the old fable have been far more ambitious than any of their precedents. An animated Disney movie (1991) was followed by a Broadway play (1994) and later by a live action musical film (2017) and, I understand, a couple of European films. This is quite a step up for an ancient fable. Or is it? The American versions of the fable were different in some important ways from the old fairy tale. It is expected that the story line would be expanded in order for the simple original to fill an entire movie, but since the whole point of a fable is to illustrate a moral message, the expansion should at least include that message. The 1991 screenplay, however, was written by an ardent feminist. While it certainly carries a message, the message is totally different from that of the fable. The blurb for the 2017 movie, which follows the Broadway play, that is in turn based on the 1991 edition, reads as follows: "A selfish prince is cursed to become a monster for the rest of his life, unless he learns to fall in love with a beautiful young woman he keeps prisoner." It's obvious on even casual examination that this is a turning of the moral of the old fable on its head.

Since the writer for the Disney film is a feminist, ideology replaced art in her product. It starts with the witch who transformed the prince into a beast. She is evil in the tale, and vengeful because the prince rejected her. In the movie she isn't so bad and the arrogant and selfish prince had it coming. In the fable, Belle is quite realistic in an ideal sort of way, an innocent of sweet disposition and good heart who is able to overcome her terror of the fearsome appearance of the beast in response to his kindness. She has virtue that enables her to learn how to look behind the beastly surface and see the prince within. The beast has the inner nobility and patience to open her eyes and lead her to love. The simple moral of looking for truth beneath the surface is illustrated cleanly and clearly, which is what a fable does best. In the film, Belle is no more complex than the Belle of the fable, but much different in character. She is, in fact, a typical modern feminist, strong-willed, independent and self-righteous. The beast really is rather beastly, with the character flaws of the film's prince. So instead of the beast's teaching the beauty how to love despite outward deformity, the beauty teaches the beast how to overcome his flaws. In other words, the moral becomes: men are pigs, but strong women can reform them.

The contemporary metamorphosis of *Beauty and the Beast* exemplifies a general trend in our society to turn traditional truths and values on their heads. Examples abound; there is almost an embarrassment of them, but a few may serve as representative of the whole trend, of established virtue overwhelmed by fad and what was thought to be eternal absorbed into the ephemeral. One of the most striking is patriotism, which has now been replaced in the minds of the elites by globalism. Americans' unabashed love of their country was legendary (or, to many Europeans, notorious) throughout the nation's history. It is difficult to say exactly when it declined, but its death knell was sounded by President Obama, who refused to accept American exceptionalism in principle. He stated outright that everyone from anywhere thought his own country to be exceptional, and backed it up by refusing to perform the usual patriotic acts such as hand over heart during the national anthem, wearing a flag lapel pin and so on. Patriotism became the last resort of the deplorables, the vanity of simpletons, a narcotic for the clueless. The sophisticates of the world, the intellectuals and anyone with pretensions to respectability, are now citizens of the world, far above boorish patriotism.

Similarly, family values, as they were understood, have been subsumed into the politically correct version of lifestyles. That is, they are still marginally acceptable as a *bourgeois* option for commoners but no longer by any means to be preferred to any other lifestyle. Similarly, the old American ideals associated with individualism and self-reliance have given way to the welfare state. Dependency on the government, once stigmatized, is now respectable, and those who earn their daily bread by toil and pay taxes are looked upon, in some vague way, as naïve, or even losers. One of the most socially divisive examples of the demise of the old values is the death of the "melting pot" concept. Formerly, immigrants to the U.S. were admired for learning the language, working hard, adopting American cultural norms, becoming good citizens and raising families that contributed to society. This ideal has been overcome by multiculturalism, and the ideal immigrant is one who remains in his heart a citizen of his former country and, in many cases, actively despises his adopted country.

In this environment, there can be little wonder that the Constitution of the United States is being dismantled. One thinks of the confirmation process of Supreme Court Justice Sonia Sotomayor, during the course of which she declared that the Court was badly in need of "the wisdom of a Latina woman." This was heard with little thought and less objection, but there was a time when that statement alone would have served to disqualify her. It would be understood that there was no need for the wisdom of any ethnic group; we need jurists with a knowledge of American law and an understanding of how to apply it to specific cases -- and the wisdom to put their own class and ethnic biases behind them in the process. The divisiveness that has been cultivated by the Left for decades has taken over the old values that united American society. It has become a major factor in the century-long progressive campaign to turn the Constitution into an ever-changing "living document"-- which is to say, no Constitution at all. It is ripping apart the fabric of our society. We are drifting into chaos.

At its core, the modern vision of society is one of turning from the fixed to the ephemeral. Relativity is the new social principle. Traditional ethical standards of all sorts are rejected; old ideals are scrapped in favor of the relativistic void of personal standards, which in turn can be modified or discarded at will. It can be seen in all of the examples cited above (and many more are available) that the movement is from stability to disorder, in our personal lives and in society as a whole. In fact, it is exceedingly difficult for any individual to maintain harmony and stability in his own life when exposed to a society of constantly increasing disorder. Unless we become hermits we are dragged into the vortex of chaos in the course of everyday contact with others. Those who resist are hounded by the social justice warriors who roam the halls of every American institution -- education system, legal system, workplaces of all sorts, bureaucracies, even churches. But even that is unnecessary: social pressure to conform to the modern paradigm of precipitate change is universal and inescapable.

The situation described above begs at least two vital questions, proper answers to each of which require far more space than is available in this essay. One is that, in the course of the long march of the progressive Left that left so many of the levers of power of this nation in its hands, and of its blatant power grabs over the last decade, where was a populace that is renowned for its fierce sense of independence? What happened to our self-reliant citizens when the Left was taking over so much of their public lives? Obviously, most of us were pottering about with our own careers, families and other private concerns, but that's a thin excuse. Frankly, we just weren't paying that much attention when it was happening. There is no real excuse for that sort of passive obliviousness. But the answer to the question doesn't belong in this particular essay. One that references a different fable might be more appropriate for it. Perhaps *Sleeping Beauty*.

The other question is: What is the underlying cause of all this? What is behind the onrushing chaos that threatens to overturn everything related to traditional truths and values? What is "that hideous strength" (as C.S. Lewis might say) that can reverse the meaning of such an eternally enchanting story as *Beauty and the Beast* with hardly a murmur of objection? Surely someone expects to benefit from the disruption of an established and smoothly functioning society, a society many of us lived in and enjoyed not so long ago. That is a question worth asking and answering, but the answer must be the subject of another essay. Fortunately, said essay is found in the very next chapter: *Depraved New World, Part II: New World Disorder.*

3/22/20

Chapter Seven

Depraved New World II: New World Disorder

Brave New World (1932), the dystopian novel of an imagined future by Aldous Huxley, derived its title from a line in Shakespeare's comedy *The Tempest*. The word "brave," therefore, should be taken in its broader 16th century meaning, which may include the modern sense of bold or valiant, but mainly denotes splendor. "Dazzling" might be a more accurate modern translation. Both Shakespeare and Huxley used the term "brave new world" in an ironic sense. In *The Tempest* it was spoken by a young and very naïve young woman named Miranda, who had lived almost her whole life on an isolated island, upon seeing her first group of outsiders. These were some rather rascally shipwreck survivors (well, not a real shipwreck, but read the play). In Huxley's novel it refers to the World State, essentially a world government that places the highest value upon order and none at all on individuality or creativity. In the novel, science has taken over, old traditions are dead, everyone is happy. Well, not happy, exactly, but they feel no pain. First, natural birth is out: everyone is "decanted" from a tank that has been dosed with a shot of alcohol to adjust IQ downward to the predetermined level of that individual in society. That done, everyone is naturally content with his place. The rest is taken care of by free sex and drugs. No one is dissatisfied because no one knows how to be. Perfect world order follows.

Brave New World was written in large part in response to a spate of utopian books that came out around and just after the turn of the 20th century, and more following World War I. These were descendants of a long line of utopian works, beginning in ancient Greece with Plato's *Republic*. Perhaps the most influential was Thomas More's *Utopia*, published in 1516, which gave the genre its name. Others number in the dozens, most being long forgotten (and mostly forgettable). One element essentially all of them have in common is the desire for social order above all. In fact, a major contribution of Huxley's novel is to point out that order and stability, taken beyond a certain point, have their drawbacks, primary among them a loss of individuality and creativity.

Of course, everyone likes to live in an orderly society, one that honors the rule of law and provides a measure of predictability for one's endeavors. In fact, the very purpose of the old traditions and societal values that pervaded the most prosperous and livable societies of history was to establish a degree of order. At their best, they were surprisingly (to us moderns) successful in doing so without excessively restricting the opportunities of their people to develop their own personal potential and to innovate. Yet, there has always been a countering tendency for forces within a society to enforce other measures designed to impose greater order through increased control of the populace by certain individuals or groups. Such measures include royal decree, dictatorial edict, theocratic mandate, legislative law and bureaucratic regulation. Those who issue the commands can be summed up by the term "elite." The imposed measures enacted to augment order by increasing the control of elites beyond that established by custom and tradition almost always unduly inhibit individual freedom and have a smothering effect upon creativity. This is the price levied by utopianism.

The original Progressive Movement of the late 19th and early 20th centuries was a form of utopianism purportedly based on science. The central idea was to trust government to a cadre of experts, a sort of techno-elite that would allocate labor, goods and services according to scientific principles. The object was efficiency in the use of resources as well as social order and stability. Another stated objective was to establish a system wherein the individual could attain maximum potential. Although it was not often openly acknowledged, the logical endpoint of the movement was a new world order, which itself called for centralized world government. This explains the old progressives' avid enthusiasm for the League of Nations after WWI. Among other benefits, they touted the impossibility of war with such a unified government (presumably forgetting America's own Civil War) and the ease of spreading wealth across all the peoples of the world. Everyone would be sufficiently cared for, self-actualized and happy. There would be a New World Order. In a word, Utopia.

The goal of the Founders of the United States was to form an enduring society that achieved the best of both worlds; that is, to achieve an orderly society by basing it upon the best traditional values but also provide the citizenry maximum personal freedom. The Constitution was their chosen means to attain that goal. And for well over 200 years it has been largely successful in maintaining the fragile equilibrium between stagnation and chaos, order and freedom. This was done despite a brutal internal war, periodic economic crises and, for the last century, a sustained attack from the Left upon its very existence. It has helped us to become at once powerful, stable and innovative, the first society in history to do all that at once to the degree that has been attained. The Constitution, based as it is on a principle of natural rights -- that is, rights that are independent of government and held by all citizens -- and on a rule of law that applies to all equally, has permitted us to maintain order without annihilating freedom. The Constitution also allows for change according to its own prescriptions. The pace of change so allowed is by design restrained and deliberate enough to give the people time to consider unintended consequences of the proposed changes. This, of course, is anathema to the Left, which prefers revolution. The leftist chant is, "What do we want? Change! When do we want it? Now!" And even better: "Hey, hey, ho, ho! Constitution's gotta go!" It can be difficult to counter the carefully crafted logical argumentations of the Left.

That is what the current battle over the future of the United States is about. It is a question of controlled change that maintains order but preserves both freedom and an opportunity for innovation -- or revolution and chaos. Those of the Left believe that over 230 years of the former is enough, that the cycle must continue onward and it is now time, or past time, for its revolution phase. Conservatives believe the Founders were correct, that we do best to keep to the ways of the Constitution, keep those of our old traditions and values that still serve us and keep order in society. That is why our current partisan divide is so bitter and deep. There isn't much middle space to occupy; we must choose between tradition and order, on one hand, and revolution and chaos on the other. To be fair, chaos isn't the end objective of most leftists. They seek a brave new world, and revolution is only their way to reach it. And this time the revolution won't be just any old revolution. This will be the revolution to end all revolutions, because we now have the technology to involve the entire world of humanity at once. This will be a truly global revolution.

Which brings us to the globalists, who are in one important way a different lot from any of their revolutionary predecessors. To be sure, they mostly consist of the usual suspects: academics and the youthful firebrands they have recruited, disenchanted intellectuals, starving artists, the merely confused and so on. But the real driving force this time, which is to say the money, is vested in a group of people new to the world stage: billionaires. There have been wealthy people around for millennia, since wealth is relative, but (thanks to the order and rule of law of this last cycle) never before has there been the extreme absolute opulence of the wealthiest among us today. Oddly enough, and unlike in previous times, many of our current billionaires are among those who actively support globalism in the interest of leftist revolution. The poster boy of this group is George Soros.

A great deal has been written about Soros over the last few decades and there is no need to rehash it here. Much of it, good and bad, is false or misleading; of the internet "biographies" of the man, most are whitewash and most of the rest are hatchet jobs. Fortunately, the facts for the purposes of this essay are fairly clear. His first big splash occurred in 1992, when his financial tactics helped drive the British pound to disaster. He is now unpopular in that nation among others, many of them in Eastern Europe (including his country of origin, Hungary) and southeastern Asia. Billionaires aren't especially popular anywhere, given the human tendency toward envy, but Soros' unpopularity is enhanced by his mode of making money. He speculates in currency fluctuations and profits from chaos. Where there is no actual chaos but some potential for it, he helps it along. It was this sort of currency manipulation that first brought him to public attention in 1992: his massive shorting of the British pound destroyed the savings of a good many families -- and netted Soros a billion dollars. That was technically legal, but he was convicted of insider trading (which is not) in France, a conviction that was upheld by that country's highest court. Similar activities have contributed to his unpopularity elsewhere.

Given his history, it is no surprise that Soros money, given through numerous NGOs, official charities and other front organizations, supports mass illegal immigration in the U.S. and Europe. This is documented thoroughly by Michelle Malkin in her recent book *Open Borders Inc.: Who's Funding America's Destruction*. It may be somewhat more of a surprise to discover that Mr. Soros is not an outlier among billionaires. The old days of the uptight, conservative, cigar-smoking plutocrat are far behind us, if they were ever real. It seems that a high percentage of the billionaire crowd of today is quite comfortable following Soros' lead. Not only does mass immigration, a major contributor to societal chaos today in many developed countries, receive heavy financial support from the wealthiest people, but so does any other disruptive leftist project. Global warming, the other major item on the globalist agenda, is heavily pushed by many billionaires. Both of these projects, it may be noted, are designed to break down national sovereignty and promote centralized world government. The first is a direct assault on the principle of sovereignty; the second is an attack on the economic systems of the most productive nations.

Why would the ultra-wealthy promote chaos? Again, just look at George Soros. He has prospered handsomely through social and economic chaos everywhere. When chaos strikes (naturally or with a little boost), many small investors and savers lose, but the money they lose doesn't evaporate. It disappears into the ample coffers of those who are poised to take advantage of the situation, which is generally the ultra-wealthy. Since the perception of wealth is relative, the very wealthy feel even wealthier as they survey the fallen masses beneath them. The globalism sought by most of the Left today is presented as a route to order and stability: a New World Order. No more war, its proponents proclaim, no more poverty, no more gap between wealthy and poor. The truth is precisely the reverse. As in Soviet Russia and every other socialist experiment in history, the division between elites and the masses would be greater than ever. The globalists' promise of order and stability is false: they offer chaos as well as slavery.

The destruction of established customs, values and truths is the destruction of the roots of our culture. It is a necessary predicate to our taking the path to the idealists' Brave New World -- or to the globalist monolith of the ultra-greedy. In either case, the reality will be a depraved new world, and the new world order will inevitably turn out to be the new world disorder. That is what the bitter partisan struggle for the soul of our country is about.

"They who can give up essential liberty to obtain a little temporary safety deserve neither liberty nor safety."   Benjamin Franklin

3/29/20

PART II

On Socialism

A case can be made that trying to convince someone that socialism doesn't work is a waste of time. It's not a difficult case to make, but anyone to whom it has to be made in view of all the abundant evidence available must be either willfully ignorant or a hopeless fanatic. Either way, that individual does not want to be convinced against socialism and no combination of facts and logic will change his opinion.

Nevertheless, we must try, frustrating though it may be. The whole concept of socialism may be obviously fallacious, but it is no less dangerous for that. One has only to look at the numerous socialist experiments recorded in history, and even around the world at the present time, to understand how dangerous that idea is. We cannot begin to comprehend the magnitude of human suffering it has caused in the last century alone, and its terrifying work is not yet done.

There are sundry labels that have, over time, been attached to the basic leftist scheme – progressive, collectivist, communist and so on – but for the most part I prefer to subsume them all under the name of socialism. It is appropriate to use one of the other terms when that is what is used by those to whom we refer, but socialism sums it up. Its basic feature is central planning of the economy (and ultimately everything else) by a core group of experts. Naturally, coercion of all the common people by the state in order to enforce the plan (and everything else) is an essential feature of socialism. Democracy, of sorts, can be a feature of a socialist state, but always under limitations. People may vote on all sorts of details, but not socialism itself, which, once instituted, remains until the government that is built upon it falls.

Among the articles that follow, the *Free-for-All* series addresses questions concerning why socialism cannot work even in theory. *Doing the Math* explains how the mathematical concept of chaos condemns socialism to failure no matter what is done to enhance its implementation in practice. *In Praise of Chaos* addresses the relationship between capitalism, socialism and free markets, and explains why a free market inevitably performs best in practice. The more subtle and complex issue of the morality of the contrasting systems is covered in the third part, *A Free Lunch*. Among the other articles, *Feelin' the Bern* covers the common defense of socialism that argues it will work if we just do it right. The rest of the articles discuss sundry aspects of socialism and its effects on individuals and society.

It isn't enough to rely on appeals to freedom and demonstrations of past failures when discussing socialism with either its acolytes or its enemies. Emotion is a weapon of the Left and it is not befitting to an intelligent person of the Right to resort to it. This section is devoted to providing facts and logic to counter the siren song of the mythical social paradise. Nothing else will serve in the end.

Chapter Eight

Third World, Seventh Heaven

Everyone wants to be happy. Versions of what happiness is vary from person to person, but we all want it, whatever it may be. It's even listed in the Declaration of Independence among the "certain inalienable rights" that are "endowed their Creator" upon all humans, namely "Life, Liberty and the pursuit of Happiness." You may notice that Jefferson didn't promise us happiness itself as a right, only its pursuit, no doubt in recognition of its elusiveness. The pursuit of happiness goes 'way back in the history of mankind; it was identified as desirable at least as far back as ancient Mesopotamia. Babylonian thought found its way to the idea of Seventh Heaven, a state of total contentment or extreme bliss that also relates to Judaic theology and its division of heaven into seven levels. Islam borrowed this feature as well and reserved Seventh Heaven as the abode of Allah and the angels (and presumably the most favored of human souls). Now the idea of Seventh Heaven has been incorporated into the common parlance as a state of perfect earthly happiness.

Most of us have been forced by the slings and arrows of real life into a degree of cynicism, which degree varies depending on an individual's nature and history of pains and disappointments. We realize that complete happiness, whatever we conceive it to consist of, is the stuff of dreams and not reality. We nevertheless pursue it, as is our constitutional right, or at least pursue some such reasonable facsimiles of happiness as wealth, a good spouse, lots of friends, excellent health, religious salvation or a late model Ferrari. Some of us, however, not satisfied with such personal sources of happiness, seek it on a larger scale. We seek Seventh Heaven not in dreams but here and now on the surface of planet Earth. We seek an ideal social structure, a kind of government under which all citizens live in perfect harmony, enabled to enjoy bliss in their everyday lives that other poor mortals can only achieve in dreams. We seek, in short, to immanentize Utopia.

Thinkers through the ages have pondered what the perfect society might look like. The first of these of whom we know was Plato, who around 380 B.C. described his ideal city-state in the form of a Socratic dialogue we know as the *Republic*. This has been followed by dozens of emulators, each offering his own view of the subject in the guise of a novel or other literary device, even in some cases a sort of travelogue. One of the latter, written in 1516 by Thomas More and entitled *Of a republic's best state and of the new island Utopia* (translated from Latin), gave its name to the whole genre. Strangely enough, none of the numerous utopian visions, produced over millennia by scholars of highly variable backgrounds, looks anything like the most successful real society of human history. I refer, of course, to the United States, a statement that is eminently defensible but will give rise to hysterics among the leftists of the world (mostly those of the U.S. itself).

In fact, essentially all utopias of literature, including Plato's original version, have one characteristic in common: they are dominated by socialist elements. There is much that can be made of that observation, starting with the tendency throughout history of academic types to idealize authoritarian government in principle while condemning its reality. Which is to say, in current terms, that socialism is fine as an intellectual exercise but, for reasons too complex to cover here (but which are covered in detail in the three articles of the *Free-for-All* series herein), is an unmitigated disaster in actual practice. It's a pipe dream which the mind can spin into an imaginary earthly paradise. Communists used to explicitly refer to their goal as a "workers' paradise" and only dropped the phrase after it became a standard joke. In any case, it's no accident that the utopias of literature and the socialist schemes of current politics have so much in common: socialism sounds wonderful in the abstract if it's not analyzed very closely. When an attempt is made to transition it from the dream world to reality, the dream rapidly becomes a nightmare. Perhaps that's why More chose the name for his fabled island: Utopia is made up from Greek words meaning "nowhere."

The utopian idea appeals to most of us in its dream form, where we don't have to think too hard about it. To some it appeals more strongly than as just an airy conceit with no anchor to reality. These would include rootless idealists, those without much ambition or energy and, in some cases, lonely people who lack a spouse or other human support and visualize government in that role. It might be said that people who have a strong need for security and a weak mind for analysis are most vulnerable to the socialist lure. This is all harmless enough, but unfortunately socialism also attracts some predatory characters who have an excellent appreciation for its impracticability combined with a keen eye for the main chance. By exploiting the idealists and others they seize the opportunity to gain power and wealth. They realize the impossibility of translating the utopian dream to reality but take advantage of true believers to feather their own nests. They understand how to manipulate the dream to find a fat niche at the top. Lenin spoke of "useful idiots" who allow themselves to be used by their masters. The thin veneer of the Venezuelan ruling caste lives very well indeed atop the compost heap of the useful.

The simple fact is that paradise on earth is a false dream, but the dream has its uses for power seekers. It's a common saying that socialism is contrary to human nature, and in one sense the saying is true. Certainly a strong feature of human nature, and a positive one, is the desire to better one's fortunes through work and creativity. That is generally defined as ambition. But there is a darker side to the same feature that is just as much a part of human nature, and that is unbridled greed. Greed, in its ugliest form, exists to a greater or lesser degree in all of us, and therefore in all societies. In a society with a free enterprise economy that is founded on a robust rule of law, this destructive side of the ambition-greed element is internally controlled to a great extent. If all people are forced to play by the rules, and all are competing in a climate of freedom, pure greed cannot thrive in the long run; it eats itself in the give-and-take of the marketplace. A socialist society, in contrast, is ultimately dependent on coercion. Socialism simply cannot exist without it: goods and services must be taken by force, explicit or implicit, from some to be given to others. This is an inevitable corollary of its underlying principle. The basis in force administered from the top provides the opportunity for certain energetic but unprincipled individuals who seek power and wealth for themselves to let their greed run free. Since they jostle themselves into position as the wielders of force, as they work their way to the top, and since once there they *are* the law, as it were, they can gratify their greedy proclivities without restraint.

We have been contemplating heaven and earth. Heaven, as noted above, is, according to some religions, divided into levels ascending upward in number to seven. Earth, on the other hand, is divided in common usage into stages numbered the reverse way. That is, First World nations are at the top economically (and most other ways as well, although globalists will argue with little evidence that all cultures are equal). There are only three widely recognized real-world levels, with the Third World at the bottom. Actually, since the Third World is said to consist of "developing" nations a case can be made for a Fourth World made up of Haiti, Bangladesh, some African nations and maybe a few others, but coming in third in tragic enough. It's a remarkable fact that the freest countries, economically and otherwise, tend to find themselves toward the top of this order, with the Third World nations dominated by authoritarian regimes. It would appear that there is a pretty firm correlation between how free a society is and how prosperous it is. Tyranny, in whatever form, has not worked out well for the citizenry.

One may argue that communist China, an authoritarian state by any measure, has attained First World status, which disproves the foregoing observation. In reply, I would point out that a single exception only proves the rule, and anyway China only achieved economic growth in proportion to how far it was able to disjoin its relatively free economy from its tyrannical political regime. The fact is that the Chinese economy under the burden of Mao's despotism was miserable despite the proven tremendous potential of the nation. There have been other unique factors in China's economic rise as well, primarily the help (much of it involuntary) of the United States over the decades since Mao's death. It was President Trump's attempts to level the playing field between China and the U.S. that led to the former's contributions to the successful coup against him. Finally, the game isn't over; there are basic weaknesses in China's economic and industrial structure that may yet have a decisive effect. So China is in several respects an outlier in the economic-political regression analysis being considered here. A far more pertinent example for this purpose is Venezuela.

As recently as the turn of the millennium Venezuela was one of the richest countries in the Western Hemisphere. Its wealth was based in large part on huge oil reserves, but it is also blessed with a good climate, ample agricultural resources and an industrious and well-educated population. There was an excess of political corruption, but the population enjoyed a high level of economic and political freedom. Much was being done right. Significantly, the nation's oil wealth was in good hands. PDVSA was a model for national oil companies, well run and professionally staffed, and operating on excellent terms with its international partners. Then, in 1999, dissatisfaction with governmental corruption led to the election of a socialist president who made big promises to crack down on the malefactors. Unfortunately but predictably, he cracked down on everything but corruption, and within a decade the country was in serious trouble. Free elections became a thing of the past, also predictable for a leftist regime, and upon the socialist dictator's death he was followed by more of the same. Now the nation is a wreck, one of the world's basket cases, despite its oil and other advantages. Socialism was a one-way ticket to the Third World.

So it goes. Seventh Heaven is doubtless a great place to be, but dreams of paradise here on earth are far more likely to lead to a Third World hell. Workers' paradise achieved through bloody struggle doesn't ever work out too well. Somehow, we never seem to make it through the struggle part to reach the paradise. Invariably, we find ourselves in a worse situation than the one we escaped. Starting with a traditional First World society, the path to socialist paradise is clearly delineated. Personal rights are the first to go, thus the socialists' disdain for any constitution that protects them. Individuals are therefore subsumed into groups based on race, sex, ethnicity or whatever, and so forced to rely on group identity for protection and preference. These groups then struggle against a supposed common oppressor group and, ultimately, among themselves for dominance. Such balkanization of a society is hardly conducive to prosperity, and it descends to chaos and despair. The socialist dream of Seventh Heaven never becomes reality. If we follow the lure of the dream we will awaken to find ourselves in a Third World nightmare.

It is better that we give up dreaming of Seventh Heaven and satisfy ourselves with living in a dull old First World nation. We can tweak it here and there to make it better. We can work to minimize government corruption, poverty and crime. We can strive to eliminate disadvantages imposed on fellow citizens by unfair and unreasonable forms of discrimination. We can improve our health system and broaden its benefits. We can do many good works gradually and unspectacularly and avoid violence and revolution in the process. But most of all, we can appreciate the enhanced lives we enjoy in a stable First World society. Our earthly lot may be boring compared to Seventh Heaven dreams, but a bit of prosperous boredom surely beats Third World tumult and misery.

12/25/20

Chapter Nine

Free-for-All I: Doing the Math

It is always tedious to try to explain to someone that socialism doesn't work. Not because it's difficult to do -- the examples of socialism not working are abundant and tragic, and those that show otherwise few and fleeting -- but because it must be done at all. No one could seriously believe socialism to be a viable economic system in view of all evidence to the contrary unless he really, really wants it to be. And if he wants socialism to be a workable system that badly, trying to convince him otherwise, simply using evidence of which he's already aware, is … well, tedious. And almost certainly unproductive as well.

The reason for the attraction of socialism for many otherwise intelligent people is that it is the quintessential *clair idee fausse*. It really should work, when you consider it in an intellectual vacuum. It sounds very virtuous, very straightforward, very orderly. It sounds as though the only reason it hasn't worked in the past is that it has never been done right. In other words, the problem with socialism must not be with socialism at all, but with the people who mess it up in actual practice. If we could straighten out the people, we'd have a perfect system for an ideal society. Right?

Thanks to that shallow spin that poses as thinking in our academic institutions, the word "socialism" has become quite popular again in certain segments of our society. One recalls the famous quote attributed to George Orwell: "Some ideas are so stupid that only an intellectual could believe them." A problem is that Orwell thought himself a socialist, at least at times. His comment was directed mainly at communists. So what's the difference? What separates, or binds, these various leftist ideologies?

My own thinking is that the leftists themselves know who they are and we should listen to them. The post-WWI country that covered much of Europe and Asia was universally accepted, by itself and everyone else, as a communist state. It called itself the Union of Soviet Socialist Republics. Did its people not know the difference between communist and socialist? Nazi Germany is now touted by the Left as the epitome of a right-wing regime. Its full name was the National Socialist German Workers' Party. Did they not know what a socialist was either? When you read it over, does that name sound like it represents a bunch of conservative crazies to you?

In fact, I don't care what the leftist groupings call themselves or what obscure criteria divide them from one another. They are progressives, liberals, socialists, communists, whatever -- for simplicity's sake, let's just call them all socialists for now. The only fact that matters in this particular conversation is the one feature that binds them: centralized planning. That is the single factor common to all, whatever the current popular name.

Planning is a word that sounds just fine: decisions of great difficulty concerning arcane and complex phenomena are made by those who know most about the subject. They are made by the experts, not the *hoi polloi* who can hardly count, much less solve a differential equation. What's not to like about that? Well, there's nothing not to like about it in the abstract, which is what makes the whole argument for socialism (and all its siblings) sound so reasonable. It's what makes the argument specious -- that is, false but deceptive, and convincing for those willing to be deceived.

So here we are with an economic and political system that looks like it should work but doesn't. Its proponents preen themselves for being enlightened in every way. They congratulate one another for their escape from the chains of ignorance and superstition, for their reliance on science to solve society's problems and for the mathematical pragmatism of their methodologies. The only regret they have for not believing in God is that there's no one but themselves to thank for being so amazingly superior to the deplorables. Are they right? Is there no convincing theoretical basis to challenge the Left's claim to ownership of science? I have good news: there is. It is only necessary to do the math.

Chaos theory is a latecomer to the panoply of mathematical concepts. It was only in 1963 that Edward Norton Lorenz, now called by many the father of chaos theory, published a paper entitled "Deterministic Nonperiodic Flow," that laid chaos theory out in the form of a series of simple (for a mathematician) equations. Several other papers by Lorenz followed, notably, in 1972, by one that could be understood by normal humans: "Predictability: Does the Flap of a Butterfly's Wings in Brazil Set off a Tornado in Texas?" The title was a deliberate exaggeration, but perhaps not much of one. Let us briefly examine the nature of the theory.

Lorenz came upon his theory by an interesting route. He was an Ivy League-educated mathematician who was assigned to a weather prediction job in the WWII army. He became so interested in meteorology that he got his M.S. and Ph.D. degrees in that subject after the war at MIT and stayed on at the university in that department. In the course of his work, in the early '60s, he noticed that weather predictions, no matter how carefully or confidently made, were surprisingly inaccurate beyond about a week into the future. This led him to chaos theory.

The first thing to know about chaos is that, in mathematics, the word has a different shade of meaning than in general usage. It does not refer to riots and violence, but rather to uncertainty. Basically, it states that sensitive dependence on initial conditions in a nonlinear deterministic system means that a small variance in one state can result in very large variances in a later state. To put it into more commonplace terms, when you input variables into your computer program (e.g., for weather prediction), if there is a very minor variation between what you input and what exists, or if some very tiny detail is unaccounted for, down the road in time there will be a deviance from your prediction that could be profound. In highly complex systems, such as one deals with concerning weather, it is virtually impossible to account for every tiny factor. Thus the little line about Brazilian butterfly wings and Texas tornados.

Lorenz was a pioneer of chaos theory, but he wasn't its only parent and meteorology isn't the only discipline to which it has been applied. In practice, just about any complex, nonlinear system that is sensitive to its initial conditions is subject to the chaos effect. That means almost anything one can think of that involves large numbers of human beings, including economic systems. When one thinks about it, chaos theory, stripped of its mathematical trappings, is entirely intuitive: small causes may produce large effects over time, and tiny differences in initial conditions may create a very different outcome from one predicted by the most ambitious computer program.

Although meteorology is a natural system and economics is a human construct, the two are similar in their nonlinearity and extraordinary complexity. The economic system of any modern nation involves many billions of decisions every day at every level, from how many quarts of milk from which dairy to order for a mom-and-pop convenience store to how many aircraft from which manufacturer to order for a major carrier. Central planners can approximate many of the mega-inputs for their predictive programs but cannot begin to account for all the initial conditions that, according to chaos theory, may result in major variances over a few days, weeks or months. It isn't difficult to understand why the various Soviet Five-Year Plans went awry. Things won't get much better with the most powerful computers, given chaos theory. There are simply too many variables that can skew the results of the most sophisticated predictions.

Let us summarize what we have so far. All societies that follow leftist principles, which are herein placed under the socialist label for simplicity, base their economic systems on central planning. Central planning, in whatever form it takes, is in turn based upon prediction. The predictability of a nonlinear system of great complexity (which is what the national economy of a developed nation is) is subject to the limitations of chaos theory. According to chaos theory, there will inevitably be large and increasing variances between predicted results and reality as time passes. Without reasonable predictability, central planning will fail and the economy will suffer.

Not much work has yet been done by chaos mathematicians specifically on economic systems, so it isn't feasible at this point to calculate with mathematical accuracy how far out time-wise one must go before an economic plan at the national level will collapse entirely. What real-life examples we have indicate that it isn't far -- certainly well within a small fraction of the five years favored by the Russian communists. As indicated by history, problems will show up within a few weeks and only get much worse with time. Chaos theory tells us that predictability won't be helped even by highly sophisticated computer programs -- the variances are inherent. The bottom line is that no matter how expert the experts who do the planning are, and no matter how powerful and elegant the computer programs they use, central planning of an economy on any meaningful scale is doomed by mathematics. Since planning is the economic basis for socialist economies, it is unrealistic to expect those economies to succeed. If the economy of a country fails, the country itself is headed for a train wreck. Simple math.

It is good for an advocate of human freedom to be able to point out so many examples of the failure of socialism and the success of free enterprise. It is better for the advocate to be able to elucidate the mathematical basis for this disparity. That is to say, from a scientific point of view, the identification of a phenomenon should be the first step in the discovery of why said phenomenon exists. In this case, the greatest satisfaction (for those who take satisfaction in such things) may be to show those who boast of their reliance on science for their political choices that science may not be on their side after all.

P.S.: The description of chaos theory given here is necessarily sketchy, to say the least. I would encourage those whose interest in the theory may have been kindled, including non-mathematicians, to read a book written by James Gliek over thirty years ago, entitled *Chaos: Making New Science* (1987). Much work has been done on chaos theory since, but that book is still a good place for the non-specialist to start.

12/3/19

Chapter Ten

Free-for-All II: In Praise of Chaos

There is chaos and there is chaos. Mathematical chaos, the absence of predictability, makes central planning impractical and therefore dooms socialism as a successful basis for a national economy. Chaos in the more general meaning of the word, which is mass confusion of some sort, may, on the other hand, be the salvation of national economies. The first part of that enigma was explained in Chapter 9, *Doing the Math*. This one will address the second half.

The question is, if socialism by its very nature cannot be successful, where do we go for success? A common answer would be capitalism. That is not really an alternative, however, because capitalism, in its most general meaning, can be a comfortable partner of socialism. Nazi Germany, a socialist state by any measure, stood fast in total war against most of the world for years, despite socialism's deficiencies, because of its embrace of capitalism as well. One might look to modern China for another example. What capitalism requires is a respect, even if limited, by government for property rights. The catch is that those property rights are held, under a socialist government, conditionally and by selected individuals and enterprises, not indefinitely and by all citizens. Perhaps socialism's recognition of limited property rights constitutes its only real difference from pure communism.

Capitalism is therefore a tool, not an ideology. One may even say it is something of an economic prostitute, ready to adapt itself to any system that wishes to use it. It is indispensable to free enterprise in a healthy polity; that is, one with minimum governmental involvement with the economy. Both require respect, on the record, for property rights, but free enterprise extends that respect as nearly universally as possible, and requires social freedom as well. Still, although they are mutually supportive, capitalism and free enterprise are not the same thing.

Free enterprise and freedom are like lungs and oxygen. The former cannot function without the latter, and function less well the more the latter is restricted. Most people agree that a certain modest degree of government regulation, judiciously applied, is beneficial even though it may hold back, slightly, the vigor of an economy of unrestrained free enterprise. The trade-off of some regulation in exchange for a bit of growth is considered worth it in order to cut down on fraud, deception and outright criminal activity. But in reality, the prevention of that sort of thing is what the law in general is for, and enforcement of the law on businesses as on individuals should suffice. Excess regulation and other forms of government intervention focused on businesses alone are killers of economic growth. In essence, regulation is a milder form of centralized planning, and the results are similar to those of the notorious five-year plans, if correspondingly less dire. One has only to look at the first year and a half of the Trump administration, marked by exuberant economic improvement that can only be attributed to a rollback of the onerous over-regulation of the previous eight years.

It must be emphasized that free enterprise, in the context in which it is treated here, does not mean ruthless, robber baron-style plundering. Enterprise is not free if it is unmoored to the rule of law and, preferably, to a general respect for basic ethical standards by society as a whole. Free enterprise therefore prospers best in a culture that has developed these traits; in the stony ground of societies that have long suffered under despotic regimes, where a dog-eat-dog mentality still rules among the populace, enterprise may be unshackled but it is not really free. That is where capitalism takes a different course from free enterprise. True free enterprise is open to any energetic soul who respects the law and his fellow man. It is free for all -- all who are willing to play reasonably fair.

Why has free enterprise been so consistently advantageous for national economies? The answer is easy: chaos. Chaos, that is, in the common meaning of absence of imposed order, not the mathematical chaos of lack of predictability. As noted above, absence of imposed order does not imply the absence of any order at all: a clear framework of law must be present and there must be general adherence to those laws, preferably willing but always enforced. However, the extreme complexity of a large economic system and the absence of comprehensive planning superimposed by a third party (i.e., government) gives the whole system the distinct look and feel of pure and simple chaos. And that's a wonderful phenomenon.

The reason free enterprise works so well in the right environment is sheer numbers. Where centralized planning is in place, perhaps a dozen people make the critical decisions for a whole country (they have hundreds of technicians and advisers, of course, but I speak of actual decision makers). They may be the very best people in the entire country (well, probably not, but it wouldn't matter), but they are by definition few. In a pure free enterprise system there are millions of businesses, large and small, and therefore millions of decision makers. If each one of these micro-decision makers makes just ten decisions per day, many billions of micro-decisions will be made each year. No one is making macro-decisions that cover entire industries, but macro-decisions are resulting from the process. One might say the macro-decisions are being made by chaos itself.

The relatively few decision makers in a centrally planned economy produce the macro-decisions remotely and well in advance of actual events. That is difficult enough, but we know from chaos theory that no matter how competent, even brilliant, the planners may be, no matter how excellent their algorithms and powerful their computers, the predictions upon which their plans are based will go wildly askew in the course of the first month or two. The plans will be obsolete by about the time they are put into effect. The economy that tries to follow those plans will founder. We who keep an eye on history already knew that, but chaos theory tells us why it happens, and that it is theoretically (as well as practically) inevitable.

The micro-decisions made by the billions in a free market, on the other hand, are certainly not all brilliant, and may not be especially impressive even on average. However, each one is made on the spot to solve a very limited problem by someone who has "skin in the game." The individual decisions may be trivial in terms of an entire national economy, but they are very important in a personal way to their makers. Even better, many of these decisions are made daily, and even the longer-term micro-decisions can in many cases be modified as events unfold. That gives the chaos-made macro-decisions of free enterprise powerful flexibility. The macro-decisions of central planners, in contrast, are pretty well set in concrete. Changing them to suit unforeseen contingencies down the road is like trying to turn a supertanker in a canal. In addition, the micro-decisions are self-correcting in a more permanent way: the worst of them, or unluckiest, lead directly to the removal of the business from the market altogether. There is an element of survival of the fittest involved.

In that regard, the efficiency of chaos in the making of macro-decisions in the economy has long been established. Among the millions or billions of micro-decisions made daily are those that recognize new technologies and changing times. Somewhere shortly after the turn of the 20th century, for example, small-scale buggy makers (of which there were examples in about every state and most towns of any size) saw some horseless carriages roll past their shops and decided to start making something else instead. If our economy had been controlled by central planners, who are far more sensitive to political pressures, there might still be a few buggy makers around to compete with the government factory that's still churning out Ladas (for one of which you might have to wait six years and bring more money than it's worth).

Speaking of which, the fact is that from a political standpoint the very strengths of free enterprise comprise a major weakness. The ferment of constant decisions and their consequences, the loss of failed businesses and obsolete industries, even chaos itself, are sources of discomfort to many. But we are not discussing the political or moral ramifications of socialism and free enterprise here; that awaits the next article in this series. When the actual economic effects of the two opposed systems are considered the conclusion is clear. Socialism simply does not, and cannot, be successful in the long term, nor in the short without both capitalism and coercion. Free enterprise is well suited to a complex national economy and leads to sustained high standards of living for the populace as a whole, although there are always those individuals who do not reach the overall standard. After all, by definition half of all the people in the country will make a living below the average, regardless of the system. The point is that under free enterprise that average is far higher than under any collectivist system.

Finally, there is a little more math. There is an interesting explanation of the above phenomena in the branch of mathematics known as statistics. Unlike chaos theory, statistics is a very old discipline, originating from the study of probability. Its most common application today in industry and elsewhere is to determine the minimum number of samples necessary to determine a defined result within a given degree of certainty. For example, how many widgets need to be pulled from an assembly line for testing in order to establish the percentage of defectives with a 99% level of confidence? Similar statistical models are designed in a political pollster's efforts to figure out who is ahead in an election campaign (so far, I might add, with less than stellar results). There are statistical models available for a wide spectrum of circumstances, from a Poisson distribution in cases where only a few samples are available, to the classic Student's "T" test to distinguish between two populations, to intricate models for specialized industrial applications.

One element common to all statistical models is the so-called "n" value, the number of samples needed or available. Two factors influence this number: the quality of the samples and their total number. Intuitively, it is evident that the more representative each sample is of the whole population, the fewer are needed to give an accurate result. Similarly, the greater number of samples, the less attention need be paid to their representative values. The analogy to our comparison of centrally planned and free enterprise systems is obvious. The few central planners are expected to be very bright and well-educated economists, so perhaps fewer are needed to fill the bill. But a few dozen in a population of hundreds of millions? The micro-planners in a free enterprise economy, on the other hand, are so overwhelming in number that, from a statistical point of view, their macro effect should be spot on.

That analogy may actually be overly favorable to central planning, because even though the few planners are possessed of advanced degrees and can speak impressively and in opaque jargon about all manner of arcane economic subjects, it is doubtful that any of them could run the Italian grocery on the corner as well as the Italian himself. The grocer may know little of economic theory, but he knows vegetables and he knows what's best for his little shop. The same can be said of the bicycle repair shop, the barber shop and General Motors (well, maybe not the latter...). All of these businesses (even GM) focus on their own issues like lasers in a way a central planner could never dream of, and the planner is in any case theoretically limited by chaos theory. So are all businessmen, one might reply, but many of their decisions are made day-to-day anyway, where chaos rules but chaos theory does not. And their longer-term decisions can in many cases be altered easily enough when chaos theory kicks in. When they do make an unfortunate big decision, they might have to shut down and do something else: painful and fatal to the business, but only painful to the person.

It must be hard for those who boast that they reject the traditional and embrace science and free thinking to accept that science has turned its back on their fondest beliefs and they are themselves acolytes of failed and obsolete gods. It must be, but apparently it isn't. Socialists, progressives, communists, all the members of the Left seem capable of ignoring science and mathematics while praising them, and of going along their old intellectual paths without giving the facts much thought. If directly presented with arguments such as those above, they reject them without reflection and immediately abandon all pretense of science to seize the moral high ground instead. They claim to defend the downtrodden and accuse us deplorables of forsaking the poor and minorities for mere filthy lucre and cold, soulless numbers. They generally end up calling us racists. Therefore, to add balance to this discussion, the third and final chapter in the Free-for-All series will be devoted to the subject of morality and human values. It shouldn't be necessary, but I suppose it is.

12/10/19

Chapter Eleven

Free-for-All III: A Free Lunch

In 1972, shortly before his death, Saul Alinsky gave a long interview to *Playboy* magazine. It is still often quoted, since it effectively summarizes the life of the man who founded the profession of community organizer and whose writings remain a cornerstone of radical leftist operational doctrine to this day. Alinsky attained a god-like stature in the pantheon of the radical Left in his lifetime and has been closely studied ever since by such as Barack Obama (who was a true acolyte) and Hillary Clinton. And no wonder: the man's accomplishments in organizational campaigns of the previously unempowered were beyond impressive and his books still constitute a leftist bible for his successors.

The *Playboy* interview was lengthy enough to cover much of Alinsky's personal life and history as well as his professional career. He was remarkably candid throughout, almost as though he sensed the end approaching, and his life stories provide some striking views of his character. One anecdote, in particular, is revealing. Alinsky had graduated from the University of Chicago not long after the onset of the Depression and was still hanging around there, cashless and doing odd jobs to pay the rent. One day he was sitting in a cheap cafeteria having coffee when an idea struck him for a simple scam. One paid the bill by taking the check to a cashier, so he claimed he'd lost the check for his coffee, paid the nickel for it and took the check to another cafeteria in the same chain. There he bought a full meal, paid for it with the nickel check for coffee he had pocketed and threw away the check for the meal. He invited others to join the scam, and soon had a following that operated all over town, wherever the chain had cafeterias. As he said all those years later, "We got the system down to a science, and for six months all of us were eating free."

Of course, they were not eating free. As the old aphorism goes, there's no such thing as a free lunch. The lunch he didn't pay for came out of others' pockets, in the long run those of all the working class patrons of the cafeteria chain. What is interesting is that forty years later, at the end of an active life, he still didn't seem to recognize that simple fact, or care to. One thing Alinsky never lacked was ego, and he considered his scam to be brilliant. It really wasn't particularly brilliant at all; it was merely dishonest. But it was typically leftist in its refusal to examine the real effects of the action. There truly is no such thing as a free lunch; it is only a question of who pays for it. If the person who consumes it does not, a person who did not eat must. Listen to any socialist anywhere and you will hear the same thing: a refusal to worry about how to pay for a good idea.

In the first two articles of this series we reviewed the mathematics and the facts of the free enterprise versus socialism debate. Add in the actual history of national economic systems over the past century or so and free enterprise comes out a clear winner, at least if economic well-being is weighted heavily in a quality of life comparison. It is at this point that the socialist retreats to the high ground of moralism and security. He begins to speak of equality of result (never opportunity) and a good life for everyone, even those who are less successful in worldly pursuits. He glows with a sense of his own virtue as he extols the social justice of leftist ideals. Let us be honest about it: socialism does sound good when seen from that perspective. So let us take the debate to the socialists' own ground and examine its moral dimensions.

First, Saul Alinsky's story from the *Playboy* interview speaks for itself. He was proud of his act and considered it his first step in developing the art of community organization. But it was an act of thievery. He and his followers stole from the company that owned the cafeterias. He stole from the shareholders, and from the working folk of modest means who ate in the cafeterias and paid for their food with their hard-earned cash. One of two things had to happen if the scam had continued indefinitely: the prices would have to be increased for all who were honest, or the chain would go out of business. In the latter case, everyone from the company officers and employees to the patrons would be damaged to a greater or lesser degree. Even the scammers would lose in the end: they would go from free lunch to no lunch. The next place they would be forced to patronize would likely be one they couldn't afford.

Alinsky gave another quote about the same caper: "There's a priority of rights, and the right to eat takes precedence over the right to make a profit." Two precepts of progressivism lurk in this one short sentence: the proliferation of lesser rights and the subjugation of individual property rights. It seems that any idea approved by socialists becomes a right, many of them at the expense of what the Founders considered natural, or God-given, rights. Natural rights are immutable and permanent, whereas the rights raised up by progressives are conferred by a beneficent government, and can therefore be taken away arbitrarily by the same. Eating is certainly a good idea and to be recommended to everyone. I would go so far as to say that all of us should help feed our needy neighbors who are down on their luck and without resources.

But a "right" to eat? There is an essential difference between rights to be left alone (sometimes known as "negative rights") and a right to demand a good or service from someone else ("positive rights"). The natural rights protected in the U.S. Constitution are of the former kind and serve to protect the individual from his government. Those beloved of socialists and promulgated by them as occasion arises are of the latter sort and serve to bind the individual to the government. It is the severance of natural rights from governmental authority that socialists find repulsive. They don't want people to be independent and protected from government; they want them to be beholden to it. And the right of individuals to be secure in their property and have a clearly delineated right to it is fundamental to both constitutional law and to free enterprise -- and therefore lower in the "priority of rights" of the socialists.

Given the above, it is hardly surprising that the socialist Saul Alinsky placed the "right to eat" above property rights. Property rights and the laws that record and enforce them are a cornerstone of individual liberty. The Founders of this country proclaimed and reiterated that precept most forcefully, in the structure of the Constitution and in their other writings. It is a prominent feature of the Federalist Papers and one of the basic features of the American polity that all of them -- Madison, Adams, Franklin, Jefferson, Hamilton and the rest -- could agree upon. The strong and universal protection of property rights is, to repeat, essential to the freedom of the individual citizens of this nation.

But socialists are pretty ambiguous about individual freedom. In fact, all in all, they don't really like the idea very much. They are far more taken with the idea of collective improvement of the group than of maximization of the liberty of an individual within that group. If an individual isn't especially anxious to be improved in accordance with the current prescriptions of his socialist leaders, he must be improved anyway, for his own good and that of society. Coercion is outwardly decried by many well-meaning progressives, but it is a vital tool for the implementation of socialist programs. Socialism simply cannot exist without coercion of individuals, and coercion outside the bounds delineated by such philosophers as John Stuart Mill and Adam Smith is inimical to liberty. Therefore, individual freedom and socialism are mutually incompatible. There is no way around that fact.

This returns us to the subject of which economic system, socialism or free enterprise, is superior in terms of morality. It must be conceded that the strength of free enterprise, which is the controlled and focused chaos that gives it direction and flexibility, is also its primary weakness from a public relations point of view. Socialists point to the people whose businesses fail in the free-for-all and those whose jobs are lost, and laud the perceived personal security of their system. There's no question that some companies, for reasons of incompetence or reasons beyond control of the managers, go out of business and lay off their people. Other businesses spring up to take their places. It is that very ferment and turmoil that keeps the free economy buoyant, but it can be hard for an individual, at least for a while. On the other hand, one can look for a handy alternative in government work, which is nothing if not stable. It is also nothing if not inefficient, dull and (for most) unsatisfying.

The fact is that there are winners and losers in every economic system. With free enterprise the criteria for success are set by the market, and include efficiency, innovation and execution. In a centralized planning system, the criteria are set by government and are arbitrary, political and opaque. Both systems can include an unfortunate dose of nepotism, bribery and cronyism, but somehow in a government-run economy these tend to be more prominent. Both, of course, also involve a certain degree of luck, but in a free market that factor tends to cancel out in the long run and is always more transparent than the manipulated "luck" of a centrally planned economy.

For many people, the chaos of free enterprise, however efficient in the big picture, is vexing. They would prefer stability at the price of lack of freedom and fulfillment. Others enjoy the excitement and opportunity that go with freedom. However, no system lacks risk. The risks of a free market are open and calculable; a businessman surveys the market, calculates the chances and ponies up the stake. The risks of socialism, on the other hand, are less visible but just as real; its celebrated security is deceptive and ephemeral. Political risks have an arbitrary quality about them, and when the whole economy falls to tatters, security of any sort is no more. Benjamin Franklin wrote that those who would trade freedom for safety deserve neither. He could have added that they will receive neither.

In the end, most of us prefer solid individual property rights to government promises and prefer a government that fulfills its constitutional duty to protect those property rights to one that binds us with gifts that are coerced from fellow citizens. Is it immoral to wish to be free? As far as the inevitable casualties of free enterprise, every civilized society that has embarked upon a free economy has provided a safety net for temporary victims of free-for-all chaos. Some nets have been deeper and broader than others, as is the case with Sweden, and the protective net has been confused with socialism. Sweden is often proclaimed by socialists as an example (the only one?) of success of their system, but it is a mendacious claim. Sweden has always had a free enterprise system, and over the last couple of decades, as their safety net has proven too extensive, they have backed off it somewhat. But the country is and has been one of freedom, and they shouldn't be saddled with the socialist label for merely trying to be more compassionate toward the current losers in the system.

To summarize, math, facts and history take us to the conclusion that property rights are fundamental to economic freedom, economic freedom means free enterprise and free enterprise leads to prosperity. Property rights-based free enterprise also maximizes the potential for individual liberty, political as well as economic, which most of us view as a good thing. It is also, despite the chaos, eminently moral. There is inherent immorality in socialism, which takes away both freedom and prosperity in order to force people to conform to the vision of improvement of an elite class. That vision, according to the socialists' own philosophy, changes with the times, and in retrospect, the current vision isn't always (or often) savory.

The original progressives of the first half of the 20th century had to change their name to "liberal" because of the promotion of such improvements as eugenics. Margaret Sanger, founder of Planned Parenthood, was a pioneer in that field, but many of her fellow progressives supported it. There has been a rather desperate attempt on the Left to rehabilitate her name by claiming she didn't really mean it, but in reality eugenics, which seeks to improve the human gene pool, is entirely agreeable to the overall progressive mission. The American version employed enforced sterilization rather than the genocidal proclivities of their spiritual cousins in Nazi Germany, and for that I suppose should be given due credit. Most of us, however, are not impressed with the high moral imperative of eugenics in any form. Nor should we be impressed with the morality of socialism in general, with or without eugenics and some of its other social remedies.

That socialism is undeserving of the moral high ground its acolytes love to claim removes its last defense. More significant to the people it purports to help is the fact, demonstrable in theory and practice, that its system is at the root unsustainable. There is nothing moral about plunging entire populations into poverty, as most recently with Venezuela, nor is there any practical value in doing so. By this time, the double meaning of the title to this series, Free-for-All, should be clear to the reader. On the free enterprise side, it refers to the jubilant chaos of open competition and change. As to socialism ... well, the meaning is all too obvious. Nothing about a real-life economy is free, lunch included. Look to Russia, Cambodia, Venezuela and so many others to understand socialism's promise of "free for all." The truth is that, as with Alinsky's scam, a free lunch is a very short step to no lunch.

12/16/19

Chapter Twelve

Feelin' the Bern

Nothing is more puzzling to the rational deplorable than the recrudescence of socialism as a political movement. Only a few years ago it was an historical artifact, dead and buried, safely entombed in the proverbial dustbin. Nothing much has happened since then to affect one's opinion of it, unless one wishes to add the implosion of Venezuela to the tragic litany of socialism's failures, and that would hardly serve to revive its reputation. Socialism, which to my mind subsumes communism, fascism and other leftist nostrums, especially in their more extreme forms, lived only in the hearts of a few harmless academicians and other retro-dabblers. That was a few years ago.

Fast forward to the present: in some quasi-intellectual circles, socialism is almost respectable. For the most part it isn't entirely respectable, and if it were it wouldn't be as popular. It's still just disreputable enough to be cool. It has some of the "radical chic" that made anarchistic random violence (as in Weathermen, Symbionese Liberation Army and so on) attractive a half century ago to the sort of people who like to be perceived as intellectually daring. But although that is doubtless an element in socialism's revival, it can't entirely explain why avowed socialists are actually being elected and are presenting some of their bizarre notions as serious proposals for public policy. And more to the point, why those proposals are apparently being taken seriously by a small but significant percentage of the population (including some who are campaigning for the highest office in the land). Obviously, something else is working in favor of this odd political aberration.

A recent remark from the unlikely leader of the current socialist charge, the doughty septuagenarian from Vermont, Senator Bernard Sanders, gives a strong hint as to the answer. When Bernie finally deigned to address the example of Venezuela, currently touted by sensible observers as an embarrassing (for those capable of embarrassment) reverse-poster child for socialism, he commented without embellishment that Venezuela isn't socialist. That was it: case closed. Only successful economies, apparently, qualify as socialist for Bernie, regardless of what they consider themselves to be. And since there are no successful economies that are truly socialist, and never have been (no, Sweden is not socialist), we are dealing with a blank slate.

A blank slate is in fact the key to the question of socialist popularity. We must hearken back to the time of that first flush of socialist respectability in the West, the first three decades of the 20th century. Starting with the Fabian Society, which flourished in England from the 1880s, intellectuals in the West became fascinated with the ideas of the European philosophers Rousseau, Hegel and Marx. These ideas, now classified as historicism and scientism, were presented as the basis of modern utopias, ideal societies guided by gifted experts trained for the administration of complex and technologically advanced cultures. Such administration was to feature detailed central planning of all facets of life, especially the economy. Readers of the "Free-for-All" chapters, above, know my opinion of the practical and moral value of central planning and utopia.

But the intellectuals of the early 20th century had an excuse: there were no real-world examples of socialist societies against which to evaluate these utopian ideas. The Soviet Union came into existence just after World War I, but the results of its communist experiment were not yet understood. Problems could be attributed to growing pains, and the real atrocities, such as the Ukrainian genocide initiated by Josef Stalin, were covered up rather than revealed by the media (do an internet search of Walter Duranty). The German National Socialists and Italian Fascists rose later in the period and were actually lauded by many intellectuals for economic achievements and held up as proof of the value of the socialist model. The fact is, there simply wasn't much real information out there to enable an honest intellectual to evaluate the effectiveness of socialism as the basis for a national economy.

On the other hand, everyone was familiar with the free market; it was all around them. It had given them the highest standard of living in the history of the world and they saw it, warts and all, on a daily basis. And there were warts, as there always are with any human endeavor. There was poverty. It was relative, since even the impoverished lived better than their ancestors, but there were some people who lived much less well than others. There was pollution from the same industrialization that gave people jobs. There was shady dealing and corruption in high places. There was chaos, that bred fear in the timid among us, the same chaos that led to growth for the whole economy. These, and other results of a free market, are warts. And warts are what you notice. If you met, at a party, Helen of Troy, the most beautiful woman in the history of the world, and she had a wart on her nose, what would catch your attention first?

So the progressives of that first third of the century had an advantage. They could compare a real-world free market economy, focusing on the warts, to a dream. They described their ideal socialist state in the pristine form of pure theory and set it against a genuine and known system that, for all its glories, had the usual share of human deficiencies. The intellectuals of the time, whose mental state tended toward the visionary mode as a matter of course, were easily seduced. Even as hard-headed an intellectual as George Orwell was attracted to the socialist utopia. It was inevitable.

Nowhere in the strange interlude between the world wars were intellectuals more radical than in Paris. The radicalism continued unabated into the post-war generation. France was master of most of Indochina, including the ancient land of Cambodia, until Japan conquered it in 1940. After WWII, the region returned to the colonial administration of France, although more tenuously. Thus it was that, in 1949, a contingent of 21 young Cambodians from the upper class went to Paris for advanced studies at the university level. Among them was a rather marginal student named Saloth Sar. Many of them were concerned about the political status of their native Cambodia, especially its prospects for independence from French hegemony. They were unsophisticated in the ways of the West and knew little about its philosophies. Young Sar came to Paris to study radio engineering but soon fell under the spell of French intellectuals.

Others in the group of Cambodian students lived with Saloth Sar in the Latin Quarter, then a hotbed of student radicalism, and formed close friendships with one another. They also formed an association with native communist activists and found leftist political theory quite compatible with their dreams for the future of Cambodia. Influenced by the intellectuals of the Sorbonne and other institutions, they joined the French Communist Party and, without intellectual defenses against it, bought into its dogma uncritically. Most of them took revolutionary names to match their new political religion. Saloth Sar is thus better known to history as Pol Pot.

Pol Pot was never a successful scholar and did not learn French well, much less engineering. Distraction by politics took its toll on a student already challenged by his studies, and he eventually lost his scholarship and had to return to Cambodia uncredentialed. His radicalized companions, some with their degrees and some without, drifted back over the following months as well. They found their country in the midst of change. When they'd left, four years previously, it was already in turmoil. France was still in charge, but in reality the French had little concern for Cambodia. The linchpin of the French Union of Indochina was Vietnam, and they had their hands full with that country. There was no stomach for another conflict in Cambodia. France granted independence in

November, 1953, shortly after Pol Pot returned, and the transition was relatively smooth. However, political roiling among the Cambodians continued with even greater force.

In the end, Pol Pot and several of his radicalized companions from Paris days joined some insurrectionists in the remote northeast jungles. These were nominally communists, somewhat affiliated with the Viet Minh of the neighboring country (who had kicked out the French in 1954). They were, however, different: less practical, more theoretical, more idealistic. Pol Pot was a purist, indoctrinated in the communist theories of the most fervid French radical intellectuals. He was largely innocent of any other intellectual tradition and perhaps somewhat unmoored from reality. He'd been told by his radical hosts in Paris to ignore the problems with existing socialist regimes because they weren't truly communist (Hello, Bern?). He'd picked up the ideas of Peter Kropotkin, especially that revolution must be carried out to a final conclusion with no compromise if it were to succeed. He and the rest of his group believed the story that *real* communism had never been tried. They determined, if they ever gained power, to do communism right, from the bottom up.

Unfortunately for Cambodia, they did gain power. After the long wilderness struggle, Pol Pot led the forces of the Communist Party of Kampuchea, better known as the Khmer Rouge, into the capital city of Phnom Penh on April 17, 1975. Cambodia was now the guinea pig of true communism. It wasn't going to be pretty.

In their zeal to ensure that communism was finally done right and to ensure the ideological purity of their regime, the Khmer Rouge determined to eliminate all potentially subversive elements from the country. Such elements included any intellectuals that were not part of the Left at the time of the takeover. In practice, that meant just about everyone who was educated or involved in any commercial activity above the peasant level. Many of these were murdered outright. To be certain, no professionals, capitalists or other bourgeois types remained at large. The cities were largely emptied out and their residents turned into the countryside. There the survivors of the purge were committed to labor camps and farms for re-education. Communism was to be instituted in all aspects of national life, from bottom up as promised. Joy of any kind was strictly prohibited, on pain of death.

Enforcers for the Khmer Rouge were mostly very young and all were very vicious. Armed teenagers, some in their early teens, did the heavy lifting for the regime's resettlement programs, and they did it with uninhibited enthusiasm. Especial attention was paid to those of non-Khmer ethnicity -- Vietnamese and Chinese -- although native Khmers with educations or any tendency to resist fared little better. The death toll was stupendous, officially well over a million souls and in reality some multiple of that. Estimates of the toll of the Cambodian genocide in less than four years under Pol Pot come to as much as 25% of the original population of the nation, which percentage-wise dwarfs the totals in all the various other socialist regimes of the 20th century. Stalin, Hitler and Mao would blush at their inefficiency. Communism was finally done right.

What lessons for the present do we learn from this appalling past? First, it is important to note that, in their lack of world-wisdom, the Khmer Rouge leaders were led into the abyss by ideas which their ignorance did not permit them to repudiate. They were told by their intellectual mentors in Paris that true communism, which inevitably yielded utopia, had never been attempted. If, they were convinced, a regime should institute a genuine socialist system and stuck to it with determination, the revolution would succeed and an earthly nirvana would result. Although their actions were evil in the extreme, the intentions of those simple rubes who engineered the Cambodian genocide were pure. They were indeed villains, but those who indoctrinated them, bloodthirsty (in theory) leftist intellectuals who had never executed anything more than a cockroach, must share the obloquy.

Which brings us back to the Bern, and to the unlikely enthusiasm for socialism we find, dominantly among younger people, today. We are speaking of people who have endured, by the time they graduate from college, sixteen years or more of indoctrination into leftist thought patterns through drearily rote teaching methods. It is no coincidence that acceptance of socialism increases with years of education in America today. The meme of today echoes that of yesteryear: socialism has never really been tried; it is a new approach that will bring equality and fulfillment to all people; it is the wave of a brilliant future for the nation. The same lie (I mean "line") that the utopian dream of socialism must be compared to the dirty reality of the free market is sold today as it was in the '20s. The dream always looks better to those who don't know better.

Permit me to end with a quotation of that most delightfully ambiguous of all history's socialists, George Orwell: "So much of left-wing thought is a kind of playing with fire by people who don't even know that fire is hot."

2/3/20

Chapter Thirteen

The Inexorability of Gravity

Once upon a time there was a neighborhood tavern in a midwestern city where, late every Wednesday afternoon, four older guys sat on stools around a nicked-up round wooden table in a corner by a window and discussed affairs of the world. They were a diverse lot in many ways, including religiously. One was a devout atheist, another a lapsed Catholic, the third a son of a black Baptist preacher and the last a lay Baptist. There was plenty of political diversity among them as well: they were socialist, political agnostic leaning left, standard conservative and populist libertarian, respectively. They were also firm enough friends with sufficient mutual respect that religion and politics were very much on the table as subjects of discussion. The conversation did get a bit hot at times, needless to say. That just gave the sessions a little spice.

One afternoon the conversation drifted, not in a particularly serious way, into matters related to divine punishment. The atheist, a generous and open soul despite the rigidity of his opinions, realized that the subject was being treated in a spirit of levity and refused to take the bait. He nevertheless took the trouble to point out that none of it applied to him in any case. "I don't believe in God" was his response, with a wave of the hand, an indication that as an atheist he didn't have to worry about stuff like sin and life after death. The populist's comment was, "I don't believe in gravity, so I guess I can fly." That rejoinder was (typically) a bit caustic, but it had a valid point. If God exists, a person's opinion about His existence is totally inconsequential. He will receive God's judgment, whatever it may be, even if he doesn't believe in Him. Unbelief does not shield him from judgment (in fact, in that particular case, unbelief is, shall we say, highly detrimental to his chances). Similarly, ignorance or rejection of natural laws of any kind do not relieve an individual of their constraints. Gravity is a good example of a physical law that will be obeyed whatever one's opinion of it.

The concept of gravity as we know it – that is, as a force describable as a field – began in an English apple orchard in late summer of 1666. Young Isaac Newton was home on his mother's farm during the closure of Trinity College, Cambridge University, during a resurgence of the plague. One evening, as he sat under the trees in a contemplative mood, he heard an apple hit the ground nearby. He thought about the force that drew the apple to the earth and wondered if the same force extended outside the bounds of the earth and into space. Might the force that drove the apple also control the courses of heavenly bodies? The seed of gravitational field theory was thus conceived, to be developed off and on in later years. Newton was to work out the mathematics of the phenomenon and eventually publish it as part of his grand opus, the *Principia*. The science of physics was born, founded upon the manifest reality of an important natural law. The bottom line is that a theory that conforms to reality is useful and stands up to the test of time. Any belief that defies a natural law is fallacious, no more than howling at the moon. Only belief that conforms to reality is worthy.

A corollary of that rule is that theories that purport to be scientific but do not conform to reality are eventually rejected. Examples include the phlogiston theory of flammability or the aether theory to explain transmission of certain forms of energy. Such ideas that vary from reality may do actual harm: the theory that one's health depends on a balance of four humors in the body led to the practice of leeching, or bloodletting, as a cure. This not only delayed the development of better medical treatments but did actual harm to many patients at the time. Lysenkoism virtually destroyed Russian genetic research in the Stalin era. The Catholic church stuck to the ancient earth-centered theory of the universe for nearly a century after Galileo's introduction of the Copernican view; the result was detrimental to both science and religion. Its rejection of Galileo's discoveries also placed the Church in a backward scholarly position relative to northern Europe for generations. It had chosen errant belief over reality, to its detriment.

The principle outlined above applies to all natural laws, including those involving the human psyche as well as the physical and natural sciences. Thomas Jefferson understood that when he referred to "the Laws of Nature and of Nature's God" in the opening paragraph of the Declaration of Independence, and that the Founders were cognizant of the principle is demonstrated throughout the text of the Constitution. In politics, therefore, any theory that runs counter to basic human nature – which is to say, does not conform to reality – is doomed to failure in the end. It will trigger an inevitable tension between belief and reality that increases in proportion to the variance between the two. The longer a society operates under a belief that is in conflict with reality, the more irrational the situation will become. We see the consequences of that irrationality in Venezuela today, in the deterioration and collapse of the Soviet Union in a previous generation, in the disaster of Cambodia under the Khmer Rouge; in fact, in what has happened with any society that has attempted to impose a socialist structure upon its people.

Bad theories in the realm of the sciences – those that don't conform to reality – cannot succeed in the long run, but like phlogiston, the humors and Lysenkoism, they may have their run of popularity. Similarly, in the political arena certain ideas run contrary to human nature and are therefore doomed, but they may, at a particular point in time, gain enough support to be voted into effect even in supposedly enlightened democracies. Socialism is a prime and recurring example. The German National Socialist Workers' Party (a.k.a. Nazis) entered power in the 1930s on the wave of a popular vote. So, in 1999, did the Venezuelan regime that has left that nation in ruins. True, the Russian and Chinese communists took control through military power, but even they had widespread popular support at the time of the takeover. Once in power, socialist regimes of all stripes tend not to leave gently; the old adage, "One man, one vote, one time" must be taken literally. But socialism, which is a theory alien to human realities, must fail in the end and leave a society in tatters in its wake.

It might be added that socialism is all too compatible with a darker element of the human psyche; to wit, greed and a sinister will to dominate others, to one's own benefit and their doom. However, that element is itself incompatible with the higher and (fortunately) more powerful human desire for freedom – freedom for all and not just for the free play of one's own dark lusts. The result for the longevity of a socialist society is the same.

The inevitable conclusion is that beliefs are only beneficial to the degree that they are consistent with reality, and that acceptance of beliefs, or theories, that are out of step with reality can have painful consequences. There is an old country song that I can remember nothing about except its refrain: "I fought the law and the law won." This is often the case with man-made law, and always the case with natural law. Laws of nature, including human nature (and laws of God, if He exists) simply cannot be ignored with impunity. The effects of ignoring natural laws are generally immediate and dire: gravity is a stern master.

Dire effects of embracing beliefs of a human nature that defy reality can be temporarily obscured by mendacity in one form or another, as the mass media has shown with the recent Trump-Russian collusion hoax (and the current Ukraine/impeachment hoax), but reality catches up in time. The organized mendacity of propaganda kept socialism alive (if not well) in Nazi Germany, Soviet Russia and elsewhere for quite a while, and has propped up socialist sentiment in most of the West over the last century. But reality can't be obscured forever, even with the most stringent efforts of adherents of beliefs that reject it.

Smoke, mirrors and disinformation can keep false beliefs more or less afloat in the short run. The longer they succeed, the worse the eventual effects on society. But fail they will, when all is said and done. Try as hard as the true believer may, in the end gravity always wins.

1/27/20

Chapter Fourteen

The Haves and the Hopes

Back in the day there were no programs in universities with names that ended with "studies." Nevertheless, even then there were subjects honored by classes that were eminently forgettable. We joked about a mythical class entitled "Underwater Basket Weaving," but some of the actual classes weren't too much more valuable than that to one's educational enrichment. Then again, there were legitimate subjects that did have academic virtue but lacked relevance to one's own interests and career objectives. So it was that many years after graduation I applied for a job that required the provision of transcripts. I looked over the old KU transcript before placing it in the package and saw, lo and behold, that I'd taken a course in Economics that I didn't remember taking at all. Then it hit me: the class included a lab (a lab in Economics?), and the lab instructor was a little, chubby, loquacious middle-aged guy. I remembered him because from his ruby lips dropped one of those pearls of wisdom one tends to recall after all else is lost. He told us what you need to get rich. It's not a high IQ, or tremendous energy, or numerical genius, or personal looks and charisma, or even great luck. It's just that you have to *want* to get rich. That's it.

I've thought about that a lot over the years and have decided that it's one of the few things I've learned that is really worth knowing. There are exceptions to every rule, but few to that one: most people aren't rich because getting rich isn't worth it to most people. Sure, almost everyone, if you should ask them, would say they'd like to *be* rich, but *getting* rich is something else altogether. Think of all you have done that you would have missed out on if you had dedicated your life to getting rich. To put it another way, to gain riches in money you would have had to give up a great deal of the richness of life itself. Those who are wealthy, and who made it themselves, made that bargain, and as far as my personal knowledge goes, most are happy with it. Making money was a joy to them, apparently as much as listening to classical music, reading great literature, playing sports, partying and all the other activities and studies others have chosen to do were a joy to them. For the large majority of us, having money is very nice indeed, but our life enrichment lies elsewhere. For us, getting rich simply wasn't worth giving up all the rest.

It has long been noted that succeeding generations of those who have accumulated great wealth rarely have the dedication of the founder of the fortune. In fact, the great man's kids more often seem to be downright wastrels. But given the foregoing, should that come as a surprise? Why should an ordinary person sacrifice sizeable swathes of his life's essence to increase a fortune when he's already rich? A very large percentage of us would choose to enjoy to the maximum that which we already have. The more we have, the less incentive there is to increase it. When one looks at it logically, who is more dysfunctional: the "wastrel" kid or the billionaire who has more than he can spend in ten lifetimes but is still grasping for more? Not everyone has a lifelong avocation dedicated to making money for its own sake (for which I'm very thankful), but except for a few hermits and ascetics we all enjoy spending the stuff. The paradigm of the rich person's children blowing the pile seems perfectly normal to me.

Be that as it may, the self-made wealthy tend to take their riches seriously. Perhaps just to give meaning to a life spent accumulating riches, a desire for dynasty-founding tends to accompany the overwhelming urge to make money. Therefore, the wealthy devote a significant portion of their energies to raise legal barriers to ensure their kids cannot dissipate the fortune. Laws are enacted at their behest to accomplish this – laws involving trusts and other limitations on the heirs' ability to access the corpus of the lucre. The wealthy have also rigged the tax laws to try to ensure the perpetuation of the dynastic fortune. The graduated income tax has been sold to the underclasses as a way to "soak the rich," but it is not a tax on the rich at all. It is, rather, a hindrance to getting rich. By taking increasing percentages of revenue from those who are most likely to become rich, the already-wealthy siphon off money flows that productive and ambitious future rivals could have reinvested in their enterprises. They therefore protect the place of the dynasty at the top by both limiting the ability of their heirs to dissipate the capital and impede the competition from climbing to replace them. The idea is to both lock in their wealth and decrease the social and economic mobility of society.

The objective of the wealthy class to preserve their dynasties is imperfectly achieved in a relatively free society. We frequently see statistics showing the gap in wealth and revenues between different economic layers of the population, usually accompanied by moaning about its increase. What is less often shown is the percentage of individuals in the current revenue categories who have changed categories over a given period of time. It is remarkable how many people at the top levels are different at any point in time than those who previously occupied it. On the other hand, a good many of those at the wealthiest levels before have dropped downward to make room for newcomers. In other words, over the period of time during which the data has been gathered (and presumably long before) there has been a high degree of economic mobility. The heirs of departed tycoons have tended to become less wealthy, despite the measures noted above, while more energetic, ambitious and (above all) hungry entrepreneurs and professionals have moved upward. That chubby little econ lab instructor was absolutely correct.

That brings us to one of the most critical – and unheralded – differences between socialism and free enterprise. The former tends to produce a fixed society, one in which a child is fated to spend his life within a narrow range of the social and economic stratum in which he initially finds himself. Central planners rather like the predictability and social stability of that system, as do most people who value security above opportunity. There is a multitude of those people, who do not wish to strive in a competitive situation and would rather that everyone live comfortably in a predestined role in life. They aren't especially interested in getting ahead and would be happier if those who were would quit making waves. They would feel better about themselves if others didn't expect them to exert themselves to better their economic status. It should be added that many other not-so-ambitious individuals are nevertheless good workers, loyal employees, decent citizens and excellent parents and neighbors. They would simply rather live out their lives tranquilly and dispense with the thrills, and are happy enough to be around people who feel the same way. Most of them aren't socialists – many are fine with more ambitious colleagues and realize they make life more prosperous for all. But a certain percentage are vulnerable to the siren song of socialism.

Free enterprise is no walk in the park. Its price is a turbulent marketplace and a highly mobile society. Mobility sounds good in theory but it does contribute to discomfort and a sense of insecurity. The prize, however, is a society that tends to prosper both materially and in terms of cultural growth. Freedom is always a little uncomfortable, in society as a whole and in our personal lives. To be free means there are responsibilities to carry and decisions to be made. But it also means there are opportunities to be seized and satisfaction to be gained. To be free is to be alive; insofar as we are not free we are that much dead. After all, who is more comfortable than the dead? Americans generally have always chosen freedom, with its burdens, over serfdom with its suffocating comfort. That is why those who would be our masters, the progressives of old and now the globalist elites, try always to change us and the Constitution that enshrines our rights. As lovers of freedom, we are not good material for their envisioned slave societies. We do not go gently into Orwell's *1984.*

There has been a lot of talk about "haves" and "have nots." There's even a TV show called "The Haves and the Have Nots," which sounds like a sort of soap opera, although I've never watched it. The idea behind the expression (and perhaps the TV show) is of a society that is stratified, more or less permanently, on the order of those of the Middle Ages. It pretty well summarizes the situation in a socialist society of the present day, with its permanent underclass overlain by a thin veneer of elites who run everything from the top down. The resulting "haves-and-have-nots" structure of socialist society is thus in stark contrast with the mobility of a society based on free enterprise. The latter may be described as having a "haves and hopes" structure, since with pluck and luck – and above all the desire to get rich – a person of any financial or social status may rise all the way to the uppermost of either. Not everyone is born a "have," but anyone in a free nation may have hope. One cannot say that of those bound in a nation based on socialism. Hope is a rare commodity in the socialist underclass.

There is one exception, of sorts, to the above. The socialist underclass is itself stratified, with a bureaucracy of lackeys (aka "experts") who handle the nuts-and-bolts functions for the elites. It's true that a citizen of a socialist state can aspire to rise from the lowermost masses to the technician level. Beyond that, advancement is risky and based on qualities much different from those required in a free environment, but it can and does happen. It might be pointed out that even in medieval times there were peasants who, one way or another, rose out of the stations of their origins to wealth or power. These cases were rare, however, and most of them involved the same sort of skills and temperament as with socialist societies today. There are indeed those who rise above their lowly origins in any socialist society – but this essentially never happens because of hard work, entrepreneurial skills or productivity. Advancement to elite status requires instead that a person be brutal and ruthless rather than entrepreneurial or productive. Charisma and intelligence may help but are of little use to an ambitious socialist if unallied with the darker traits. I would suggest that a doubter of that statement read Boris Pasternak's *Dr. Zhivago* (or watch the movie) for corroboration of it.

Apart from the inevitable brutality factor in socialism, there is some degree of security. Unfortunately, whatever security exists in socialism benefits the elites only, much as the income tax and related laws benefit those who are already wealthy. So much of leftism hearkens back to medieval times, from the technology of windmills to the stagnation of society. A strictly stratified society can be genial only to those at the top. For those born into less favored circumstances, stability and security can only be confining and dismal, an ephemeral gift of government rather than a natural right. A socialist state must by its nature be one of the haves and the have nots. One must look exclusively to free enterprise for a societal structure that allows for mobility of the populace in terms of wealth and privilege – one of the haves and the hopes.

1/17/21

PART III

The Left

Have you ever wondered what is the source of that fascination almost everyone feels when wandering through a zoo? Why should looking at creatures in the flesh that we otherwise can only see in movies, videos and picture books bring us that sense of awe? We all know what a rhinoceros looks like, or a cheetah or giraffe. But when we look upon a real one it's like we've been transported to somewhere else, somewhere mysterious and exotic. After all the time I've spent in the local zoological garden and arboretum, I still get a thrill from seeing the actual, living animal. There is even a kind of warm feeling of fellowship that goes with it, an understanding that we are strange companions on the same planet.

Oddly enough, I get something of the same sensation when I encounter a social justice warrior or particularly militant socialist – absent the warm feelings, of course. It's difficult to actively dislike someone just because of political differences, but it's also hard to shake the impression of something strange, different, almost alien. This is not the case with the everyday, garden-variety liberal, although that person's opinions certainly differ from mine over a wide range of topics. No, I speak of the true believer, the dedicated acolyte of the Left. Somehow, I can meet a Greenland Eskimo and feel more of a sense of common humanity than I do with a hard-core leftist native of my own hometown. To repeat, I feel no antagonism toward that individual, even during a heated discussion, but find it difficult to relate to the person as a member of the same species that I belong to. Something like the zoo.

The articles in this section concern aspects of the Left in a general way. The key article is *The Righteous*. That one, with its two related righteousness chapters, is central to understanding any of the other leftist features and foibles that are discussed in this book. The overwhelming certainty of their own righteousness that is common to essentially all committed leftists explains nearly everything political that they think or do. It is the *sine qua non* of their very existence. Its importance to any thoughtful analysis of the current situation of this country, or indeed anywhere touched by Western civilization, cannot be overestimated. If that sounds overblown to you, read on ....

Other chapters in the section cover some of the typical characteristics of the Left, as well as some of its effects on our society. *Machiavelli and the Snowflakes* exemplifies these, but all show some side of the leftist paradigm. Much more could be written about the Left, its mindsets and objectives, and in fact much about the Left pervades many of the articles of this book. The fact that it is the Left that dominates here probably derives from the same fascination with strange things described above. A plain old conservative, no matter how intelligent and interesting, can't compare in exotic qualities to a militantly shrill social justice warrior. You know, kind of like the zoo.

Chapter Fifteen

The Righteous

"Opinions are like bellybuttons: everybody's got one." That old platitude (slightly cleaned up) isn't entirely true. Some people don't have opinions on a particular subject; others have more than one (a condition known as cognitive dissonance). Actually, the joke is about the worthlessness of opinions in general, their insubstantiality and transient nature. But there are opinions and there are opinions. Some derive from that antiquated discipline called logic, carefully thought out and based on observation. Some are arrived at impulsively and based on ephemeral emotion. Others are borrowed from other people, perhaps a favorite professor, a social group or (worst of all) a Hollywood celebrity.

The problem is that, however they are acquired, some opinions matter. Not all do: an opinion about whether the Cubs will ever win another World Series doesn't matter – unless, of course, the holder is laying a substantial sum on it. Others, such as whether the Christian God exists, matter a great deal to an individual but perhaps few others. But some, like who should be the next president, have wider consequences. People vote, politicians are elected or rejected, and the politicians who are elected do things. They do things with other people's money – our money, in fact. And the things they do have an effect on more money yet, and on many occasions on much more than mere money. Thus, some opinions, taken in aggregate, end up mattering a great deal to all of us.

Therefore, opinions differ as to their importance to ourselves and to society as a whole. As far as the significance to ourselves goes, even though opinions may vary widely on the same question we all believe our own opinion to be correct. How could it be otherwise? If we don't think our opinion is right, we'll change to another opinion. But there does seem to be a divergence between Left and Right on this point. Conservatives may be as stubborn and difficult to convince as anyone else when it comes to their treasured opinions, but they do tend to have more than a grain of respect for different opinions, or at least for the right of another to hold a different opinion. There seems to be little such willingness on the Left. And why should there be? Why should one respect opinions different from one's own, or the people who hold them, when one is Righteous?

There are also differences between individuals as to the effects of their opinions upon others, in the cases that those opinions have any effect. In a nutshell and as a generality, people of a conservative political bent worry about results on those occasions when their opinions are put into effect. People of a leftist bent tend to be concerned about getting their opinions put into effect but not so much about actual results once those opinions are implemented. Leftists don't have to worry about actual results; they are primarily concerned with motives. If their intent is pure, what happens after is of little concern. In many cases, they don't even seem to recognize what the consequences of their implemented opinions are. Their opinions spring from noble hearts and that is what matters. They are Righteous.

A mega-example of how Righteous motives commonly lead to dire consequences is found in President Lyndon Johnson's War on Poverty. It is instructive to read the many writings of economists Walter Williams and Thomas Sowell that describe, with an ample catalog of irrefutable facts, the frightening effects that series of programs, the centerpiece of Johnson's Great Society, had upon the black community nationwide. The lost opportunity cost has also been immense: in the forty years from its initiation in 1964, a conservatively estimated $15 trillion dollars in taxpayer funds were spent directly on War on Poverty programs (Cato Institute}. The bloodletting continues. Despite the more or less official end of the war in 1981, many of the programs continue today. Secondary costs were, as always, far greater. All those resources, that could have been directed to vital needs, gave us little but desolation for millions of poor people's lives. Even now, when leftists bother to address the issue at all they ignore the informed analysis of Williams, Sowell and others in favor of bland statements of support for the failed programs, backed by obviously specious statistics. Why should they worry? They are the Righteous.

Other examples of leftist initiatives that have wreaked havoc among both supposed beneficiaries and unwilling benefactors, all without much angst felt by their designers, are legion. Among them is affirmative action, an overt embrace of racial discrimination that evolved from the worthy concept of equal opportunity. The various programs implemented under the affirmative action label have diminished the genuine achievements of some people while putting others in a position of certain failure. It is highly questionable if much good has been done to compensate for these human tragedies. Progressives are proud of affirmative action anyway and continue to try to find ways to work around legal barriers that have sensibly restricted it. They don't even think about apologizing for it. To mangle a famous quote from the movie *Love Story* (1970), "Righteous means not having to say you're sorry."

It would be tedious to try to list all the leftist programs over the last century that have not only failed in their objectives but caused heavy social damage in the process. The multitude of New Deal projects alone that fit that bill could fill a book. In fact, they have filled several recent books, of which the best is probably *The Forgotten Man: A New History of the Great Depression* (2007) by the estimable Amity Shlaes. The disaster of the New Deal is proven by modern scholarship to have extended the misery of the Great Depression by almost a decade beyond its normal expiration date. It was, in fact, only brought to an end by the even greater disaster of World War II. Progressives are still proud of it; Paul Krugman (yet another living embarrassment to the Nobel Committee) claims FDR's only mistake was not spending enough! The concept of FDR and his associates and enablers was sublime, so who cares about mundane consequences? One must be concerned not with results but with Righteousness.

The bottom line for all the Left's economic and social engineering adventures is ... well, a terrible bottom line. We have little to show for them but economic and social impoverishment. Among Mark Levin's recent books is *Plunder and Deceit* (2015), which quotes the government's own figure for the federal debt as just over $18 trillion at the time of its writing. It is somewhere in the vicinity of $22 trillion now, just four years later. It was "only" $10.6 trillion when President Obama entered office in January, 2009. Levin's thesis is that we are well into the process of not only wrecking the economy of our own generations but plundering our descendants. Actually, in the same year of 2015, economist Dr. Laurence Kotlikoff pointed out that the real debt problem is far worse: counting "off the books" obligations, the country's fiscal gap (a more realistic picture of the debt) was $210 trillion. We are not only broke now, we have already burdened the future beyond reasonable ability to recover. And all the progressive Nobel Laureate Dr. Krugman can say is that we should have spent more. But he can say that sort of thing and escape censure: he is Righteous.

Massive debt is not the only downside of the Righteous schemes, and it may not be the worst. There is also a massive loss of fundamental freedom that is invariably associated with them. In fact, the loss of freedom and what Jefferson called the "inalienable rights" of American citizens is considered by the Left to be routine. It is impossible to carry out wide-ranging social engineering projects without infringing on individual liberties, and the Righteous think that's a small price to pay for the implementation of their Righteousness. Since the U.S. Constitution is specifically designed to guard the individual liberties of the citizens against government, it is a deliberate impediment to progressives which they want curtailed, if not eliminated. Even the progressives themselves will be unfree, but they will be Righteous.

A corollary of the taking away of freedoms that have traditionally been thought of as inherent to humanity and thus untouchable by government is the necessity of coercion. Formerly free peoples tend to resist the loss of those basic freedoms, and such resistance is anathema to socialists. After all, if one is Righteous, how can anyone who isn't justify such resistance? There may be some pain involved, but that's the way a Righteous world works. There's some Righteous mumbling about eggs and omelets and the great works of socialism move inexorably ahead. In fact, for all the platitudes about tolerance and inclusion and diversity on the Left, coercion is part of the very fabric of socialism in all its forms. A socialist society cannot long exist without it, and none ever has. The cost in human quality of life has been immense in every case where socialism has been instituted as a form of government, and such will always be the case. But should you resist? Your egg may be broken and the resulting omelet inedible, but look on the bright side: your masters will be Righteous.

Assuming that one does wish to resist the onset of socialism and to reject the siren call of all that "free" stuff, how does one go about it? If you are a deplorable, which can be defined as anyone so unrighteous as to turn down the offer of a socialist to run his life for him, how do you resist? There are a number of possibilities. A common expedient in countries that have already adopted socialism is passive resistance. One goes through the motions in a minimalist manner, sabotaging an already creaky system in small ways as opportunity arises. This is reflected in the old Soviet maxim, "We pretend to work and they pretend to pay us." A more direct approach is armed resistance, either civil war or rebellion, depending on the circumstances. This is thought of by most of us as a last resort, as it should be, but violence in defense of freedom is, as Thomas Jefferson famously noted, at times sadly unavoidable.

A far better way to resist the Righteous in their push for a socialist society is persuasion. There is ample evidence that socialism doesn't work in practice no matter how good it may sound in theory, and in fact it can be demonstrated that it can't even work in theory (see the articles in the *Free for All* series). Surely we deplorables can subdue the progressives in each of our orbits through rational argumentation, bring them over peacefully to our way of thinking and avoid resistance, passive or active, altogether. It is altogether more pleasant to convert those who hold malign opinions to a more rational way of thinking than to bludgeon them into it, or (worse) be bludgeoned ourselves into socialism.

Unfortunately, the history of the efficacy of reason in this regard is not encouraging. The problem is Righteousness. Leftists don't argue with those who disagree with them, no matter what the issues or substance of the arguments may be. They only accuse. It's rather frustrating, actually. Just as a deplorable begins to enjoy the argument, just as the issues are clarified and developed, the progressive drops out, like an intellectual party pooper. He gives up all pretense of debate and calls the deplorable a racist, or perhaps some sort of phobe, depending on his mood. That is a sign of surrender, of course, but it's a victory that is deeply unsatisfying to someone who enjoys intellectual infighting. Besides, the leftist doesn't even recognize his surrender; in his own mind he has simply declared victory through inherent moral superiority. The bottom line is that the Left is wrong most of the time, but it doesn't matter. A socialist doesn't have to be right – he is Righteous.

So all of us have opinions and most of us are quite fond of them. Most of us also realize they *are* opinions, and not handed down as graven stones from on high. But those of the Left seem to visualize *themselves* as engravers of those stones. Philosophically, for the Left humans are gods, and special humans are Righteous. When a Righteous person pronounces an opinion, deplorables must defer to him (or her, or it, or X). In the true socialist pantheon, there is no god but Man, and government is his (or hers, etc.) prophet. It is this sense of Righteousness that underlies all the intolerance and will to coercion of the Left, all the foibles, large and small, that terrify or irritate the rest of us. It explains a great deal about the everyday behavior of your leftist friends and acquaintances. Without the conviction of Righteousness and their own good intentions there could be no socialism.

The final verdict is that the Left is lethally dangerous to your freedom and your prosperity, and to your life, liberty and pursuit of happiness. But that is as it should be, for it is Righteous.

10/21/19

Chapter Sixteen

Righteousness Redux

The New York Times has rarely been accused of nurturing a sense of humor, but I suspect its editors must have one. Otherwise, how could it publish an article in its On Tech newsletter like the one of April 23? The title gives it away: "What to Do When Your Uncle Believes Coronavirus Conspiracies." It explains, in the most patronizing manner, how you can rehabilitate "loved ones" who don't believe whatever Pravda West and the various experts it worships are peddling on any given day. How can you rescue the poor gullible souls from the siren messages they may read on the internet? How can you bless them with your own superior intellect and moral superiority, not to mention the message *du jour* of the techno-experts of our infallible bureaucracy? The author's ideal is for the "helper" to avoid outright mockery of the deluded family and friends who endeavor to think for themselves, but rather to set a noble example and refer them to trusted individuals such as sports figures and celebrities. The key word is "trust," and the Righteous must lead them to enlightenment.

The article drips with leftist Righteousness. It bemoans the fact that "trust in authority figures [is] falling," without, however, mentioning another fact; to wit, that the Left has been working full-time since at least late 2016 to undermine all authority figures to the political right of Karl Marx. It quotes an Ivy League professor "who studies misperceptions about politics and health care." What sort of idea do you suppose would be defined as a misperception by the good professor? My guess is anything he (or Shira Ovide, the article's author) would disagree with, which is to say anything anti-socialist. The article also suggests, with that sublime lack of self-awareness found in nearly all devout leftists, that we should "look behind the curtain for people with a political message and others who have incentives to fan our fears ...." That is especially rich, since the people she is so dedicated to reforming are precisely those who are looking behind the leftist curtain at socialist authority figures lurking behind said curtain with their own political and health care agendas.

So the NYT editors apparently do have a sort of Teutonic sense of humor (and please don't tell me such a sense doesn't exist: I personally knew a German who told a joke once – anyway, I think he thought it was funny). If they don't have a sense of humor they are at least capable of arousing one in the rest of us. Surely we can laugh when we read about Ovide's desire to "help" her lesser fellow humans get over the dangerous tendency to ignore the NYT, the prissy bureaucrats and ego-bloated politicians, the fellow-traveling Hollywood celebs, red professors and other such Left-think worthies, and drift without wise leftist guidance into unorthodox opinions. It's inconvenient, of course, that orthodoxy on the Left is kind of difficult to nail down: if you ask five leftist experts about anything, you'll get seven mutually contradictory opinions. If you ask tomorrow, you'll still get seven, but all five experts will have different ones from the day before. It's like a game of musical chairs, except instead of one chair short there are two extra. I suppose one just has to keep reading the NYT to know how the Righteous should think to keep their orthodox creds up to date. (The reader is referred to an article from a couple of years ago, *The Righteous*, to understand my definition of this fundamental phenomenon of the Left.)

There are strikingly childish aspects to leftist Righteousness that can be frustrating as well as humorous, the almost universal self-unawareness referred to above being a prominent one. A childlike tendency to trust adult figures who are outside the mainstream of the individual's culture is another. The opinions, however toxic, of teachers and professors are valued far above those of parents and childhood mentors. So are those of certain designated government techno-experts who have impressive titles and little else. At the very bottom, some poor leftists even value the opinions of Hollywood airheads, especially those who become more loquacious as they fade from former celebrity. The current propagandists of Pravda West err by trusting each other. How many cases have there been over the last several years of hordes of "journalists" parroting the mendacious "news" story of a colleague at another outlet without checking it? It becomes difficult to keep up with them, and even harder to find the retractions when the truth is eventually revealed.

But there is worse, much worse. Children are cruel before they are taught better, and those who are never taught better become cruel adults. Leftists seem to miss out on socialization (if not socialism) more commonly than normal people, and the mixture of lack of socialization with Righteousness is a lethal one. Socialist excesses of just the last century include the massive examples of the Nazis, Soviets, Maoists and Khmer Rouge. Lesser (but still vicious) atrocities, such as those of communist Cuba, abound.

Conservative governments may bore certain dissidents of radical temperament to death, but at least they don't gas or bayonet them. What nasty examples might be cited for liberal democracies throughout history tend to count casualties in the dozens or less, not dozens of millions. Even when bad deeds are committed in our republics, they are aberrations carried out by renegades, not cold-blooded programs carried out by mainstream regimes.

A certain suspension of disbelief accompanies Righteousness and self-unawareness in leftist minds that, even in our own republic, leads to distortions in our political processes. Supreme Court nominations, for example, need to be taken seriously but do not need to be turned into circuses of character assassination. Suspending disbelief about the most questionable allegations (please refer to Chapter 27, Part IV, *The Incredible Dr. Ford*) for purely political ends is both unseemly and destructive. Impeachment of a president should be taken very seriously as a last resort response to actual criminal activity, not as a temper tantrum of political partisanship. Again, suspension of disbelief to permit patently bogus and manufactured story lines to rise to the level of "high crimes" results in chaos and pointless obstruction.

The same sort of suspension of disbelief that thrives on the Left and vexes our politics is similarly able to distort science. Perhaps the classic example of that phenomenon in recent history is the sad tale of Lysenkoism in Soviet Russia. Perhaps it is inevitable that when the Left substitutes Science for God it must also politicize it out of all recognition, and the adoption of Trofim Lysenko's crackpot notions as official science by the Russian Communist Party in the 1930s is an outstanding example of the certain result. No genuine biological scientist could have been convinced of the truth of Lysenko's "science," but under a socialist regime, suspension of disbelief is always attainable. Nor should scientists of the modern West look upon their Soviet predecessors with too much disdain – government money has suspended the disbelief of a great many of them in the cause of anthropogenic global warming. More recently the same sort of thing seems to be happening in medical science with the coronavirus panic. Such incidents couldn't occur except in an atmosphere of Righteousness, and may be expected when all is politicized and Science becomes religion.

Speaking of which, it is said that Christians are, collectively, the greatest detriment to the proselytization of Christianity. This isn't entirely true: most Christians do not at all fit that pattern. The adage refers to the others, a small minority, one hopes, of self-righteous and holier-than-thou types who are capable of turning off just about anyone. The Deacon, a character in the old Pogo Possum cartoon series, epitomized the breed. With the deft touch of the inimitable Walt Kelly, the dark and sinister Deacon was as close to a villain as the series possessed. The repulsive traits of that unfortunate kind of professed Christian were based on the same sort of Righteousness that marks our current social justice warriors and their allies in academia and media. We call it political correctness, and no one could have it without a deep-seated sense of superiority over the common run of humanity. Without Righteousness, Shira Ovide could not have penned an Op-Ed of the kind described above, nor would she have had the degree of self-unawareness to permit herself to reveal that disgusting self-righteousness.

But that is the least of it; that is but a moment of quiet inner laughter for the rest of us. The problem is that without Righteousness you could not have had the atrocities that socialist regimes have perpetrated upon the human race repeatedly over the last century. You could not have had the unprincipled grasping for power of the Left here in America the last three and a half years. You could not have the amoral plotting for domination that goes on in the shadowed lairs of the Deep State at this moment. In the end, Righteousness is not a joke.

5/11/20

Chapter Seventeen

Fauxbiaphobic

The word *phobia* is derived from the Greek word for fear and has traditionally been used in the English language as a stand-alone noun meaning a persistent irrational dread of something; It is also commonly used in a combined form with another Greek root that denotes the thing feared. *Acrophobia*, the fear of heights, is a common example, although *arachnophobia* is more exciting (it was the title of an old B-grade fright movie). A related adjective is *phobic*; it also can be stand-alone and is also commonly used in combined form, as in an *acrophobic* trapeze artist (also known as a tragic loser).

That's the traditional usage of the word. It is probably no surprise to anyone that the Left managed to alter reality in a manner very much at variance with original intention. The word *homophobia*, which formerly took its meaning from literal Greek as fear of boredom, or fear of the same ol' thing, was re-introduced in 1969 to mean hatred of homosexuals. Notice the shift from fear to hatred. There is no nuance of meaning in the word *phobia* in its original language to indicate hatred. It was simply convenient for the Left to assign that meaning.

The transition of the meaning of *phobia* from fear to hatred is significant, given the Left's obsession with the latter. After observing the level of vituperation in the antics of many progressives since the 2016 elections, it is tempting to attribute to projection their common practice of calling almost any activity of conservatives a manifestation of hate. Progressives are capable of finding dog whistles and esoteric symbols of white supremacy in the most innocent comments and gestures imaginable. Even as we resist this temptation to practice pop psychology, we must be aware that the hate obsession is not confined to the social and political spheres. It now has important legal ramifications as well, as explained in Chapter 40 herein, *Hate Crime and Punishment*.

Before we examine this problem further, we should seek to clean up a linguistic issue concerning the word *phobia* itself. After all, a major function of language is to distinguish between different essences, and surely there is a major difference between hate and fear. For the sake of clarity, therefore, I would propose to coin another word for phenomena motivated by hate rather than by fear. Since the Greek root of *phobia* refers to fear, and the historical use of it is for fear-related phenomena, it is reasonable to retain that definition and find another word for hate-induced effects. I would prefer, if possible, to keep the pronunciation the same but have a distinctive spelling. Fortunately, such a word is available simply by changing the *ph* to *f,* which also gives it a nice French twist. Henceforward, let us call the irrational emotional state based on hate, rather than fear, *fauxbia.*

Let me hasten to assure you that this proposal is made entirely in good faith. It is no more than a vehicle of convenience, to distinguish two phenomena that are indisputably quite different in nature. We can therefore continue to use *homophobia* for the irrational fear of boredom, or indeed of homosexuals, and can use the word *homofauxbia* for the irrational hatred of or aversion to homosexuals (which latter is what we usually mean these days). Therefore, if I'm afraid of all foreigners for no reason other than their citizenship, I would be xenophobic. If I harbor irrational hatred of all foreigners, I'm xenofauxbic.

Of course, not all accused phobes or fauxbes, whether homo-, xeno-, Islamo- or whatever- (as Hillary might say) are justifiably so labeled. If I have an aversion to certain illegal aliens because they are criminals, or simply because they suck up welfare money, flood the schools and hospitals and can't pay, and demand everything while contributing little or nothing, those are rational bases for fear (of criminals) or hate (of any of the above). If I'm nevertheless accused of fearing them or hating them simply because they're foreign, that would be an unjustified charge of either xenophobia *or* xenofauxbia. My aversion may be uncharitable or even nasty, but it's still rational, and therefore neither phobic nor fauxbic.

I'll try to summarize the above confusion. First, *phobic* is a meaningful and legitimate psychological term that has been hijacked by the Left for its own political purposes. My coinage of the word *fauxbia* is an attempt to correct that particular leftist atrocity, at least in part, by differentiating the emotions of fear and hate that have been conflated by the hijacking. I consider it a step in the right direction, but incomplete. In fact, the entire animus of the Left remains unexposed at this point. Why would progressives bother to hijack that simple word *phobia*?

The answer is painfully obvious. It has been neatly encapsulated just this past week by a CNN commentator, who stated that we (meaning President Trump) must stop demonizing people – and proceeded to demonize the entire Caucasian male race in the very same sentence. He was cheerfully and typically unaware of the irony. So the Left as a whole has no problem using technical psychology nomenclature to disparage those who disagree with its politics. Anyone who, for any reason, fails to support one of their favored "protected" groups or characteristics must be labeled a nut case. He has a phobia. There can be no other explanation for opposition to the progressive agenda.

So what is someone who objects to illegal immigration into our country? Well, he's a racist, of course, but that hardly counts; everyone a leftist doesn't like is racist. More to the point, he's a xenophobe, because the Left has to import foreigners to make up for the votes it's losing among citizens. What is someone who objects to being blown up by Muslims? Easy: an Islamophobe, because the Left needs Islam....for what? This is a trickier question because Islam represents everything progressives abhor. Its adherents murder homosexuals, treat women in the most vile manner and are rigidly religious. Ah, you say, but they also despise Christians! The enemy of my enemy is my friend, right? It so happens that Muslims commonly aren't fond of leftists as well, but, following the adage of their forbear Ralph Waldo Emerson, progressives consider consistency to be horridly uncool. Go figure.

Anyway, I have, to borrow a phrase from Jonathan Swift, a Modest Proposal. It's quite simple: why let the Left have all the fun? Not to be selfish, let's give the progressives a few fauxbias first. How about deplorofauxbia, in honor of Hillary, or bimbofauxbia in honor of Bill? The Left can certainly identify with those terms, as well as nazifauxbia, which they feel for just about anyone they don't agree with. But we should be permitted a few of our own, since even on the Right, patience has limits. A favorite of mine is sophistrifauxbia. Those specious arguments progressives constantly indulge in drive me nuts. Even better is pharisaismofauxbia, for those of us who are weary of our progressive friends' overwhelming self-righteousness. It has the advantage that both ends of the combined form are French. Anyway, you get the idea. Roll your own.

Actually, I'm personally not very fauxbic about most of the usual topics. For example, I'm not in the least xenofauxbic. I did most of my business in Latin America, Eastern Europe and elsewhere around the world for years, lived in the south of England and maintained an office in the Polanco district of Mexico City. I had cordial relations with a great many people who are not Americans. Some of my best friends, both in the U.S. and in their native countries, are Hispanics. None of them are illegal immigrants (although one once was). Neither am I homophobic, nor homofauxbic. I've never discriminated against any LGBTQX individual, and have high regard for several, without particularly approving of their lifestyles. I have a straight friend who's a serial adulterer and I don't approve of his lifestyle either, but that's not especially relevant. Neither the gays nor the straights care much about my approval or the lack thereof, nor should they. The point is, one can get along with a huge variety of people and not agree with them on every issue without being any kind of fauxbic.

What I *am* fauxbic about is phobia, as defined by the Left. I abhor the term as it's applied to anyone with whom progressives disagree. Remember back in the salad days of the '60s when the hippies started the big move to the left? Remember their disdain for the practice of "labeling," and how they hated the application of certain terms to themselves? Now, when they find themselves in the driver's seat of cultural influence, the whole labeling thing takes on a different aspect. The labels are coming fast and furious, and the labelees are us deplorables. What a surprise.

I suppose this makes me phobiafauxbic. I just don't fit comfortably into any of the phobic categories of the Left, and I'm not comfortable when someone tries to make me fit into them. Neither do I fit many of the "isms," but that's a different and more complex subject of its own. Suffice to say that I'm definitely not racist. If I were, Janus, my black blog-writing colleague, would no doubt have flattened me long ago. He probably could do it, too, especially at this time of year. I just had a birthday and, notwithstanding his status as the Old Geezer, for the next three months he will be younger than me. I'd best tread lightly.

1/20/20

Chapter Eighteen

War Against the Statues

As of New Year's Day of 2015 there were, by one reliable account, 718 monuments and statues around the country that memorialized the Confederacy. There were in addition over 800 other Confederate memorials such as plaques and historical markers. Most of them were, as one would expect, located in the states that comprised the old Confederacy. Most were also in Confederate cemeteries, with many around statehouses, courthouses and public parks. There were two periods of time in which a large majority of these memorials were established. The first was the last two decades of the 19th century and the first two of the 20th century; the second was the decade following the mid-1950s.

As of today, there are several dozen fewer statues and memorials dedicated to the Confederacy and figures associated with it. They have been removed, either through mob action by radicals or official action by leftist politicians, following a couple of highly publicized incidents. The first of these, in 2015, was the despicable mass shooting of members of the congregation of a black Christian church in South Carolina by an unbalanced young neo-Nazi and white supremacist; the second was a riot in Charlottesville, Virginia, in 2017. The first was an act of sheer individual lunacy with the avowed object of starting a race war. The national trauma that resulted led to the escalation of the war against Confederate statues, although the killer's attachment to the historical Confederacy was exceedingly tenuous. The second incident involved the proposed removal of an actual statue and was seized upon by those already intent on eradication of all Confederate-related memorials to accelerate the anti-statue movement.

There is a good deal of support for the War Against the Statues in the usual quarters of academia, media and left-wing radicalism in general, but a good deal of pushback as well. In fact, public support for statue removal is, for the most part and in most parts of the country, weak at best. Nevertheless, removal goes on, here and there, and is accompanied by related activity such as name changes of streets, schools and so forth from Confederate personages to people of more politically acceptable groups. These enterprises continue, although the rate of progress appears to be slowing. And there has been, predictably, a touch of what might be termed mission drift. Not all the statues and memorials currently being attacked have anything whatever to do with the old Confederacy. The knives have come out for all sorts of new targets. It appears that these days anyone with a grudge can declare himself "triggered" and demand the extinction of a piece of American history.

A fine example of the latest phase of the anti-statue war took place in the town of Arcata, in northern California, early in 2019. After a long period of grumbling and rabble rousing by Native Americans, a statue to President McKinley that had graced the town square for more than a century was removed (at public expense) and carted off to Canton, Ohio, the man's hometown. It is not entirely clear what specific crimes that president had committed to earn him the scorn of the populace, since he'd never been near Arcata -- or even California, I suspect. However, he did have something to do with the American legacy of Manifest Destiny, having approved the expansion of the U.S. into various lands in western North America and Hawaii. These had been lands occupied by Native Americans, whose descendants are now getting what revenge they can. Since all of the continent had been occupied by Native Americans when some English settlers showed up on the east coast in 1607, we can expect a lot of statues to go if the country follows Arcata's example. As for McKinley, he has been further dissed by the official removal of his name from a mountain in Alaska, replaced by an earlier Indian name. Poor guy: he had an excellent presidency, except for getting assassinated by the radical son of an immigrant.

Mission drift in the war against statuary has taken a much broader turn in New York City. A male member of the city's Public Design Commission has issued a call to remove a bunch of statues of men in Central Park. Apparently, he got wind of the triggering of certain feminists as they jogged through the park and had to look at the oppressive bronze and stone figures of males. Strangely enough, this is not a joke, although it may have been taken as one by the vast majority of the people of that fair city. In any case, no action on the suggestion has been taken to date. It would certainly solve the problem of Confederate statues if it were to become a movement, and that of oppressors of Native Americans and most other problematic groups as well. Most non-problematic groups too, if such still exist.

There is an air of unreality in the statue affair, as in most of what happens in the fantasy universe of the Left. But there is a deadly serious aspect to it as well. Destroying chunks of metal and stone may strike one as a rather feckless enterprise in itself, but viewed in the larger context of denigration of the nation's historical legacy it is disturbing. The roots of the movement are found in a spurious hypothesis promoted by leftist historians that insists the American Civil War was begun and fought exclusively to end slavery, and that the ongoing struggle against racism is the continuation of that war. If that were true (which it manifestly is not), the justification of the war against the statues would be both valid and obvious. The two periods of statue-building mentioned above, according to leftist gospel, coincide first with the heyday of Jim Crow and second with backlash from the civil rights movement. This proves, to the Left, that the statues are no more than a means to intimidate blacks and support white nationalism. Dog whistles, maybe.

But there are other cogent reasons for the timing of monument-making. The first period also marks the invention of new techniques of production that lowered the cost of statues dramatically. It is no coincidence that the erection of many statues that had nothing to do with the Confederacy (including a goodly number to Union officers and to heroes of other wars) occurred in the same time frame. In fact, statues were being mass-produced, so the stone or bronze Union soldier in the square of a town in Ohio looks strangely identical to that of the rebel soldier in a similar town in Georgia. As to the second phase of statue-building, it coincided with the celebration of the centennial of the war and includes plenty of Union representatives. The simple fact is that, with few exceptions, the statues are no more or less than memorials to valor and self-sacrifice in a time of national trauma. The current mission drift of the war against them is evidence that the true purpose of statue vandalism, official or riotous, is far broader than to relieve sensitive souls from triggering. The War Against the Statues is one small piece of an anti-sovereignty movement that began with Marxism, if not before, and has waxed distressingly in recent years.

The movement in opposition to the concept of national sovereignty, commonly known as globalism, has been around a long time, but it has gained a huge surge of support since the turn of the current century. It has many elements, all trending toward the desire for a centralized world government and an integrated international economy that transcends (but certainly includes) mere free trade. Antagonism toward statues and any other physical reminder of a nation's history and exceptionalism is striking and demoralizing (and at times comical), but it is hardly the most damaging aspect of globalism. Far more dangerous is the attack on the very borders of a country, which has reached a peak in Europe and the United States. Mass immigration has, in the last few years, radically changed in terms of character as well as sheer numbers, and has taken on the features of invasion. Unlike the periods of large-scale immigration in former times, immigrants now are motivated not by famine, political persecution or the desolation of war but simply by a desire for economic improvement. What quicker way to improve one's lot than to move into a more prosperous land and simply take a share of its wealth?

The darker side of current immigration is that a large percentage of the immigrants have little intention of assimilating into the host country's culture.

A striking feature of the mass immigration of this century is the arrogance of the new arrivals. Whereas older illegal immigrants "lived in the shadows," today's illegal aliens seem happy to declare their presence quite openly. They demand not only complete acceptance but also a place at the front of the line for all the benefits that accrue to citizens. Many make no effort even to learn the country's language, much less cultural patterns. They expect the country to accommodate itself to their own. This sense of entitlement is just another aspect of globalism as we now know it. The new immigrants' attitudes reflect what they are told by numerous NGOs and other government-supported agencies, the mass media and various religious organizations. They feel justified in their expectations by the massive propaganda that, in many cases, prompted them to migrate in the first place. "Open Borders" is a mantra by which many on both sides of those national borders that are under attack have been seduced.

There is a Latin phrase, *cui bono?*, that has been used among lawyers for centuries. It means "who benefits?" and is a logical question to ask when seeking the perpetrator of an act, criminal or otherwise. One consistently good way to seek an answer to that question is to follow the money. In the case of mass immigration, a great deal of money is involved in the movement of whole populations from one place on the earth's surface to another. Tracing money movement on this scale is arduous, wearisome and time-consuming, and few of us have the research resources to do a thorough job of it. Fortunately, it has been done for us, with the results published in a recent book by Michelle Malkin : *Open Borders Inc.* (2019). The funding network for mass immigration advocate organizations is huge and intricate. I would encourage everyone to read the book itself for the full picture, but will reveal the two outstanding culprits here: the Catholic Church and George Soros and his merry band of billionaires. That hardly exhausts the support framework for the movement, but it covers a good deal of it. Again, read the book.

Other support for the movement, financial and otherwise, comes from sources such as the Democrat Party, unions and chambers of commerce. These are odd bedfellows, one might think, but there are reasons for it. People who fund something like an open borders campaign expect to receive something for their money. How do Soros and other billionaires benefit? A look at Soros' history suffices. His billions were gained, for the most part, by creating chaos. A favorite technique is placing financial bets on the collapse of certain currencies; he is notorious for severely damaging the Bank of England in that manner and collecting over a billion dollars for the effort. Nor is he above taking measures to promote social and financial instability to improve his odds. As a result, he is *persona non grata* in much of Europe and elsewhere, including his country of origin, Hungary.

The other billionaires who support open immigration and other leftist causes do so for similar reasons. The ultra-wealthy always want more and are largely protected by their wealth from ill effects of their activities.

But what of the Church? Are the bishops not motivated by the teachings of Jesus rather than greed? Well, not so much. They do defend their actions by cherry-picking certain quotations of Jesus without much regard for His larger teachings, but there is a more substantive reason for the stance of the Church's leftist elements on immigration. Congregations of the faithful have been dwindling in America lately, and what better means to replace people in the pews (and cash in collection plates) than by importing good Catholics from Latin America? Labor unions have a similar motivation: their ranks have thinned alarmingly since the glory days and large numbers of bottom-of-the-barrel workers comprise a potentially fruitful recruiting pool. The Democrats' motive is all too obvious: they need voters to replace the working class voters they've alienated and the black voters they will soon lose. Chambers of commerce are happy to see a supply of cheap labor for their members. None of these groups, it may be noted, are thinking too hard about the long-term good of the nation and their society as a whole. In each case, the focus is on short-term benefits and little else. Greed is good, is it not?

So much for the beneficiaries of mass immigration and the anti-sovereignty movement in general. Who are the losers? The answer is, pretty much everyone else. Regular citizens who can no longer walk the streets of their own cities in Europe, working people in the U.S., everyone who is not shielded by wealth and power from social and financial instability, all are hurt by mass immigration and globalist chaos. George Soros made a bundle in the Bank of London caper, but many thousands of ordinary people, not just British citizens, lost a goodly chunk of their hard-earned savings to line his pockets. Faithful Catholics have their offerings used against them in a direct way, but all taxpayers contribute unwittingly to the Church's support of open borders immigration. As Malkin demonstrates, large amounts of U.S. tax money supplement the coffers of the many Catholic charities that support the immigration invasion.

The erosion of national identity of all countries has profound negative effects on their populations (excluding the elites). But there are far more ordinary, working citizens than there are billionaires and bishops. How do the globalist elites muster sufficient popular support to effect their cause when it hurts a huge majority of the people? Are the nations of the West not democracies, and do people not campaign and vote to protect their own interests?

The foot soldiers of the anti-sovereignty movement are the usual suspects: social justice warriors, brainwashed college students and graduates, their professors who want to feel important by being (sort of) associated with the elites, celebrities who want to be trendy and fit in with their crowd, people in all walks of life who feel they must virtue-signal. They are encouraged by the propagandists in the offices of what used to be news organizations. They support globalism because, short-term, it makes them feel important, or smart, or virtuous. Long-term they will suffer with the rest of us, but that's then and this is now. You might also refer to Chapter 5: *Little People.*

In summary, the War Against the Statues seems silly on the surface but is on a deeper level an attack on the national fabric of the country. It is unlikely that most of those involved in or supportive of the attacks realize the underlying significance of what they are doing. If they did, some would continue anyway, because they have been taught to despise the country and all its traditions. They believe patriotism is an antiquated relic, that the sophisticated people are citizens of the world. They embrace chaos without recognizing it. Those who do recognize it and work to achieve it are the few who will benefit from it at the expense of humanity.

And as an aside, there is one problem that the modern iconoclasts are only beginning to see. The expense of removing statues is much higher than most of them thought (when they thought about it at all). It can cost a municipality as much as a teacher's salary for a year or more, which can put a dent in local budgets. But what then? There is still the matter of a pedestal, sitting there on the town square lonely and bare, a reminder of the very thing we're all supposed to forget. The cost of removal of that ugly structure can be even higher than that of the statue itself!

"The most effective way to destroy people is to deny and obliterate their own understanding of their history"
George Orwell

1/6/20

Chapter Nineteen

Righteous Privilege

As was mentioned several chapters ago (in *Righteousness Redux*), an adage among evangelists is that the worst enemy of Christianity is Christians. This saying is intended as humor but has a hard edge of truthfulness, and refers to a certain type of "holier than thou" church member. Also as mentioned, most Christians are cheerful souls, tolerant and kind toward those of other beliefs no matter how sincere their own faith. The problem, from an evangelistic point of view, is with those of inflexible mindset who take every opportunity to condemn anyone who might not rise to their lofty standards of morality. Those people may obtain much satisfaction from their self-preening attitude but, as the adage indicates, make it difficult for laborers in the vineyard of the Lord to convince lost souls to come to the faith. Another old adage is that it's easier to catch flies with honey than with vinegar, and while I certainly do not wish to compare non-Christian humans to flies, and don't think of converting them as "catching" in the entrapment sense, the point is evident.

If certain repellent Christians give the church a bad name, characteristics similar to theirs occur in most groups of humanity, and nowhere is that more evident than among those of the political Left. So much of the holier-than-thou mentality traditionally associated with churchy types is now exemplified by leftists that it's hard not to think of socialism itself as a religion. That may sound odd considering that a high percentage of socialists are atheists or agnostics, but Righteousness can be found in people of all persuasions and nowhere can it be found in a higher concentration than on the American Left. Righteousness has been a common topic in these pages, and for good reason. It is the key to many of the foibles of the Left, and much of its success as well. The Left couldn't be effective without it. Few leftist nostrums for society can be defended with logic, so Righteousness substitutes for reasoned argument. That may sound harsh, but it has worked for leftists for decades. Righteousness allows a socialist to feel confident in his opinions; It gives him power. It confers upon him privilege -- Righteous privilege.

When one thinks of all the vices that flow from Righteousness, none is more prominent than hypocrisy, and nowhere is the joy of hypocrisy celebrated more robustly than on the Left. There is an embarrassment of riches when one looks for examples to illustrate that assertion, but a couple concerning the current Democrat candidate for the presidency will suffice for the present. Let us compare the treatment of Mr. Biden when accused of sexual assault with that of Mr. Kavanaugh during his confirmation hearing. Keep in mind that the accusation against the latter was not only weak on its face but carefully constructed so as to preclude a fact-based defense. It was also totally uncorroborated by any source, even by the sources cited by the accuser. In contrast, the accusation against Mr. Biden was defined as to time and place and had at least some reasonably plausible corroboration behind it. His record of public behavior around women doesn't help him, either. Treatment of the two cases by Democrats and their press was shockingly different, with no shame or apologies. Kavanaugh is still mentioned in the same sentence as "impeachment"; Biden's case has been dropped into a memory black hole.

Further, the current president is constantly excoriated for dilatoriness in dealing with the coronavirus "pandemic", including by Mr. Biden whenever opportunity arises. Yet it was Biden who was sharply critical, with cries of xenophobia and racism, when Trump placed an early ban on travel to and from China. You might be forgiven for forgetting that; it hasn't been mentioned in Pravda West or by a Democrat politician in a long time. Speaking of the virus, a more recent example of arrant hypocrisy might be mentioned. Churchgoers were harassed and vilified during the hysteria, and accused of endangering the public by attending services. Not long after, mobs of BLM rioters did their thing without a single whimper of criticism from a Democrat -- pundit, journalist or Biden. Presumably, the mobs weren't a menace to society like the churchgoers. As I've noted before, the takeaway must be that it's OK to go to church as long as you're going there to burn it down.

The most blatant examples of leftist hypocrisy have to do with First Amendment rights to free speech. It's hypocritical enough when the Left invokes the Constitution to defend anything, since normally they hate the Constitution and all its works with a white-hot hatred and have been working diligently for over a century to destroy it. To invoke it to defend their right to riot, commit vandalism and burn the flag is even worse, since any speech (I mean actual s-p-e-e-c-h) they don't want to hear is condemned as hate speech. Perhaps leftist hypocrisy concerning free speech has something to do with the monopoly over most public speech they held for decades with their dominance of the three big TV channels and most of radio. The rise of conservative radio and social media eroded that dominance, and although the Left labors tirelessly to restore their monopoly, far too much actual free speech still gets through to the deplorables to suit them. Us deplorables are getting dog-whistled all the way to freedom, and it has to be stopped! This festering frustration of the Left can be understood in terms of privilege. They are Righteous, and a monopoly over speech is simply a usufruct of Righteous privilege.

Iconoclasm is an especially fun duty that derives from Righteous privilege. Since part of that privilege is not having to put up with anything that tends to trigger those of the Left, which is anything they find disagreeable, and since our forebears lacked the virtue and intelligence of the current generation of leftists, and since our history is therefore not up to standards, it is necessary to change history to what it *should* have been. This solemn duty leftists of all stripes perform with vigor and enjoy every minute of it. Since no one is perfect -- at least no one other than social justice warriors -- and since no statue, plaque or other memorial should exist for any historical figure who fell short of SJW perfection, which is all of them, before long not a single statue will be left in America. Well, there may be at least temporary exceptions made for people of color, but even they will have to overcome a high bar. Righteous privilege knows no bounds.

The most important of the many benefits of Righteous privilege is an absolute right to set the terms of any discussion. This ability to control all discourse is what gives the Left its power in our society today. Without it, the Left is impotent; with it the Left cannot be defeated with any normal discourse. It is the pinnacle of Righteous privilege. Its effect is to declare a leftist the winner in any argument before the argument begins, which is useful indeed when the premises from which said leftist must argue are indefensible by regular logic.

And why should a leftist not be blessed with this advantage? After all, if one is Righteous, what is the point of discussion in the first place? What can a Righteous individual learn from someone who disagrees with him when said person is not only wrong but also un-Righteous, which is to say evil. The Righteous person does better not to talk with a deplorable at all, except to excoriate and condemn him, which is what generally happens. For decades now, conservatives have hesitated to speak up in public for fear of being labeled horrible persons who would do better to be struck by a meteorite and perish from the earth by disintegration into basic molecules. They live in terror of being called racists, homophobes and every other "ist" and "phobe" the ingenuity of the Left has devised. So they stay silent while the leftist crows.

Domination of public discourse by moral intimidation, supported by most of our public institutions, has given the Left free rent for its occupation of the moral high ground. The Left has supplanted the worst of the old-time religious bigots in that respect. As with the latter, most ordinary citizens of the country, some of whom may even agree to some extent with leftist policies and political nostrums, have little but contempt for the most rigid and unforgiving of the social justice warriors of the Left. Even so, with a few courageous exceptions they avoid confrontation because of a certain reserve about violating Righteousness. Among the courageous, none are more so than that exceptional handful of blacks who have embraced conservatism and are willing to face the most outrageous slander and obloquy rather than compromise their principles. If any are to lead us out of this morass of moral straitjacket and intellectual bigotry, they will be at the head. Let us hope there are enough of the rest of us to follow them.

So Righteous privilege allows the possessor to lie blatantly, to be an egregious hypocrite, to slander and libel any who disagree with him and wreak havoc on other people and their property, and to be praised and defended in the process. All that is protected by the First Amendment right to free speech when committed by the Righteous, but criticism of it by a deplorable is condemned as racist or whatever, and prosecuted as hate speech. You will search in vain through the Constitution and its amendments for wording to that effect, but no matter: Righteous privilege is clearly included in the Left's new constitution, which is in any case far superior to the old one. After all, the old Constitution was crafted by a bunch of dead white heterosexual males, some of whom were even slave owners. The new constitution is a much better reflection of Who We Are. Or perhaps I should say "who we will be," if the Left continues to have its way.

Righteous privilege may be a major pain for the rest of us, but it is wonderfully liberating for those who have it. Those privileged souls can do almost anything and not only get away with it but feel good about themselves in the bargain. The current wave of riots and vandalism, in the course of which perpetrators are sanctified and police are vilified, is proof of that for anyone who may still need proof. The only line anyone remembers from the old movie *A Love Story* is "Being in love means you never have to say you're sorry." That may or may not be true, but there is no doubt that having Righteous privilege means that, even to himself, he who has it never has to admit he is wrong.

7/5/20

Chapter Twenty

The Dog Whistlers

The usefulness of dog whistles is based on the fact that dogs can hear sound waves of shorter wave lengths, which is to say higher frequencies, than can humans. If one lets go a blast on a dog whistle, therefore, no human being around will be bothered by it, or even know it has been sounded unless he is very close, in which case it will only be a soft hiss. Of course, it might set off all the neighborhood dogs as well as one's own, but one can't have everything. A dog whistle is commonly used in the training of an animal or just to signal a pet without arousing human attention. In fact, the dog's owner has to be careful when employing the device; if it's blown too vigorously it could be quite painful to his furry buddy without his knowing it.

Somewhere along the line, certain social justice warriors of the human species picked up the idea of the dog whistle for an entirely unrelated purpose. Those sensitive souls decided that various deplorable humans (or perhaps sub-humans), mainly those of the white supremacist persuasion, were using esoteric signs and phrases to signal their fellow miscreants -- signals that were hidden from good people. These signs and phrases, which they called dog whistles, were being used (they theorized) to encourage bad behavior and forbidden thoughts generally, and specifically to instigate foul actions against racial, ethnic or religious minorities. The idea is that these racists, xenophobes, homophobes, Islamophobes, etc., could coordinate terrorist activities in secret, sort of like Indians making bird sounds to let one another know the situation as they sneaked up on unaware settlers. The SJWs, ever vigilant and always protective of the poor helpless minorities, are wise to the devious machinations of the fascists and ready to warn the potential victims of looming danger. The world is dangerous, but safer for disempowered prey because of the virtue of the SJWs.

There's one (at least) curious anomaly in that noble scenario. It's that the "dogs" in question -- i.e., despicable deplorables -- are totally oblivious to the supposed dog whistles of their supposed leaders. In fact, the only people who appear to be able to detect the signals are the very people that are presumed not to be able to detect them. Although I am myself a deplorable by most leftist definitions, I don't personally know any overt racists or white (or any other color) supremacists or even fascists other than those of the standard left-wing variety, and don't want to. But all of the ordinary deplorable types I do know, of any race or ethnicity, are unaware of the existence of dog whistles and oblivious if they see or hear one. I rather suspect that the same may apply even to most right-wing extremists. In other words, the only people who can see or hear the various nasty dog whistles are the very ones whom the whistles are intended to deceive. What good is a dog whistle that dogs can't hear but humans can?

I flashed a familiar hand sign at my friend and fellow blogger Janus at the bar a year or so ago and asked if he knew what it meant. He looked at me as though I'd gone dotty and answered, "The OK sign, of course. But it dates you; everyone has used thumbs up for at least twenty years." When I told him it was now some kind of racist dog whistle, he just shrugged and had another sip of his favorite beverage. We went on to talk about the football playoffs. It must be admitted that Janus is black, and so presumed to be helpless, not too bright and dependent on the protection of the SJWs. Presumed so by the SJWs, that is -- no one who knows him would be under any such illusions. Besides, the very savvy Indian bartender wasn't aware of the racist dog whistle either. If none of us knew, nor any other white or black or Latino conservative I asked, it's a safe bet that that particular hand sign wasn't working too well as a dog whistle. The only person with whom I am acquainted who was familiar with the whistling effect of the old OK sign was a white female student of very leftist leanings. It may be safe to infer that the OK and all the other arcane signs and phrases are actually reverse dog whistles, activating not the dogs but the SJWs.

Looking past the strangeness of the theory of right-wing dog whistles to the probable genesis of the theory, one sees immediately a familiar leftist eccentricity: a penchant for the art of projection. It is the SJWs themselves who are sending a constant stream of signals to their acolytes and allies, so naturally they look for the same in their conservative adversaries. But the "dog whistles" sent out by the Left are as odd in their own way as those the leftists attribute to the Right. They constitute a veritable barrage of sound that can be heard all too clearly by everyone: their own followers, the deplorables and people who just don't care. The commands of Maxine Waters to SJWs and leftists of any stripe to hunt down and harass all people to the right of Karl Marx, to drive them out of restaurants and any public venue, to never give them a moment's peace, are signals for certain. If the commands were sent out stealthily they would manifestly be dog whistles. As it is, they are more like dog bugles. So it is with most of the signs given by leftist leaders to their acolytes to pursue the persecution of the political enemy. But if the signals are supposed to be dog whistles, which apparently they are, they fail to qualify by sheer volume of sound.

So what's going on? The right-wing leaders fail to connect with their supremacist followers because the latter can't hear the signals, but at least they're presumably trying to signal the correct crowd. The leftists are sending out blasts that everyone can hear, even those who aren't listening, so how is anyone to know who the intended recipients are? Which is to say, how do the intended targets of these ear-crushing dog whistles know they, specifically, are being whistled at if everyone alive can hear the whistle? Some of them, of course, know for certain. The SJWs and the Antifa thugs have no doubt that they are being summoned to action when the peals of virtuous thunder ring out. But how about various other groups that are being appealed to by the ear-splitting demands of Waters and her colleagues, people of a more pacific nature who are less accustomed to violent activity? And who are they, in fact?

Democrats have long considered themselves the patrons of a mosaic of demographic classifications. The idea of victimization is the glue that binds their coalition together. In return for protecting these presumed victims of white supremacists from their oppressors and giving them handouts (of other peoples' extorted money), they expect a few services in return. Primary among those services is voting for any Democrat on any ballot, early and often. So while Maxine Waters' stentorian dog whistles are clearly directed at certain activists, there is a plethora of other whistles, just as obvious, that go out regularly to a broader base. When Joe Biden says, "If you don't know who to support, me or Trump, you ain't black," that's a pretty loud whistle to the whole black electorate to perform on their collective duty to the Democrat party. Not too many days go by without the issuance of dog whistles of that sort, and no particular care is taken to hide them from anyone anywhere on the political spectrum. They are definitely signals, but as dog whistles they leave much to be desired. Or do they?

Looked at another way, even though they can be plainly heard by everyone, perhaps those signals are not so lacking in dog whistle value after all. Biden didn't have to say, "Vote for me or the white supremacists who are lurking everywhere will lynch you and tar and feather your families." It was implicit in what he did say, implanted by decades of leftist propaganda aimed at the black community. It is no longer necessary to say outright that minorities will be endangered if Democrats aren't in power, or that the SJWs are the only entities standing between them and destruction. Blacks have been dog-whistled for decades in this manner, ever since the Depression years and FDR's New Deal. Whistling on this theme only intensified with LBJ (a notorious racist himself) and the Great Society.

The dog whistle isn't hard to hear, it's just coded. The code is decipherable only by history, a long history of real oppression of black people.

The only problem, as it happens, is that the wrong people are doing the whistling. It has been sort of forgotten by the Democrat politicians and their house media that the people doing the actual lynching and oppressing back in the day were, essentially all of them .... Democrats. Even after the Democrat Party reformed, in its way, the nostrums it advanced, as detailed by Candace Owens in her book *Blackout* (2020), didn't do the black community much good in the long run. What they did do was disrupt black society and chain a huge majority of black people to the Democrat political plantation, seemingly forever. They sensitized the black population to their dog whistle and by freely blowing it took command of a huge percentage of black votes. By means of that key voting block they gained both national and local political power without actually having to do much for blacks except shovel out to them a few bucks of other people's money. Rather clever, wouldn't you say?

Leftist dog whistling worked so well with black people that the Democrats have taken up the technique with other minorities. Hispanics are now supposed to believe they would be deported *en masse*, whether here legally or otherwise, if not for the heroic actions of their leftist protectors. True, more illegals, Hispanic and otherwise, were deported during the Obama regime than under Trump, but the whistle still belongs to the Democrats. Other minorities respond to whistles designed by SJWs for them, and there's even a majority that gets dog whistled. There are more women in the US than men, but they have a history of oppression also -- nowhere near that of black people, but enough to design a few whistles for them. Again, the whistles for women aren't so subtle and can be heard by everyone. Neither are they as effective for women in general; they mainly work on single women. Movies like *The Handmaiden's Tale*, restructured scripts such as those for the various *Beauty and the Beast* plays and films, novels with a feminist slant, and most of all alteration of the English language to emphasize gender distinctions -- all of these send signals to the vulnerable.

It won't end there. If any new divisions within the human race are identified, the Left will politicize them and invent a dog whistle or two to take advantage. Meanwhile, those ever vigilant and hyper-sensitive SJW saviors will continue to hear ghostly dog whistles emanating from the ghostly leaders of the deplorables of the Right -- and blow the whistle on them.

Chapter Twenty-One

Machiavelli and the Snowflakes

There's an idea among historians that every century begins about a decade and a half late. It may be more appropriate to say that each one ends a decade and a half late. You may think it's the same thing, but there seems to be more clarity to endings than beginnings. Perhaps that is only because we don't know something has begun until we see it in retrospect.

An example of that is the real beginning of the 15th century, arguably in the year 1415. That was the year of the famous Battle of Agincourt, the victory of English archers and men-at-arms against all odds over an overwhelming force of French armored knights. It marked the high tide of English success in the Hundred Years' War, an era that belonged to the last part of the 14th century. Although rightly celebrated as a spectacular English victory, it was in reality the end of the period of English military dominance on the continent. That means it was also the beginning of the consolidation of France as the first real nation-state. No one knew that at the time, of course. It is only by looking back, only when it had become history, that we can see the meaning of an ending – and thus the beginning.

Similar late endings mark the 17th century (end of the religious balance in Europe and outbreak of the 30 Years' War in 1618), 18th century (death of Louis XIV), 19th century (Waterloo and the end of the Napoleonic and French revolutionary eras) and the 20th century (outbreak of the Great War and end of the age of kingdoms and empires). One might go back even further, to the end of the 14th century (start of the Great Famine in 1315, which ended the period of European growth known as the High Middle Ages) and of the 13th century (signing of the Magna Carta in 1215 and the end of the untrammeled power of the king in England). All of these events are genuine landmarks of European history; the delayed-century pattern is real. As far as the rest of the world goes, centuries may or may not conform to their own patterns.

You may have noticed that I left out the 16th century from the catalog. That wasn't from lack of a suitable event: when an Augustinian monk nailed a piece of paper to a church door in Wittenberg in 1517, more than a millennium of the total domination of Rome over the religion (and much of the politics) of the West came to an end. It was because I was saving for last a less obvious late-century occurrence than any of the above, the writing of a short book (actually little more than a tract) in 1513 in Florence. Its title was to become *The Prince* and its author was Niccolo Machiavelli.

Machiavelli wasn't really such a bad person, certainly not as bad as his eponym: "Machiavellian". Does that word bring up some ugly feelings in you? It should. It's the ultimate adjective for brass knuckles, take-no-prisoners, cynical and manipulative politics. The book was written when its author had just left Florence to go into exile on his small family estate south of the city. It was a blessing in disguise, because it gave him time to put some of his thoughts into writing. They were pretty good thoughts, because Niccolo was a pretty good diplomat, and the book is generally considered to be the foundation stone of modern political science. But it came up a little short on the professed ethics of the day and the Catholic church banned it not long after its 1532 publication. Now it wouldn't be thought so evil; modern *realpolitik* and actual practices follow it closely. Machiavelli was a pragmatist above all. He described what a ruler must do rather than what he "ought" to do. His advice was for a prince who had to run his country first and could think about going to Heaven later.

But this article is about Machiavellianism, not Machiavelli. It is about cynical manipulation of government institutions for tendentious ends, about unethical practices by government officials who have been given responsibility to do their duty to the public and have betrayed their offices. It is also about the end of the 20th century. Did the 20th century end late, like so many before it? If you were to do a poll of the American public now, I suspect most respondents would say the end of the century occurred on September 11, 2001, almost on schedule. I disagree. My proposal is that it ended on the usual late schedule, in November, 2016. That was an ending, something that we can see: the death of democracy in the world's leading democratic state. It was also, perforce, the beginning of something else, but what that is will only be known to our descendants.

On Tuesday, November 8, 2016, Donald Trump, Republican, was elected President of the United States of America, immediately triggering a movement to overturn that election. For only the second time in American history, major elements of the losing side in a national election refused to accept its results. The first time, Lincoln's election in 1860, was different in several significant ways and led to an organized war between two geographically defined nations. It was not a civil war in the normal sense of the term: the warring parties were not striving for control of the same government. In the present case, in contrast, the struggle is indeed for control of the U.S. federal government, and we are involved in a true civil war. So far, and let us be thankful, it is a cold war.

What is interesting about the recalcitrant 2016 election losers is the speed with which the winner was rejected. An article published on the internet by a Joshua Holland on February 6, 2017, lists several dozen "resistance" organizations then in existence. Donald Trump wasn't inaugurated until January 20 of that year, only eighteen days earlier. A large majority of those resistance groups were formed before he even became president, and all of them before he had a chance to do anything. Even more interesting is that powerful elements in what we know as the Establishment, including within Trump's own administration, constituted a resistance inside the walls, so to speak. This two-pronged attack on the current president and his administration, the Machiavellians inside and the snowflakes outside, together make an interesting subject for study.

Let us address the former first. If no other benefit has ensued from the political vitriol of the last two years, at least we can count as one the revelation of the existence of the Deep State. An important element of this nebulous force behind the Establishment power structure is, sadly, the Intelligence Community (IC) of the U.S., and prominently within the IC, the Federal Bureau of Investigation. Not the entire FBI, it can be said with hopeful confidence, perhaps not a very sizeable fragment of it, nor of the IC as a whole. But the corrupted element was unfortunately at the very top of this justly famous organization and included directors, former directors and high-level officers. The FBI is part of the Justice Department, which still has people at and near the top who are very much part of the Deep State. The Justice Department belongs to the Executive Branch of the government, which is headed by the president. This means, of course, that a significant number of the people who are attempting to bring down the president are members of his own administration. This would have made Machiavelli proud, if he really had been as bad as some of his critics declare.

Perhaps the apex of this mountain of deceit and manipulation was revealed in a celebrated New York Times article that purported to be (and probably was) written by a Republican official in the administration who was also proudly Deep State. This anonymous soul described his daily routine of actively obstructing the work of the president at every opportunity. We must conclude that the willful sabotage of the president's agenda is not a merely partisan effort. The Establishment as a whole is closely involved, although not every individual associated with it. Their elite status, their revenues and perks, their self-esteem, all that gives them the privilege to look down on the deplorables is at stake. Trump came to Washington to break something (at the behest of his voters), and the Establishment does not want any piece of their smug little lifestyle broken. Let us look briefly at some of the Machiavellian devices its Deep State agents have used.

The Clinton campaign and the DNC hired a law firm and opposition research team to, in turn, hire a foreign national to use Russian contacts to compile a phony dossier to discredit their candidate's opponent. They later took that bit of salacious fiction, along with some drunken bar boasting by a minor Trump campaign functionary, before a FISA court to have a special counsel appointed and assigned to find evidence of collusion of Trump's campaign with Russia. The special counsel used this as an opportunity to examine the last two decades of Trump's activities in minute detail and to squeeze anyone he might have known to bear witness against him. Deep State operatives too numerous to name, and in many cases not yet publicly identified, used the Department of Justice, CIA, FBI and NSC to obstruct, first, Trump's candidacy, then his team's transition efforts, and finally his presidency, in every possible way. In addition, these elements within his own administration tried to influence the Electoral College and sued to change vote totals in several key states in an attempt to reverse the election results.

These same people have from the beginning leaked anything and everything that might be embarrassing to Trump and his administration to a willing media, the journalists of which can themselves be fairly considered Deep State operatives. Every week or so these newshounds drop another "bombshell" story that is highly incriminating against the president. Every bombshell is accompanied by cries of joy by other journalists: "That's it! Now we've finally got him. This is impeachment material for certain!" Every bombshell proves to be fabricated, of course, but is either retracted at the bottom of page 31 or is forgotten and never retracted at all. Between bombshells, the "news" reports not only continue at a 90% level of negativity against the president but manage to subliminally slip in a few little gratuitous jabs as lagniappe. Taken all together, the activities of Deep State agents within government, the federal courts and the media are purest Machiavelli on steroids.

Enter the snowflakes. The amazing rapidity of the formation of a "resistance" was described above. It was mostly nonviolent, but certainly there were threatening aspects to it, as with harassment and stalking of conservative politicians and commentators, and some truly ugly actors also appeared, notably the fascistic Antifa (I'm aware of the irony) lot. Then came the 2018 midterm elections and the snowflakes marched in on the big stage. Actually, the Left didn't do tremendously well overall, given their advantages and the expectation of a Blue Wave. Democrats did gain a House majority, as expected, but lost ground in the more critical Senate. It was rather a draw, but any gain at all energized the Left. What is more, the new Democrat faces in the House are largely new indeed: young, brash and unabashedly leftist. The most vociferous among them are proudly socialist, in fact. And they are flakes of snow to the fingertips.

One of the bold new representatives, Rashaida Tlaib, made a fearless cry for impeachment of the president that will resonate in every snowflake heart. "Each passing day," she intoned, "brings more pain for the people most directly hurt by this president, and these days we simply cannot get back. The time for impeachment proceedings is now." Now, President Trump, for all the naughtiness he has committed, has never, to my knowledge, been accused of physical assault, so she must refer to his tweets or speeches. Just think, something Trump said has ruined an innocent victim's whole day! The beast! It melts the coldest deplorable heart. That quote might be set to music as an anthem for the snowflakes.

So there we have it: a resistance to the administration; a refusal to submit to democratic norms; the declaration, in effect, of a cold war. The constant desire of leftists of all stripes is for impeachment. Among them, the Machiavellians of the Deep State are traditionalists of sorts: they realize there must be a constitutionally acceptable reason to impeach a president beyond just not liking him. They have been working most diligently for over two years now to unearth such a reason – any excuse will do.

The snowflakes don't see it that way. They've been taught (in a system designed by the Left) that their safe spaces are sacrosanct, that they have a right not to be disturbed by statements or ideas with which they disagree. They can't understand why any reason is needed for impeachment beyond their own discomfort. The incoherent speeches of Maxine Waters, that aging snowflake precursor, consist of little more than hysterical screams of "Impeachment!" and the young snowflakes seek no further. So we have a two-pronged attack on the presidency of Donald Trump – Machiavelli and the snowflakes. The former try to provide legal means; the latter provide emotional momentum. The media mediate, so to speak: they labor to undermine the president by working both ends, by fabricating stories of legal transgressions, hoping something will eventually stick, and by providing sympathetic support to the emotionally distressed.

To return to the beginning, where will that century that started on November 8, 2016, lead us? What will historians of the 23rd century think of the 21st? I doubt that anyone alive today will really know, although the youngest may gain some idea if they live long enough. Of course, this beginning is a double one: it is also the beginning of a new millennium. If our American republic fails to survive as either a republic or a liberal democracy, who knows where the world will be at the end of this young millennium?

I end this article with a short line from T.S. Eliot's *Portrait of a Lady* that seems especially appropriate: "But our beginnings never know our ends..."

Chapter Twenty-Two
The High Ground

The Left seized the moral high ground for good in the 1960s. Those who are old enough to be cognizant of what was happening then remember the '60s as an age of turmoil and social division. University campuses were ground zero for the uproar of the time, as students dressed in semi-military looking brown shirts (inadvertent symbolism?) and carrying bullhorns roused their fellows to action. Besides posing for news reporters, most of the action had to do with pot-smoking, booze and sex, but that was a lot more fun than slogging through a jungle in some far-off part of the world while being shot at. Better yet, not going to Vietnam not only was safer than doing one's civic duty, it made one the hero in the scenario, while the people playing soldier were conscienceless baby killers. True, there wasn't much studying going on among those who went to college for little more than fun and (most important) draft deferment, but with all that *was* going on there wasn't much time for study anyway. And they were on the moral high ground while having fun.

The high ground wasn't invented in the 1960s, of course. It has always been around as the preferred resort of those who couldn't make a decent moral argument for their actions (or lack of actions) in the usual ways. Through the course of history, a goodly percentage of its occupants have been of various religious persuasions. Indolent wearers of the cassock and their prelates used the high ground as a cover for their sloth and sins in the Middle Ages and beyond – by no means all churchmen or even a majority, but enough to paint an enduring image. More recently, a certain minority of the deacon class of modern churches have forgotten that we are all, yea every one, sinners, and taken to looking down on us normal people from holier-than-thou perches. But politically, at least since the French Revolution, the high ground has been a sanctuary of the Left. With the coming of the Fabian Society and the onset of the Progressive Movement, the high ground became the

Left's exclusive province, although it was taken over in subtle ways in those days. Since then the Left became bolder in its seizure of the high ground, and the ground has gotten ever higher since the epic consolidation of the Left's position thereon in the '60s.

The Left's right to own the high ground is based on its sense of self-righteousness, referred to merely as Righteousness in many previous chapters. It is based on no facts, and certainly not on logic. The Left stakes its claim to the high ground as a kind of innate right, much as Thomas Jefferson invoked natural rights as a basis for his Declaration of Independence. When one is Righteous, one holds the high ground as a matter of course, without having to justify it by any sort of argument or indeed anything whatever other than Righteousness itself. It is a religious sort of thing, the substitute for religion of those who tend to be, on the whole, unreligious. One might say that it is a matter of faith for those who profess no faith. Therefore, leftists rarely try to justify their station on the high ground, and it is well that they do not, because they are at a distinct disadvantage in the practice of the art of polemics. The disadvantage is not so much a matter of paucity of intellectual firepower as one of a paucity of supporting facts. No one can hit a logic target with no ammunition; it is best to rely on emotion.

And reliance on emotion is what typifies leftists' arguments. They take advantage of the high ground to launch moralistic proclamations in lieu of logic as their initial gambit in most political discussions. That gives them leverage in two ways: first, it establishes their moral superiority; second, it lets them avoid any attempt at logic. The idea is that if anyone attempts to employ logic at that point, they are by implicit admission morally deficient philistines. Thus, Nancy Pelosi can shrug off any need to address the damage inflicted by illegal immigration on working class Americans simply by invoking her generosity of spirit and announcing that we must welcome illegals "with open arms." Anyone who argues with that must by definition be racist, xenophobic, greedy and uncharitable. End of argument. And if the nasty person who disagrees with the leftist continues to argue, the latter moves immediately to the second level of leftist argumentation, which is condemnation. That is, he calls the miscreant, in a fit of Righteous indignation, all the names listed above, plus a few others. If even that fails, if the poor right-wing fool continues to spout logical nonsense, the leftist, left with no more weapons except more *ad hominem* insults, may simply stalk off in high moral dudgeon. He has won the argument; if the logician hasn't the grace to admit defeat it's not the leftist's fault.

Appeals to emotion and condemnation may not be enough to persuade regular working people, especially the multitude that is basking in the joys of white privilege, to the socialist way of thinking (or, more accurately, feeling). Fortunately for the Left, there is a final backup that operates on a grand scale in this country: the Big Lie. The phrase was actually coined by a socialist of the nationalist class, none other than Adolf Hitler, in his book *Mein Kampf* (1925), although used there in a different context from the usual one that is attributed to Hitler's Minister of Propaganda, Joseph Goebbels. Its common formulation is: "If you tell a lie big enough and keep repeating it, people will eventually come to believe it." Socialists throughout the 20th century were able to wield the Big Lie by means of their control of the media, or the most important segments of it, and that remains the case today. Pravda West is even more completely under leftist domination than almost anyone realized before the accession of Donald Trump to the presidency. When all else fails, the mass media's use of the Big Lie propaganda technique effectively maintains the Left's grip on the high ground.

With this in mind, the potency of the combination of the Big Lie and Righteousness can be understood. How can a normal person withstand the sheer hammering effect of the Big Lie as delivered daily by Pravda West when to even try to resist is to admit moral depravity? As long as the Left holds the moral high ground, the Big Lie of the moment will dominate our "news" without serious opposition. No one enjoys attacking a statement that is pronounced from on high; no one wishes to be labeled a racist or another such term of opprobrium. So the Big Lie is not only big, loud and constant, but is shielded by moral privilege. The effect of the combination is to deny a victim of leftist denunciation, however outrageous, any means of defense. It's like fighting quicksand. The more one declares innocence, the more guilty he becomes. During the Trump administration, this effect has been focused on a single man, whose identity you can probably guess.

During WWII a number of psychological analyses were made of Hitler in an effort to discover his vulnerabilities. In one of these, done by Henry A. Murray in 1943, there is a passage that is eerily reminiscent of Pravda West and various Democrat politicians in their treatment of President Trump: "Never to admit a fault or wrong; never to accept blame; concentrate on one enemy at a time; blame that enemy for everything that goes wrong; take advantage of every opportunity to raise a political whirlwind." The passage described the Nazis' denunciations of the Jews, but it could just as well apply to the Left's attacks on Trump. The Russian collusion hoax raged in the media and the halls of government for years; instead of offering an abject apology when it was proven false leftists still raise it from time to time. The impeachment fiasco followed with similar result. Then a windfall arrived for the Left: a new virus strain from China that could be hyped by media and politicians into a pandemic that was used to torpedo a wildly successful economy and might yet sway the coming election. It's all Trump's fault, of course. Hitler and Goebbels would be proud.

But why would Trump be a target of such uninhibited vituperation? He's the leader of the opposition party, of course, and the Bushes before him received plenty of flack. Even the amiable Ronald Reagan was the subject of bitter personal attack, a fact that is now conveniently forgotten by many. But the sheer viciousness, the vitriol that accompanies criticism of President Trump exceeds not only in volume but in nature anything else in living memory involving political invective. There is an element of actual hatred in the Left's attitude toward Trump that is almost frightening. It is literally deranged. But it can be comprehended when one remembers the Left's treasured and hard-won possession of the moral high ground. For decades now the Left's moral ascendancy has been unchallenged. Any suggestion that it is undeserved is crushed under an avalanche of *ad hominem* insults. The Left's hatred is easily understood: Trump Derangement Syndrome is a reaction to an existential threat to its high ground.

Trump's great sin in the eyes of the Left is that he doesn't cave in to the usual barrage of moral condemnation. Unlike all the others the Left has buffaloed, Trump hits back with obvious gusto. The more unbalanced his attackers become in their blind ferocity, the more pleasure he takes in the counterattack. The real problem for the leftists, especially Pravda West's propagandists, is that they have begun to look ridiculous as well as biased. Nothing is more dangerous to a system based on moral pretension than to have people laugh at it. Trump's dogged resistance and refusal to fold threatens the very foundations of the moral high ground. This, more than anything, accounts for the profound hatred of the Left. If the high ground should begin to erode from beneath them, what is left to the leftists? Facts? Logic? Hardly. If they lose the high ground from which they have viewed the rest of us with such disdain these many years, socialists, with their Antifa thugs and social justice warriors, are finished as a real political force. The Constitution may be taken seriously again. People may return to thinking of themselves as Americans rather than members of some social, ethnic or sexual group defined as marginalized by Democrat politicians. They may even start voting Republican.

It is interesting to reflect that possibly no individual in America other than Trump could have threatened the Left's high ground so profoundly. He is a billionaire and can't be bought like the Clintons and Bidens of the political world. He spent his career in the extreme rough and tumble of NYC big-time real estate and can't be intimidated like the Bushes. He has an ego that won't yield to the threats of moralists. He isn't a politician and the weaknesses of the political class are not included in his makeup. In short, he is largely invulnerable to the usual weapons of the Establishment. His flamboyant style captures the popular imagination, both positively and negatively; otherwise he could not have incited the firestorm of hatred that has consumed the national attention. Most of all, he has been constant in his determination to withstand the storm of slings and arrows hurled from the moral high ground, and that is a mortal threat to the Left. His populism may motivate him, but populists have been around a long time without rousing such utter hatred. Even Reagan wasn't attacked with such reckless vituperation, although he was denigrated unfairly and regularly. The fact is that, for all the good he did for his country, Ronald Reagan never posed the exigent peril to the Left that Trump does.

It is ironic that the threat to the Left's hold on the high ground is in part of their own making. By attacking Trump so tenaciously in defense of the high ground, the Left has focused attention on the high ground itself in a manner that wouldn't have happened if they had ignored Trump or merely laughed at him. As it is, they are now exposed. The riots, burning and vandalism that shake some of America's great cities are not attractive arguments for moral superiority. The intemperate language used not only against Trump but against anyone who speaks well of him or votes for him is not especially suitable for a secular priesthood of moral leaders. Trump is a threat, but blame for the damage being done to the Left's moral pedestal can be laid at the feet of its own acolytes. With each day that passes, the high ground is beginning to look more like the low Swamp.

7/2/20

PART IV

The Party of the Left

The Left has its very own party these days. Yes, the oldest political party in this hemisphere, and maybe in the world, depending on how one looks at it, has been totally captured by the Left. It's a fairly recent phenomenon; as late as the turn of the century there was still room in the Democrat Party for conservatives, or at least moderates. Now a politically moderate Democrat is a *rara avis*. People point to Joe Manchin, senator from West Virginia, as an example, but although he talks a moderate game (as anyone expecting to be elected from West Virginia must), he votes solidly with his party on any substantive issue. Besides, just one example among that whole lot? One *rara avis* does not a summer make – or a non-leftist party.

Since the Democrat Party is now the official and exclusive party of the Left, it is manifest that all the comments in the previous section about the Left apply to the party as well. This section, however, is more purely political in that it addresses the effects the leftward shift has had on the party itself and its future prospects. In a sense, all bets are off as to what will become of the party as the future unfolds, because it has changed so drastically that there are no precedents to help us predict its course. The party has certainly been associated with progressivism since at least the presidency of Woodrow Wilson, but it has also been balanced by more conservative blocks of both politicians and voters. These have been falling by the wayside over the last few decades, as described in several chapters below, especially *The Emulation of Brunnhilde, Part I: The Common Man*. The entire "Solid South" of former years is now almost as solidly Republican, and although labor union leadership mostly remains under the Democrat banner, many of the rank-and-file members have deserted.

The party has managed to hold the core of its variegated coalition together, as shown by the last national election, but how long that will last is uncertain. The 90%-plus share of the black vote, for one example, may soon be a thing of the past. Efforts to shore up the coalition continue, and additions to it through encouragement of new immigration may succeed for a while, but it is evident that the party will have to wean itself from extreme leftism and broaden its base of actual issues to prosper. Most of the material in the next seven chapters is therefore still relevant. The fundamental weaknesses noted below still burden the party, the results of the narrowness of the party's strictly Left philosophical outlook. Current desperate measures being taken by the new administration to lock in the two-year Democrat advantage may not be enough to sustain the party in the longer run. It needs some new blood and some new thinking, as suggested by the following chapters.

Chapter Twenty-Three

The Key

The world is a complex place. It's big, it's diverse and it's constantly changing. No matter how old we are, from time to time we find ourselves in a new place, often a place of stupefying strangeness. There is, however, one advantage that accrues from age: we've been in so many strange places that we're no longer amazed by either strangeness or mutability. That feeling of being lost has at least become familiar. Some of us have, over the course of time, come upon a way of dealing with the uncomfortable phenomenon of weirdness. We have come to realize that there's nearly always a very simple way of looking at the most unfamiliar and apparently complex situation that clarifies it and enables us to understand it. There is, in a word, a key that, once discovered, answers all the questions that seem so opaque, bizarre and insoluble. More often than not, it's the very simplicity of the key that makes it hard to see.

The place we now find ourselves in the political life of the United States is one that no living person has ever before seen. The very foundation of our system is crumbling beneath us. I refer to our democratic tradition, which underlies our constitutional republic and the whole political structure that is built upon it. As pointed out in Chapter 20 (*Machiavelli and the Snowflakes*), widespread refusal of most of the hard-core Left of the nation (and much of the everyday Left) to accept the legitimacy of the 2016 presidential election marked the end of democratic process in the world's foremost democracy. Always before, however hard-fought an election was and however great the perceived stakes, the losing party always (if not always graciously) accepted the result. The failure of so many Democrats to do so in 2016 broke the mold. We are now in a phase of unprecedented adversarial vituperation in terms of our national politics. There have been rough times before and politics is always a rough game, but this level of hatred of a president and pure vitriol from the mass media is uglier than any precedent. The reaction from the other side, the despised deplorables, is one of undisguised contempt for the self-styled elites. Not a good situation.

Extreme language from Pravda West bombards the country daily. Leading the parade of partisan intemperance are some of the more highly respected and traditional outlets rather than the scandal sheets of former days. A couple of recent NYT articles by Timothy Egan are typical. The shorter one contains 14 brief paragraphs in which the word "evil" occurs 14 times (including the title). All refer to the president. The nasty vocabulary isn't limited to that word. Near the beginning is the statement, "On any given day, Trump is vindictive, ignorant, narcissistic, a fraud -- well, his pathologies are well known." Other words that refer to the president or followers in the two articles include "depravity," "repulsive," "creepy," "corrupt," "unstable," "criminal," "debased," "sociopath," "morally bankrupt," "lawless," and "corrupt." Nor is the invective restricted to Mr. Trump personally: "When the hate flag is flying, most of Trump's followers have stood and saluted." In fact, over the course of Mr. Egan's numerous NYT articles, "hate" is almost as popular a word as "evil." I suppose we should be grateful that his vocabulary of insults isn't more extensive than it is. There seems to be a competition in the search for intemperate language among the writers and pundits of Pravda West to use for the vilification of Trump. Whatever, they do their best to fan partisan flames in an already divided nation.

Television talk shows contribute their own heat to the fire. In general, my impression is that those on the Right make some attempt to keep to the facts and even, on occasion, present some aspects of the other side's point of view. Those of the Left do neither, and don't think of apologizing for it. I will freely admit to bias in this matter, but even friends on the Left tend to agree with that observation (albeit grudgingly). In any case, the media in general does nothing to close the gaping political divide of the country and much to exacerbate it. A result is that political argumentation is becoming more hysterical and less rational by the day. An even worse result is that Democrats in their last bastion of power on the national level, the House of Representatives, are becoming steadily bolder and less controlled by the restraints of convention and simple civility. Encouraged by their vociferous leftist base and the mass media, Democrat legislators are ignoring normal governmental functions and tradition alike in a headlong pursuit to bring down the president by any means at hand. They seem, at times, to be conscious of the danger that presents both to the interests of the nation they represent and to their own future. But they do it anyway. Why?

That is where the key comes in. It becomes clear if you remember this: *What is good for the country is bad for the Democrat Party*. That's it. There is a possible variation on the theme, to wit, what is good for the country is bad for the Left. The former version is the purely political iteration, the latter the more general one. In theory the use of "Left" is more accurate, since (for many reasons including pure habit)) not every Democrat voter is a true leftist. In practice, however, the two versions are essentially the same, since the party is currently the earthly vehicle of leftist philosophy, is dominated by the Left, and espouses leftist doctrine in every plank of its platform. The Democrats themselves appear to be vaguely aware of the key, but have unfortunately reversed it into what is neither in logic nor practice a corollary: *What is bad for the country is good for the Democrat Party.* This is doubtless true in the short run, but longer term there is plenty that is bad for both, as Democrats will someday discover. But with a quick look at history, it's not difficult to understand why the Left, and the Democrat Party with it, have taken the path they are on.

Internationalism has always been a strong element of socialism. And "always" goes back a lot further than most people realize. The International Workingmen's Association, an amalgam of existing socialist, communist and anarchist groups and trade unions, was founded in London in 1864 -- during the Civil War. The Industrial Workers of the World (aka Wobblies), composed mainly of radical socialists and anarchists, began in Chicago in 1905 and still exists today. Vladimir Lenin started the Comintern -- short for Communist International -- just after he took over the Bolshevik movement in 1919. The objective of the latter was to establish a world-wide Soviet republic as a transition to total abolition of national sovereignty. This distrust of the nation-state concept carries over to the Left of our time. President Obama seemed to think of himself as a citizen of the world rather than an American and dismissed the idea of American exceptionalism. In fact, the U.S. is condemned by much of our own academia as the source of most of the world's ills. Given the fact that the U.S. is the world's leading nation-state in many ways, such ideas are to be expected from the Left. And, given the Democrat Party's status as the Left's standard bearer, it should be no surprise that a sentiment that what is bad for the country is good for the world, and therefore for the Democrats, is a dominant theme of the party now.

The foregoing explains, among other things, the apparent irrationality of much of what Democrats, as a party, do. Let us consider the late, and not so great, impeachment fiasco as a prominent example. After over two years of pushing a Russian collusion narrative and, after pulling out all the stops -- a fake dossier to obtain irregular FISA warrants, appointment of a special counsel with a poisonously anti-Trump team, roiling the nation with constant "bombshell" flubs, inadvertently revealing the corruption of the IC and Department of Justice -- and coming up with a blank, one would think the Democrats would lay low and lick wounds for a while. But they didn't. The tears on Rachel Maddow's cheeks were hardly dry before they were at it again with an even thinner excuse: a hearsay "whistle" blown by a CIA geek over a presidential phone call. Pundits on the Right celebrate, and many of those on the Left fear, the potential damage to the

Democrat Party from the impeachment attempt. It was almost certainly a step too far, and it was without doubt a risk-filled effort. Nancy Pelosi long hesitated to launch it, citing the divisiveness it would inflict on an already divided country, but finally was pushed over the brink. When she did go forward with it, it was with nasty zeal that was unseemly or worse. It failed, but nearly all the Democrat legislators went with it, most of them quite ungraciously. They seem poised to try something else, even now. All of that is, at a minimum, irrational.

Irrationality may be expected to ensue from the use of a false key to inform one's worldview. The Left simply can't seem to grasp the notion that what is bad for the country might be even worse for their party. To this fundamental source of irrationality may be added that which derives from hysterical Trump-hatred and desperation at the prospect of further loss. The shock of the 2016 election, which ripped from them the final victory they thought was theirs, still deranges many Democrats. They are encouraged in their delusions by a mass media that both controls and is controlled by them, that feeds them propaganda and reinforces their vision of Trump as a figure of Hitlerian evil. They suspect that their political positions are unpopular with most of the American populace and despise the latter even more for that. They have no one, or at least no one they will listen to, to tell them their worldview is based on the wrong key.

But the true key, that what is good for the country is bad for the Democrat Party, proves its validity as time goes by. The Left knows perfectly well that it is correct. What damage Democrats have no power to do outright they still try to make people believe has been done. Pravda West, their propaganda organ, occasionally takes time out from maligning Trump, Republicans and deplorables in general to proclaim that the booming American economy is a disaster. Except that from time to time they admit the economy is doing well, but its success can be attributed to Obama (an argument that is so sad it can hardly be called specious). Any steps to reverse the slide of national sovereignty into oblivion are derided as either futile or diabolically effective, depending on the mood of the moment. Anything that reflects well on the country is either ignored or distorted and attributed to bad motives. The mass media is dedicated to making people feel bad -- about themselves, the country and in general -- in an effort to denigrate the Right and the nation. The Left indeed knows the true key is valid and in response works diligently to minimize whatever may be good for the country.

The Democrats are, as will be pointed out in an article of Part VII, *Bottoms Up*, on the wrong side of every current issue. Immigration, taxes, regulations, health care, gun control -- all of them -- they cannot win on the issues. Even the larger picture is against them: The U.S. is not the universal source of evil in the world; indeed, the robust American economy sustains the prosperity of the rest of the world to an impressive extent, and the

American political model is still a beacon. Socialism has failed everywhere it has been tried. Prosperity, wherever it is found all around the world, is driven by free enterprise. It is simply irrational to swim against the current of obvious and demonstrable facts. The Democrat Party is at present committed to a course that is both detrimental to the nation and self-destructive. To continue on such a course indefinitely is the definition of irrationality.

In view of the key, it would be constructive for all Americans to ask each other (and themselves) the following question: How would you like to be a member of a political party of which it can be said that what is good for the country is bad for your party?

2/10/20

Chapter Twenty-Four

The Emulation of Brünnhilde, Part I: The Common Man

The single image that defines opera for those who have never seen or heard one is that of a Viking-sized lady with long blonde braids, dressed in armor with horns or wings on her helmet and holding a spear. The image is that of Brünnhilde, daughter of the Norse god Wotan and chief of the Valkyries, that band of warlike women who sweep up fallen heroes from corpse-littered battlefields and carry them to Valhalla on winged steeds. She has a prominent role in the last three of the four operas of Richard Wagner known as the Ring of the Nibelungen. In the last scene of the Ring cycle she takes the cursed gold ring of power and rides her warhorse Grane onto the blazing funeral pyre of her lover, the hero Siegfried. The scene is called "The Immolation of Brünnhilde," and is justly famed as one of the most iconic in all of opera. The motives that impelled the formidable lady to immolate herself on a pyre with her dead lover, and their relation to the modern Democrat Party, are the subjects of this essay and the next.

It is difficult to contemplate the fiery end of the Valkyrie without thinking of the situation in which the Democrats find themselves. Even Pravda West, the mass media that is now, unfortunately, little more than the propaganda arm of the party, mostly agrees that it is in some degree of disarray. As several previous articles have noted, Democrats are on the wrong side of virtually every major issue of the day, and as a party they haven't had a genuinely new idea since the days of Franklin D. Roosevelt (and those were bad ones).

They have frittered away their recent control of the House of Representatives in a sorry exercise in obstruction and negativity. All the party's energies for the past three years, and those of its assets in the media, academia and other institutions, have been directed at vilifying the current president rather than developing a resume for governance. As the next presidential election approaches, which will also involve all House seats and a third of those of the Senate, the identity of the party's nominee for president is still a mystery. A half dozen possibilities remain in the running, and it cannot be said that any of them are particularly attractive to the general electorate. One wonders how one of the two major political parties of the world's leading democracy could find itself in such an infelicitous situation.

It was not always that way with this, the oldest political party of the U.S. and of its kind in all the world. The party was founded in the 1820s under the leadership of Andrew Jackson, although its roots go back three decades earlier. It was quintessentially the party of the "Common Man," committed to the sturdy individualism of citizens, state sovereignty and distrust of central banks and strong central government. It was, less attractively, also anti-abolition, a taint that followed it for well over a century. This, however, was not a central precept of the early Democrats; the emphasis was on laissez-faire economic policy, extension of voting rights, strict construction of Constitutional law and maximum participation of citizens in government. Opposition to rule of the elites was fundamental. Jackson won the election of 1824 and his presidency, although somewhat chaotic by standards of the time, was successful in promoting a truly democratic agenda. Jackson's democracy was well-suited to the Common Man idea. It was born on what was then the frontier and its supporters were mostly of agrarian and working class backgrounds.

The approach to the Civil War, the war itself and Reconstruction caused an upheaval and major reworking of American politics. The Democrat Party was overshadowed by victorious Republicans until 1885, when Democrat Grover Cleveland became president. This put the seal on the end of Reconstruction, which had effectively ended in a back-room deal eight years earlier. The party that took over at that point was fundamentally different than the Jacksonian party, being more concerned with issues like opposition to the gold standard than such broader principles as states' rights. No wonder that its ambitions were limited; it was a thoroughly chastened organization. In the almost three-quarters of a century between just before the Civil War until the accession of Franklin D. Roosevelt in 1933, of the fifteen presidents of the U.S. thirteen were Republican. The Democrat Party predictably went through profound changes in the effort to recover from the war and its long aftermath, which included the period of reform that dominated politics from the mid-1890s into the 1920s. But throughout the struggles and changes of the decades, the concept of the centrality of the everyday American citizen, the Common Man, was to remain the foundation principle of the Democrat Party.

During much of the party's long sojourn in the wilderness, its most prominent voice was that of William Jennings Bryan. Bryan was an odd character in American history. He was definitely a progressive when progressivism was closely identified with political reform, but he was also religious in a most orthodox way. He failed in his runs at the presidency but had a lasting effect on the soul of the Democrat Party. Although progressive in his policies he was strongly dedicated to the pre-eminence of the Common Man, was called "The Great Commoner" and was supported by the splinter Populist Party. It has been said of him that he was too progressive to be traditional and too traditional to be progressive. But he definitely led the party toward progressivism at a critical time. The most critical moment came when Bryan's leadership of the party was in decline, in the bitterly contested election of 1912. In this campaign, Theodore Roosevelt, who had been a Republican president from 1901-1909, broke off from that party as a result of his dispute with the Republican incumbent William H. Taft, whom he had previously mentored. Roosevelt ran on the ticket of the Progressive (or "Bull Moose") Party, effectively giving the election to the Democrat Woodrow Wilson.

What was critical about the 1912 election is not so much that Wilson was one of only two Democrats to win the presidency during this long period as what his election did to the party itself. All three of the candidates were, in one degree or another, reformists, which at that time meant progressive. Had the Republicans remained united they would almost certainly have won the election, and thereby taken on the mantle of progressivism for the indefinite future. As it was, Wilson's win established the Democrat Party as the party of progressivism, which it remains to this day. Prior to 1912, and despite the mixed progressivism of Bryan, an objective observer would probably have given odds for the Republican Party to carry on the banner of the Progressive Movement. Certainly the history of the two parties prior to 1912 would seem to favor that outcome. But Wilson became the second progressive president, after Roosevelt the Republican, and carried out a distinctly progressive agenda throughout his two terms. He even appointed Bryan as his Secretary of State to help him with the agenda.

Bryan did, in fact, help Wilson pursue progressive reforms, but his presence helped offset Wilson's rather elitist persona at the party's top levels (Wilson had been a prominent academic and president of Princeton University before his political career). After Bryan resigned his cabinet position over Wilson's push for the U.S. to enter the war against Germany, Wilson's ability to advance progressive initiatives diminished. After World War I, the first phase of the Progressive Movement faded in a wave of national prosperity and another series of Republican presidents entered the Oval Office. The economic meltdown of late 1929 again favored government activism and Franklin D. Roosevelt came to dominate national politics with an extreme, if eccentric, brand of progressivism. The surge to the left by Democrats abated somewhat during the tenure of Harry Truman, which was followed by the hiatus of the Republican Eisenhower presidency. John F. Kennedy, who followed, was probably the least leftist Democrat to occupy the Oval Office since Grover Cleveland, but remained populist in his appeal despite his elite aura. His time was cut short, however, by a communist assassin, an act that was to change the history of the party and the nation.

Lyndon B. Johnson renewed the Democrat Party's leftward movement dramatically with his Great Society programs. Government spending, and with it control, affected nearly every aspect of national life. It also had other significant effects, one of which was to lock in the Democrat grip on the black vote and that of other minorities. The party had relied on coalition politics since its dark age of war and Reconstruction ended, but from LBJ onward the coalition factor was emphasized. Bill Clinton was a master of the care and feeding of a coalition party, but he was also a pragmatist (a cynic might even say opportunist) in matters of ideology. In this regard, he was similar to most of the presidents of both parties between the end of LBJ's reign until the accession of Barack Obama. Only Ronald Reagan demonstrated a strong ideological bent during that 40-year span and that, of course, was to the right. The others -- Nixon, Ford, Carter, the two Bushes and Clinton -- left little real ideological stamp on the body politic. Throughout this era, in rhetoric and spirit the Democrats held fast to their image as the party of the Common Man. This image, however, was becoming increasingly difficult to maintain as the party moved leftward.

Unfortunately for the Democrat Party, there is strong natural tension between progressivism and the idea of the Common Man. The basic principle of progressivism from its 1890s beginning has been government by the elite. Specifically, this is envisaged as a techno-elite, composed of people of superior intellect and judgment who have been highly educated for their leadership roles to lead the nation to a new earthly paradise. This accounts for the Left's aversion to the Constitution, a document designed for the purpose of limiting what the federal government is permitted to do. Progressives prefer to curtail democracy. They have a vision of government wherein the people elect little more than figureheads to legislative and executive positions and the real business of governing is carried out by a permanent bureaucracy. Those who occupy elective positions come and go, preferably without doing much of anything except ritual functions, while the professionals of the bureaucracy take care of real business. An ideal president is someone like Obama, who helped politicize the bureaucracy and appointed executive branch flunkies who supported the professional bureaucrats. A president like Trump is a frightening aberration in this system.

So where is the Jacksonian Common Man in all this? Where is that concept of self-rule of everyday citizens that was the vision of the Founders and the core belief of the Democrat Party? The Common Man was the fundamental principle of the party through good times and bad, even through the progressive upheavals of the New Deal and Great Society. Even later Democrat presidencies, those of Carter and Clinton, professed a firm belief in the preeminence of the Common Man. But somewhere in the early years of the 21st century, as Republicans under G.W. Bush moved their party from the Reagan Right to the center and forced Democrats further left, the Democrat Party forgot its roots. The loss was made official in 2016 with Hillary Clinton's infamous campaign speech in which the Common Man became the "basket of deplorables." Barack Obama did nothing to dispel that idea, with his talk of desperate simpletons clutching their guns and Bibles. Somewhere during that interval the party became the playground of billionaires and other elites, of celebrities and their violence-prone minions. The Democrat coalition began to lose its core of working folk and the party now looks elsewhere, including to unrestricted immigration, to replace them.

But the greatest loss to the Democrat Party is not voters but its soul. Without its old central ideal, it has lost that which carried it through the victories and defeats of the centuries. The Common Man was the basis of the world's oldest truly democratic party, essentially its very definition. When the party transferred its allegiance to progressive elites and the ultra-wealthy, it destroyed its own *raison d'etre*. It has lost its heart.

3/1/20

Chapter Twenty-Five

The Emulation of Brünnhilde, Part II: Siegfried's Pyre

Self-immolation by fire is not a natural act. Whether it be performed by a Valkyrie of Nordic myth and Wagnerian opera or by the modern Democrat Party, such an eccentric deed seems to beg for an examination of motives. Let us attempt to discern the motives behind both Brünnhilde's legendary ride upon the flaming funeral pyre of the hero Siegfried and of the very real and present self-inflicted destruction of a major political party. The two sets of motives perhaps have more in common than meets the casual eye. Or perhaps not.

Richard Wagner is best known as a composer of music, but he was also a dramatist of no mean skill. He would hardly send his heroine into the flames without first establishing a convincing foundation for such action in the preceding musical drama and her own farewell aria. As is appropriate for such a scene, Brünnhilde's motives are melodramatic, perhaps even a bit histrionic, but straightforward. They include elements of love (since she and Siegfried were classic lovers), grief (at the murder of a peerless hero), guilt (since she betrayed her lover to his death), remorse (since she belatedly discovered that he didn't deserve it) and rejection (of the world system behind the whole fiasco). There was also an element of revenge (see the part about rejection, above) that she carried out against both the mortal enemies of her and Siegfried and the gods of Valhalla who, one way and another, brought her plight about. Thus, as she perishes upon the pyre of the hero,

Valhalla itself appears in the background in flames and the Rhine rises to reclaim its fire-purified gold from Brünnhilde's ashes and to destroy the pagan world she now rejects. At the end, the music describes the rise of a new world that will replace that of the old gods.

The sad state of today's Democrat Party is nowhere nearly so dramatic or noble as the Immolation Scene, nor is the wreckage the party leaves behind likely to be as promising. Nevertheless, certain comparisons are valid. The first part of this essay (*The Common Man*) discussed the party's surrender of its core traditions in favor of progressivism and its ensuing rush to embrace elitists and the wealthy. With that came the substantial loss of a critical piece of the party's traditional coalition, the blue collar working man, who found himself among the deplorables of Hillary's basket and didn't much like it. To counterbalance that loss, plus the anticipated loss of a good chunk of another big piece of the old coalition, the black vote, Democrats looked elsewhere for replacement blocks. The solution – open borders and unlimited immigration from the Third World – seemed promising but put them on the wrong side of a major issue. As understanding of the negative effects that result from uncontrolled immigration deepens in the native population of the country, including all ethnic and economic groups, the Democrats are bleeding even more of their old base. They have now become desperate, promising free everything to everyone, swallowing the socialist Kool-Aid in massive doses in a wild grasp to regain the affection of the Common Man. But most of us commoners know better.

Escaping from the dilemma has proven difficult. The party's sharp turn to the left in the 2008 election, propelled by previous moves to the center by the Republicans and pressure from the Democrats' own extreme wing, has built a leftward momentum that cannot easily be reversed. Socialism has become respectable among the most energetic of Democrat supporters. The entire globalist agenda, beloved of the billionaire and techno-elite classes, with its push toward climate change-related rejection of national sovereignty and lust for overarching world government, is the new bible of Democrat money sources. How can the party resist the leftward and globalist surge? Its energy is in its socialist wing, its funding in its globalists, its sheer numbers in new immigrants, most of them unable to vote legally. And what are its alternatives? The traditional coalition is in shambles, thanks to the abandonment of the Common Man (including, by the way, the Common Man of color). The new coalition is unruly and even more variegated than the old one. How comfortably are billionaires, professional bureaucrats, globalists, dream-intoxicated radicals and indigent aliens likely to co-exist in political bliss? And how long can the Common Man be expected to pay for it all?

To be called self-immolation, and not just death by fire, the act must be deliberate. This was certainly the case with Brünnhilde; could it be said of the Democrat Party?

The answer is more complex, but probably still yes, in the sense that the Democrat actors knew full well that their actions were exceedingly risky and therefore potentially destructive. One must remember that back in 2016 no one could foresee the situation in which the party finds itself today. There was little doubt in the collective Establishment mind, Democrat and Republican alike, that Hillary Clinton would be the next president. Actions were taken by many people that were based on that assurance that would never have been taken without it. Some of those actions were taken to help grease Hillary's ascension to the Oval Office, some were just in the way of old-fashioned corruption that would never be exposed in a Democrat administration. The result of the 2016 election was therefore more than shocking – it was mortally dangerous to certain individuals. Nevertheless, the collective actions of the party were taken with full knowledge of risk, in the same way a drunk driver intentionally drinks too much before taking the wheel.

Worse for the Democrat Party, once the 2016 election was lost, is that risky actions of the past led to even riskier ones. A prudent response to the lost election would have been to draw back into a bureaucratic defensive shell, throw a few low-level people under the bus and let the pet media blow smoke until it all blew over. This is precisely what the old party of the Common Man would have done. Instead, and against the better judgment of the old guard of the party, Democrats doubled down with actions that held a risk factor that made them suicidal. Why? Again, the answer is complex. Certainly the radical socialist wing of the party has over the last few years forced the party's establishment progressives to take risks the latter would have preferred to avoid. This has resulted in two major direct attacks upon the presidency, which have together consumed virtually the entire political energy of the party at a critical juncture. The attacks were abetted by the Deep State, the self-serving amorphous force within the bureaucracy and its Intelligence Community that promotes stronger central government and which, above all, fears President Trump's crusade to drain the D.C. swamp. Pressured by the Deep State and its own radicals, Democrat establishment politicians had little choice but to forge ahead with the risky attacks, even though both were founded upon absurdly weak foundations.

Again, the failure of the first attack, an obscenely partisan distortion of the already questionable instrumentality of the Special Counsel, would in better days called for a pulling in of the horns of the Democrat Party and its adjuncts in the press and bureaucracy. Instead, in a fit of self destruction, the party doubled down once more, this time going all the way to a purely political impeachment based on the flimsiest of pretexts. Failure was even more complete, as might have been expected, and the political liability for the party as a whole (and the personal liability of certain actors), while still to be determined, will be proportionate to the risk that was assumed in taking the action. That risk was monumental, and begs the question of what motivated its taking.

The blazing funeral pyre upon which the Democrat Party is now mounting is that of its own original tradition and the core of its existence: the traditional Common Man of the Democrats. There are profound similarities between that Common Man and Brünnhilde's consort, Siegfried. Both were heroes, of sorts, both were mythical in concept and iconic in stature, both are still idolized by the immolating parties – and, if nothing else, both are dead. There are also some similarities in the motives of those riding onto the pyres. As discussed in the first part of this essay, Democrats certainly have second thoughts about giving up the Common Man in exchange for a goulash of billionaires, half-mad professors, treacherous intelligence operatives, globalists, bureaucrats and greed-suffused immigrants. The grief they feel, with a touch of guilt, is not only that of losing much of their old base, and with it the 2016 election, but also for the loss of a genuinely noble cause. They also feel guilt and remorse, as is appropriate for such a bad choice, and as the Valkyrie felt for her mistaken betrayal of her lover. If they did not feel these emotions, Democrats would be as demonic as they are sometimes portrayed in right-wing outlets, the times being as bitterly partisan as they are. But let us not believe the worst of our fellow citizens. Democrats, as individuals, may be mistaken but they are still entirely human.

But there are also motives for the party's emulation of Brünnhilde that are far different than hers. The most striking difference is that the love motive is largely absent, and has been replaced by hate. Perhaps the least attractive aspect of Democrats in general, certainly a majority of their leaders, is the unbridled hatred of the current president. So-called Trump Derangement Syndrome is unfortunately real. Many Democrats are so deeply in hate (most with someone they know only through a distorted media) that they simply can no longer think straight. They are functionally insane when it comes to politics, even though nearly all are perfectly normal otherwise. This alone explains much of the irrational drive toward self-immolation on the pyre of their old ideals.

As this was being written several aspiring Democrat presidential nominees dropped out, apparently at the urging of the DNC, giving their endorsements to the candidate who is perceived as the most politically moderate. This is, unfortunately, too little and too late. Too little because said "moderate" candidate promotes almost precisely the same specific policy initiatives as the overtly socialist candidate. Too late because the party has already gone too far to turn back, both in its actions against the president and in its acceptance of an extreme leftist agenda. One is put in mind of Macbeth's famous line, after the murder of King Duncan: "I am in blood stepp'd in so far that should I wade no more, returning were as tedious as go o'er." The pyre is lit and the horse has plunged in; there is no going back at this point.

Finally, there are two related motives attributed to Brünnhilde that have not yet been considered in relation to her emulators: rejection and revenge. One must remember that her immolation included not herself alone but also the whole world from which she had come. The cosmos of the ancient Nordic gods fell into the flames along with the Valkyrie, never to rise again. The impression is strong and widely held that the Democrat Party of today may, in its desperation and rage, make an attempt to pull the nation into the conflagration of its own destruction. If this should be the case, a ruinous Democrat defeat in the election of 2020, which seems quite possible, may mark not only the end of a political party but of a great society, and the beginning not of a brave new world but an age of apocalyptic fury.

3/7/20

Chapter Twenty-Six

A Party of Poverty, Part I: In the Land of the Bland

Pravda West, the nation's mass media, has somehow been missing the biggest story of an election year ever since.... well, the last election. That story, of course, is the utter poverty of its very own Democrat Party. The tragic indigence of the party is not one of money. The Democrats are the party of billionaires; they are flush with cash. Just a few days ago, one of their favorite billionaires, Michael Bloomberg, committed a cool one hundred million U.S. dollars to buy the electoral votes of just a single state: Florida. A big chunk of that stash (to be matched by a number of other high rollers, including some major corporations) will be spent on paying off the personal debts of thousands of felons, in order that they may legally vote. If this sounds to you suspiciously like bribery, it's because it is. In the old days in New Orleans, politicians would deliver sacks of groceries around the housing projects for votes and provide buses to the polls. The Florida felons owe, in many cases, tens of thousands worth in debts. You have to feel sorry for the poor New Orleans tenants; their sponsors were a bunch of pikers. No, the Democrats aren't hurting for funds these days.

The poverty of the world's oldest living (sort of) political party is one of ideas; which is to say, the sort of ideas that win over voters. For specifics, I refer you to several previous articles that were devoted to just that subject: *Under the Lamp Post, Bottoms Up* and *The Emulation of Brunnhilde: the Common Man* are most to the point. The bottom line is that the party is on the wrong side of every major issue. On the economy, on immigration, on education, on energy policy, on everything significant the Democrats' ideas are at odds with both popular opinion and what works to the advantage of the country. I didn't mention foreign policy because the Democrats have no ideas at all about it, except to oppose whatever President Trump is doing. What ideas they do have about anything are inherited from previous generations and didn't turn out well then. Socialism, as a primary example of their "new" ideas, was trendy a century ago, until history proved it flawed as a basis for a national economy, or for society as a whole. Choosing globalism over American interests is great for the billionaire sponsors but isn't playing so well in Peoria. Exchanging real religion to embrace the worship of Science isn't working out so well either, nor is "reimagining" police forces out of existence in favor of social workers likely to lead to domestic tranquility and crime control. In short, the Democrats are out of valid ideas, and the few ideas they do have seem to be drawn from a nightmare.

Given the current state of the party, it must be conceded that the Democrat slate for the upcoming election is absolutely brilliant. It is, in fact, a blank slate, which suits the party's platform perfectly. In a recent article, *In the Land of the Blind*, a quotation from Erasmus was used to illustrate the fact that leadership qualities tend to be relative. On a ten-point scale, Joe Biden's abilities must be rated at minus three. Nor is it a matter of his apparent senility: he has never shown great potential. In the course of a career in Washington that has spanned nearly half a century he has accomplished nothing whatever except the enrichment of his family at the expense of American national interests. Unlike many other ineffective politicians, he doesn't even look good doing nothing. His gaffes are legendary and his public demeanor (especially around women) is....well. A fairly credible sexual assault allegation against him that would bring down any Republican has been papered over by the Democrats' pet media and some blatant corruption overseas largely ignored, but his bland incompetence can't be shrugged off. Bernie Sanders tries to help him out, but the best he can tell his people is to hold their collective nose and go on out to vote for Joe, just to get rid of Trump. The general consensus is that if, by hook or crook, old Joe wins, he'll be no more than a figurehead for the socialists and globalists anyway.

One of the arguments among leftists in favor of their presidential ticket is that Kamala Harris will be mostly running the show from the vice presidential office. They forget that the blandness doesn't stop with Joe. Harris, despite her very leftist political views, is hardly the firebrand that the Young Turks of the current Left seek. She simply can't stir up their juices the way Bernie can, despite his age and her relative youth. In fact, she doesn't do much for the older crowd, either, of any particular political persuasion. Even her ethnic background as sort of POC hasn't helped much: the important Democrat black demographic is lukewarm toward her at best. It can't be said that the Democrat base was ever enthusiastic about Harris; you may remember that she was one of the earliest dropouts from the large but less than impressive bunch of candidates for the party nomination. About the only splash she made in the debates was her savage attack on -- yes, Joe. This all may reflect, at least in part, her less than sterling record as top California prosecutor, and of course her method of obtaining that job. There's a great deal of baggage in that trunk, and the trunk belongs not to a 2020 Lamborghini Terzo Millenio but to more like a 2012 Ford Focus. Bland.

But the Democrats haven't entirely lost their old political slyness. They're keeping Joe hiding in his basement, probably to conceal his blandness more than his cognitive issues and even more than to avoid the gaffes. We haven't seen much of Harris, either, which also keeps the poll numbers up. The party is playing to what few strengths are left to it, mainly control of Pravda West and access to plenty of billionaire money. The former is put to use with wall-to-wall "news" that expands on every abrasive or confrontational moment Trump has ever had (lots of material there). Even more important is what the "news" does not cover, which is any good thing that has happened in the Trump administration (lots of material there, too, which means all the more work in keeping it under cover). Scattered through the bad "news" about Trump are the usual flat-out lies, now mostly about where the coronavirus came from and how Trump has presumably mishandled it. As for the money, that shows up in a tsunami of advertising that shows Joe in a rare lucid moment, trying to act like a moderate and blaming Trump for all the messes Democrats have made, past and present.

The ongoing debates between the president and Biden present another problem for the Democrats, but Pravda is deploying the usual damage control measures, also known as "spin" in journalism circles and "whoppers" among us common folk. The moderators, so-called, are, as expected, doing their best to tilt the field toward poor old Joe, and to hide the tilt as well as they can in the process. Their help for Biden will come in the form of neutral questions to him and refusal to pursue them to a genuine answer, plus a few direct slap downs of Trump when they can't help themselves. Perhaps Democrats feel that the single debate between the vice president and Harris will recoup some of the damage, in which hope they are likely to be profoundly disappointed. The highest probability for an outcome will be that Biden will avoid (with moderator help) any discussion of actual policy issues and stay alert enough so the media can forget the blunders he makes. In that case, the media can claim an even match, or even a narrow Biden victory. Certainly low expectations for Joe going in will help Pravda out immensely. In the end, it may not matter much: people will vote for the candidate they've already decided on and the final issue will depend on how many mail-in ballots Democrat agents can harvest in the battleground states.

The Democrats have caught one huge break, a stroke of luck (if luck it was) that gives them an excellent opportunity in a race that would otherwise have been lost already. Among the many imports from communist China was a virus that was spread by either incompetence or intention by the government of that nation. As it happens, it isn't unusually lethal except to a specific demographic that could be isolated and protected with relative ease: the elderly and others who are already suffering from other serious health issues. However, with the eager assistance of federal medico-bureaucrats and Democrat politicians, Pravda West was able to declare a pandemic, with the prospect of a million or more deaths across all age groups in the U.S. alone. In the panic that ensued and amid stentorian demands from all quarters (but mainly the Left) that the government "do something," governments at all levels indeed did something. They destroyed a national economy that was in the midst of a period of historically rapid growth by a series of totally useless lockdowns. Small businesses were decimated while those who could afford huge political donations thrived, or at least survived. Lives were destroyed along with the economy, no doubt many more than were saved by the shutdowns. It was a case of government malfeasance of the highest order, and it may have saved the Democrat Party from a massive defeat. Or maybe not. The people may yet be smarter than the elites believe.

The bottom line is that the Democrats are running *for* nothing, since there is nothing in their platform worth running for. They are running strictly *against* something, and that is a straw man: an image of Donald Trump that has been carefully constructed by their media over the years (admittedly with his cooperation). Would you seriously campaign in favor of an environmentalist nightmare called the Green New Deal that would wreck everything most people have worked to build (which they did, Obama's proclamation notwithstanding)? Would you campaign for unrestricted immigration that would preclude the children of citizens from ever entering the work force? Would you ask people to vote for defunding police forces so that leftist mobs could continue to threaten them and wreck their cities? Or for locking the children of the poor into failing schools with no access to alternatives? Or for accelerating the deterioration of society through enhanced divisions based on race, ethnicity, religion and sex? Or for turning the nation into a socialist concentration camp? Or for a dozen other related programs designed to restrict the people's liberties and degrade their standard of living?

This is indeed the platform of a party of poverty -- not the poverty of the elites but that of the people. And more than just physical poverty is involved here: there is a poverty of the spirit that lurks within all the Democrats seek. With this program, blandness is the best image to cultivate, and blandness is what the Democrats have in their candidates and their political message. The less the public knows of their agenda and sees of their candidates, the better, and Pravda West is helping them hide both. This is perhaps the most critical election we have seen in our lifetimes, and the strangest. Erasmus' celebrated quotation is: "In the land of the blind the one-eyed man is king." On the Democrat side, we've lately entered the land of the bland. Let us hope we don't linger there, for in the land of the bland, the half-witted man is a figurehead for disaster.

9/11/20

Chapter Twenty-Seven

A Party of Poverty, Part II: Smoke and Mirrors

With no decent ideas in their platform and no real substance in their agenda, Democrats have to resort to smoke and mirrors to promote their chances for electoral success. This isn't a matter of choice; surely the party would prefer to display an array of wonderful options to lure the public away from their conservative rivals. But such is not the case. The socialist elements that hijacked the party after a century of fluctuating successes and failures lack both validity and originality in the idea department. Their day, intellectually speaking, passed with the calamities of both the New Deal and the Great Society many decades ago. The recrudescence of the worst of old socialist notions, combined with a few ghastly pseudo-scientific environmental initiatives, forms the "modern" Green New Deal, a centerpiece of Democrat idiocy. The current Democrat presidential candidate publicly rejected that paragon of unintended humor (when he wasn't embracing it) in an effort to attract voters, which gives us some insight into their collective opinion of the political value of their own best ideas. So, enter the world of smoke and mirrors.

Let us begin with the smoke, which in this context represents rhetoric not based on reality. For Democrats, symbolism is an important element of their political message and takes the place of reason and rational debate. A photograph of a Hispanic woman, wearing rags and a soulful expression and holding an apparently underfed baby, is a symbol that saves them the need to formulate a carefully reasoned argument for their stance on the complex subject of immigration. They point to wire enclosures to symbolize their views on border control in general (not bothering to mention that these temporary holding "cages" were photographed during the Obama administration). The need to eliminate traditional policing of urban areas is proven by photographs or edited videos of police-POC confrontations, all taken out of the context of the entire incident and free of any background data that might tend to exculpate the police personnel in the scene. Symbols of the "other side" are treated as though real and made into straw men for leftist rage. Age-old statues, seen by normal people as chunks of rock or metal, are transformed into bearers of racism and white privilege and torn down in acts symbolic of the vandals' socially just purity.

This isn't to imply that symbolism is unimportant as a form of expression in our political lives. National flags are emotional anchors for citizens of all nations, and Old Glory has long waved as an important unifying symbol for all Americans (which is why it is so often burnt by divisive leftists). The reviled statues were placed on pedestals as symbolic exhortations to pursue paths of honor, courage and virtue as life goals for our citizens. Few of those citizens will claim that the United States has always been on the right side of everything or that the persons that inspired the statues led perfect lives. We view the flag and the statues as merely symbols for the best qualities of what they represent and realize that rational argumentation concerning them and whatever causes or characteristics they portray is proper and necessary. It is when a symbol is used as a weapon to eliminate the need for rational debate and logical argumentation that it becomes dangerous. As in the examples given above, and many others that could be offered if space were available, the Left tosses out its symbols to shut down debate, and even thought. At that point, symbolism is no longer a source of inspiration. It is a substitute for intellectual effort by the intellectually lazy. It is merely smoke.

Its innate preference for smoke over reality, symbols over substance, talk over deeds, is enough in itself for the Left to hate Trump, policy differences aside. Trump has a direct personality, sometimes to a political fault. He doesn't bother much with political correctness and other leftist symbolism and says the "wrong" things in an unpolished way. He's simply not a politician but a businessman with the habits of a dealer in a rough and unforgiving business. He is, in short, a man of action who tends to let results speak for themselves -- and when he does try to speak for them it's not pretty. This is a personality defect, to put it mildly, in the minds of those within the DC Establishment, and it inflames progressives against him in a way that more conventional conservatives have never done. Democrats don't like to be reminded that their results rarely match their rhetoric. Their pronouncements about how they are the protectors of black people, for a prominent example, don't stand up very well to analysis of their deeds in that respect. Against that background, men of action are, understandably, unappreciated by the Left.

So much for the smoke part of the smoke and mirrors employed by the party of intellectual poverty. The mirror part is in some ways more interesting. Psychological projection was posited by Sigmund Freud as a personal defense mechanism whereby someone denies the existence of certain thoughts, motivations, desires and feelings in themselves by attributing the same to others. Such projection of guilt thus leads to false accusations, personal or political. Later psychologists have concluded that projection may not be a defense mechanism as Freud thought, but rather a broad tendency to believe others are similar to oneself and therefore to project one's own traits and motives onto other parties. Whatever the true nature of projection, the Left has, over the decades, lifted it to an art form. The Democrats routinely accuse opponents of doing or planning precisely what they themselves have done or expect to do. One exhibit is the shrill accusation of collusion of the Trump campaign with Russia which led to an expensive and exhausting special prosecutor investigation that consumed much of the first half of Trump's first (and maybe only) term. As it happened, there was indeed a Russian connection, paid for by the DNC and Hillary's own campaign. Similarly, the bogus impeachment that muddled most of the rest of Trump's first term was based on a Ukrainian incident which, as is now coming to light, was real -- except that it should have inculpated the Bidens rather than Trump.

The interesting feature of leftist projection is its tendency to provide advance clues as to what the Left is thinking and planning. One has only to note current accusations against the opposition to predict the next Democrat outrage. For example, it is widely believed in leftist circles, and frequently stated, that Trump will not leave office if defeated in the next election. We may therefore anticipate with confidence that Democrat politicians up and down the line will vigorously contest any election, even remotely close, that they may lose. Actually, the Left has already tipped its hand in that regard. Some weeks ago, Hillary publicly advised Biden never to concede the election, no matter the circumstances, and other rumbles to that effect have since come from the Left. Several prime examples of the latter appeared in the leftist journals *The Atlantic* and *Politico* over the last few months. Ditto the reliably leftist NYT, of course: Peter Beinart wrote a NYT op-ed on the theme that Trump "repeatedly suggested that he won't accept the results of the election, should he lose." The mirror image appears in Democrat operative John Podesta's contemporary work with Democrat governors to devise ways to manipulate the Electoral College so as to swing the electoral vote to Biden, voters be damned.

As for *The Atlantic*, one article by David Frum may suffice to represent a myriad of similar examples. It recounts "war games" scenarios developed by an apparently *ad hoc* group calling itself the Transition Integrity Project. A shopping list of possible political atrocities the group expects from Trump's people is offered, with a final prediction that the only gamed scenario that does not result in widespread civil violence is an overwhelming Biden victory in the upcoming election. It is notable that any sort of victory by Trump is predicted to result in violence (yes, think about that for a moment). Therefore, everyone should vote for Biden to preserve the peace!

There is much more projection going on with the Transition Integrity Team's "war gaming" than that indicated above. The long list of potential Trump team acts of violence and political shenanigans entered into the gaming calculations is not matched by a corresponding list of such imagined deeds for leftist actors, even though anyone with a television set and a grain of common sense would know that leftist acts of violence and shady political manipulations dwarf anything of the sort on the Right, and have done so for a generation or more. The list is in fact compiled from a leftwing playbook that has been projected onto Trump and his allies. Actually, the very name, Transition Integrity Team, is inverted projection. Recall the efforts of Obama and his politicized bureaucracy (aka "the Deep State") to sabotage the incoming Trump administration from the beginning of the transition onward. Presumably, the Democrats are convinced that since they were involved in political sabotage, the Republicans must inevitably intend to resort to the same sordid methods. That's what projection is all about.

So the smoke of symbol-infused rhetoric and the mirrors of projection constitute the true platform of the Democrat Party. The stated platform, which includes the Green New Deal, open borders, end of law enforcement and rejection of the Second Amendment, is largely forgotten on the campaign trail (and by Pravda West until the election is over). On the unavoidable occasions that Biden is forced to talk substance, he largely borrows Trumpian ideas that seem to resonate well with the electorate. No wonder he's flustered most of the time: who could keep up with the political counterpoint of simultaneous mutually conflicting story lines when he's already having cognitive issues? To repeat: the only way to figure out what the Democrats are really thinking is to listen to what they're accusing Republicans of doing. Viewed that way, leftist projection is a two-edged sword that reveals intentions you will never see in a newspaper or hear on the Pravda TV channels. Analyzing the accusations is the only way to cut through the smoke of symbolic rhetoric and see through the contortions of the mirrors of projection.

Will it work? Will the smoke and mirrors fool the public long enough to carry the Democrats to victory? They may. The showman P.T. Barnum said, "No man ever went broke overestimating the ignorance of the American public." When that ignorance is reinforced by a partisan media it's a powerful aid to the Left. His handlers have apparently convinced Biden to run out the clock -- to hide in his basement and keep his mouth shut when not in sight of a teleprompter -- until November 4th. The virus has removed the danger of more debates and his "town meetings" are meticulously scripted, populated (if at all) with loyalists and carefully rehearsed. He's leading by a substantial margin in every poll. So was HIllary in 2016, of course, and scandal and past misdeeds are struggling to burst out into the light from every direction to destroy Biden's chances, as they helped destroy hers. Under a thin grandfatherly veneer, Biden is a crotchety and unlikable person, and his running mate is even less attractive. But Pravda West is doing its best to hide the facts from the people and time is running out.

The irrepressible Barnum had a few other things to say on the subject. In riposte to Abe Lincoln, he stated, "You can fool most of the people most of the time." He also said, "Many people are gullible, and we can expect this to continue." Our media has apparently taken close notice of Barnum's words of wisdom. The smoke and mirrors program has worked pretty well for the Democrats over the years and, with nothing else going for them, they aren't going to abandon it now. In the end, it works because many of us want it to work. One more quote from P.T. Barnum sums it up: "The common man, no matter how sharp and tough, actually enjoys having the wool pulled over his eyes and makes it easier for the puller."

9/18/20

Chapter Twenty-Eight

The Incredible Dr. Ford

Of all the bizarre phenomena of the latest Supreme Court confirmation debacle, the strangest, to my mind, is the almost universal acceptance of the sexual assault accuser's credibility. On the Republican side of the controversy, the mantra seems to be that she is so believable because an incident did in fact occur, but time and trauma have altered her memory as to the perpetrator. On the Left, they find her "incredibly credible" (yes, one of them actually said it), and leave it at that. At the risk of being found abysmally politically incorrect, I now state that I don't find her testimony to be credible at all. I think she was flat-out lying.

Ah, I feel the waves of opprobrium washing over me already. One isn't supposed to say such things, even if they are true. It is "victimizing the victim" and "re-traumatizing" her if she should read it. But in fact, if the woman *is* lying (as has been documented all too often in the recent past), the true victim is the man accused, and there is plenty of trauma in store for that poor wretch. In my experience, which is considerable, women lie as often as men, and they tend to be better at it (with the notable exception of a true artist such as Bill you-know-who).

I have some reasons to doubt Christine Blasey Ford's veracity, several of which are pretty convincing in themselves, and which taken in aggregate strike me as conclusive. The foremost has been pointed out by many commentators, but rarely explained in legal terms. It is generally encapsulated as "gaps in the story," but there is more to it than that simple phrase implies. It should be noted that the gaps consist of two critical items: the date of the alleged incident and the place it occurred. The reason those items are critical is that, together, they constitute the only real means by which the alleged perpetrator can definitively exculpate himself. It is difficult enough to prove a negative in the best of conditions, and far more difficult to do it after the passage of 36 years. In a case such as this, the only feasible way for the accused to establish his innocence is to have an alibi. He must show he was somewhere else at the time the crime was supposed to have taken place.

It is striking that Ford's memory is so precise about everything else (one beer consumed, etc.) but that the very items that might, just possibly, lead to the proof of Brett Kavanaugh's innocence kind of slip her mind. It is precisely the sort of thing that a lawyer who scripts the story would be careful to omit. Of course, her means of getting to and escaping from the scene of the supposed assault must also be forgotten, since they would inevitably identify the place. It is just too neat, from a legal point of view.

Actually, the point that first tipped me off that the testimony was odorous was an odd description of what happened after the poor girl had locked herself in the bathroom. She spoke of the two lecherous drunks (Kavanaugh and Mark Judge) coming out of the room of the crime laughing, and then "pinballing" down the stairs. Pinballing? Where did a person of her age hear that term? Pinball machines were a distant memory long before her time, and even an old geezer like me never heard it used as a verb. But more to the point, laughing can be heard but pinballing is a visual phenomenon. How could she see the evil lads pinballing from a locked bathroom? It is evident to me that the scripter of this tale erred in an effort to increase the drama of his (or her) opus.

But why would a young woman as terrified as Ford claims she was run to a bathroom anyway? Would she not just shoot down the stairs and out the door? Kavanaugh and Judge, by her own account, were far too "stumbling drunk" to chase her (with only one beer in her) with any chance of success, and by hiding in the bathroom she just gave them the opportunity to wait her out at the bottom of the stairs. Which, by the way, they manifestly didn't do. Instead, they just laughed and stumbled off to wherever.

The laughter of the two inept rapists has, by Ford's testimony, haunted her dreams all these decades, but it seems odd that they would be laughing at that point. Even drunk, they must have been a little shaken themselves. Again, the improbabilities here seem to be those of a soap opera: inserted for dramatic effect by the scripter. Some observers claim that these "details" add to the authenticity of the tale. I suspect they are flaws, part of an overdone effort by an amateur dramatist to attain an extra touch of heartbreak.

Other questions arise that could have been examined in the course of a competent cross-examination. For example, the swimsuit (one-piece; another detail, which also signals the wearer's virtue). It was worn under Ford's clothes, which must mean it wasn't wet. It also means the event was a pool party, so the house obviously had a pool. But she hadn't been in the pool, despite the fact that she'd been around long enough to have a beer. The boys had had plenty of beer, according to her, so presumably they'd been there awhile and probably had been in the pool. Were they still in swimming gear? Were they wet? Did Kavanaugh soak her when he supposedly jumped atop her?

The discussion above does not exhaust the catalog of inconsistencies and improbabilities in the accuser's testimony. Small details such as her declaration that she didn't tell her parents because she didn't want them to know she was drinking beer in a house with just boys (when she later identified her girlfriend as an attendee) could be added. Any one of these details might not matter, but they add up. And of course, the details that could be corroborated, including those who were present at the party (including the girlfriend) .... are not.

The swimsuit details, in particular, wouldn't necessarily either support or enervate her story, but they represent the kind of thing that could be cleared up in cross to lend a little context to the situation described. As it was, there was no real cross-examination at all. The prosecutor who questioned Ford lobbed a few softballs that avoided anything that might threaten her credibility. Even the softballs drew some blood, however. Ford was totally confused by a few unintimidating questions about who was paying the bills. It was manifest that she was closely coached for the Judiciary Committee affair and instructed not to talk off-script. In fact, her testimony in many places followed the letter sent to Senator Feinstein absolutely verbatim. Even the tears came at the right places. A real cross-examination (not permitted because of the risk of re-traumatization) would have blown her up.

Speaking of tears, I also disagree that Ford's technical performance was gripping. I'd characterize her as a C-list actress. Well, OK, maybe a B-minus, but no better. All a woman has to do is cry a little to get rave reviews from some gullible listeners.

It is my opinion that Ford was deliberately recruited to carry the flag for the Left, based on her presence in Maryland at the right time and place (maybe), her familiarity (even though not very intimate) with Kavanaugh and his crowd, and her leftist politics. I also suspect that the person who wrote her script was an older lawyer, but that's more speculative. Still, he or she was old enough to remember pinball machines and lawyerly enough to avoid the most obvious pitfalls. Time may tell how close I come here. I also understand that a substantial amount of #GoFundMe cash is floating around and would dearly love to know where it ends up. And there is also the money that remains dark.

No doubt Ford's fans will use the fact that the letter was mailed before the nomination of Kavanaugh was announced to deny that this sort of staging was possible. They probably will forget to mention that it was mailed *after* the finalists were revealed. I have no doubt that whoever organized this caper could have found likely candidates to impugn the other two finalists as well and sent all three letters in advance. After all, as we have seen, the letter was to have been held for weeks anyway, to be leaked at the most appropriate (or most inappropriate) time.

Finally, there is the question, if my conclusions prove correct, of why did she do it? I doubt that money was a prime mover, although it may have been a factor. More likely, Ford's profession that "civic duty" motivated her has more than a grain of truth. Of course, her civic duty is my felony, but the Left has an odd worldview. She is, on the record, a pink-hatted left-wing political activist.

She actually broached this line of thinking herself, when she stated that anyone who thought she "came forward" for partisan political reasons didn't know her. That, at least, is true: I think she probably did it in support of her leftist ideology, and I don't know her. Nor do I want to.

Chapter Twenty-Nine

#BelieveAllDemocrats

Hypocrisy is no stranger to politics. That is far from an original thought, and it would hardly be worth repeating except for the fact that Democrats, with exuberant support from their own Pravda West, have in the past few years set a new gold standard for an old art form. It started with the downfall of the odious Harvey Weinstein and led very quickly to a too-long-delayed movement against the sexual harassment of women by predatory men. The movement, commonly designated #MeToo, rose rapidly to prominence because it called attention to something that had occurred too often to too many people and had not been taken seriously enough. It may have taken an unfortunate turn toward the victimhood role in its fast rise, as pointed out in a post on the original blog by Patricia Fenati, *Not Me*, but it properly called attention to real and serious abuse. Unfortunately, the necessary and constructive aspects of the movement have since been compromised by partisan politics, by way of good old-fashioned hypocrisy. And this version of the phenomenon has been hypocrisy on steroids.

Whatever one's opinion of the value of #MeToo, it is inarguable that it was founded on real abuse. The same cannot be said of its offshoot, #BelieveAllWomen, which was kick-started in the hysteria of the confirmation of Brett M. Kavanaugh's appointment to the Supreme Court. Since the desperation of the Left to keep another conservative off the court was unbounded and no reasonable claims could be made against Kavanaugh's credentials, leftists had no recourse other than the tried and true: character assassination. In what has become standard procedure at this point, Democrats trotted out a woman with a claim (from decades before) of sexual assault against the judge. She was carefully rehearsed, but her story was totally uncorroborated (even by friends she'd named for corroboration) and, as detailed in the article above, *The Incredible Dr. Ford*, inherently unbelievable.

It was also a bit too carefully crafted: any detail (such as when and where it happened) that could have been found to disprove it had been conveniently "forgotten." Nevertheless, Pravda West pursued the story with breathless enthusiasm and every Democrat politician who could gain access to a mic pronounced the tale totally credible. Other women rushed forward (or were rushed by attorneys) with even less believable fabrications. We were all enjoined to believe every syllable of every charge according to #BelieveAllWomen. Unless, of course, we were willing to be thought of as misogynistic and backward apes.

It has been noticed elsewhere that the whole #BelieveAllWomen program began to fall apart when Tara Reade accused former VP and presumed Democrat presidential nominee Joe Biden of sexual assault that took place in the '90s. It took a good piece of #MeToo with it. I cannot say that Ms. Reade's accusations were categorically believable, but it is manifest that they were far better corroborated than Dr. Ford's, not to mention that the story line is inherently more realistic. Also not to mention that Joe Biden's public performances around women are not such as to lend him much support in his denials. But we need not accept his guilt uncritically, or at all, in order to raise an eyebrow at the eager accusers of Mr. Kavanaugh. In contrast to the cacophony of denunciation that accompanied the attack upon the judge, the silence surrounding the attack on Mr. Biden was positively deafening. What noise could be heard was in the stout-hearted defense of the Democrat nominee, and that noise came from the mouths of the very same hashtag believers that had excoriated Kavanaugh the most viciously. What could account for that phenomenon? Surely you would not suggest mere mundane partisan politics! Not on the part of these idealistic protectors of all womanhood, right?

I do not include Pravda West in my (in)sincere doubt that lowly politics was involved in the very different treatments of Biden and Kavanaugh. The mass media is indeed a counterpart of old Soviet Pravda: it is under the control of a political party (that would be Democrat), at its beck and call, and will reliably report as news whatever the party tells it to report (and fail to report the reverse). It is in the obvious interest of the Democrat Party that silence should reign on this subject, and whenever silence cannot be maintained the accusations against Biden must be either soft-pedaled or denounced, as appropriate. No, my doubts (if any) are about those big-hearted feminists of #MeToo and related movements whose only desire is protection of the security and well-being of other women. Among them is Alyssa Milano, spiritual founder of #MeToo, who said precisely nothing when Ms. Reade came forward with her story. When hard pressed to say *something*, Ms. Milano issued a tepidly neutral statement that the accuser deserved to be heard, nothing more. That is, almost nothing more: she also reiterated her long-term support for Mr. Biden and his candidacy. It is no doubt just coincidence that Ms. Milano is leftist and Democrat.

The Kavanaugh-Biden reversal has historical precedents, the most vivid of which occurred in the 1990s. Those of us old enough to remember will recall that Justice Clarence Thomas was confirmed to the Supreme Court in a process strikingly similar to that of Justice Kavanaugh. As with Kavanaugh, Thomas could not be attacked on the basis of his credentials, and it appeared that his would be an easy confirmation until Anita Hill came forward with a story of sexual harassment. Unlike the current situation with Biden, there was no charge of actual assault, but there was some corroboration, however questionable. Otherwise, the parallelism with the Kavanaugh confirmation is striking, and, like Kavanaugh, Thomas was confirmed on a mostly partisan basis by a narrow margin. Feminists, Democrats and celebrities were outraged and vocal. Then, a little over four years later, President Bill Clinton began an affair with a White House intern, much of which took place in the Oval Office. Clinton denied it vigorously and under oath when the intern spoke out, and was supported enthusiastically by nearly all the same politicians and celebs who had been so adamant that we believe the woman in the Thomas affair. The difference was a fluke piece of physical evidence that forced the president into a confession. He was eventually impeached; however, in that pre-#MeToo era, the only charge was lying under oath, not sexual harassment or oppression.

So there it is: two conservatives hammered (and probably set up) by feminists and the Left, two progressives (probably guilty) stoutly defended by the same. The actual evidence against the latter was in both cases distinctly stronger than that against the former. Back in the '90s, the general feeling against sexual harassment (and worse) was strong but not so well organized as at present, and one reason it didn't become so well organized until the gross stimulus of Harvey Weinstein was the rank hypocrisy of the movement revealed by the Thomas and Clinton affairs. It was all too obvious then, as now, that the imperative to believe the woman, except against a Democrat, had a political basis. The primary underlying cause of the accusers of conservatives was repeatedly shown to be abortion rights; principles that are of more general interest to a widespread base of women are secondary. Several feminists at the time stated outright that they defended Clinton because of his support of abortion rights; it was worth it to overlook his personal abuse of women. It is, notwithstanding one's views concerning abortion, entirely appropriate for anyone to support politicians and others who promote one's favorite causes. Unfortunately, many on the Left promote a cause that many others staunchly oppose by covering it with a more popular cause. The result is hypocrisy which, when revealed, is, to put it mildly, embarrassing. This is what we see today with the Biden accusations.

The role of the mass media in all this has been predictable. Attacks on conservatives are covered immediately and intensely; all are treated as breaking news and not just rumors or contrived tales. There is little actual investigation and, when a story proves false, it is commonly simply forgotten, overtaken by the next "bombshell" and retracted inconspicuously if at all. When a progressive Democrat is accused by a woman, it somehow doesn't manage to attain the status of news for an extended period, obviously in the hope that it will go away. If it becomes impossible to ignore, Pravda suddenly rediscovers its duty to investigate, to weigh all sides of the question, and finally to decide that the Democrat deserves the benefit of the doubt. With a conservative, as it happens, there is never a doubt to receive the benefit. The rule of thumb with Pravda is to take the denial of a progressive who is accused at face value and to discount that of a conservative out of hand. That's the news.

Fortunately, #BelieveAllWomen is now dead, at least until the next Supreme Court nomination. It never was a very good meme, since everyone who has occupied this planet for more than year or two realizes that women can and do lie about as much as men, and most of them do it better. Everyone with any sense of fairness and right also realizes that women have been unfairly treated at many levels, especially in the workplace, and that it is proper that this be taken seriously. But women activists of the Left can't seem to cut the cord to partisan politics, especially as the politics relate to their main concern of abortion rights. Since they can't win on that cause alone (about the same percentage of women as a whole oppose or are highly ambiguous about abortion as for men – about half or a little more), they resort to vociferous support of a movement with more general support to remove political opponents. Unfortunately, fully justified resistance to harassment and abuse of women is eroded by the blatant hypocrisy that results. It is highly unlikely to occur, but it would be more honest, and certainly refreshing, for the Left to adopt the banner they really prefer: #BelieveAllDemocrats.

5/18/20

PART V
The Media

Some readers may be surprised to find a section in a book that is mostly given over to government and politics that is devoted to the news media. They shouldn't be; the media has been recognized as part of any nation's power structure for centuries. The term "fourth estate" was used first for the media, mostly newspapers at the time, in the early 19th century by Thomas Carlyle in England. It derived from earlier use in France of "*quatrieme pouvoir*" or "fourth power," which added journalists to the traditional three major divisions of the state – the clergy, the nobility and the commoners. Many European countries use a similar term today for the news media. In the US, "fourth estate" recognizes the media as being on a par with the three branches of the federal government: executive, legislative and judicial. So even though the media is not formally a part of government at any level, it has traditionally been conceded to have political clout on a par with the formal branches. Its political mission has also been traditionally defined: it is the watchdog, assigned to ferret out corruption and bad practices and report them to the public. That is a mission and a duty that has long been recognized as vital to a democracy.

One of the more painful words in the English language is "betrayal." *Et tu, Brute?* still makes us wince in a way that simple murder does not. Down deep, we like to feel assured that there is something on which we can depend, or someone who reliably has our back. When an institution as important as the news media betrays our trust in it, it hurts. And this is exactly what has happened. The younger generations may be surprised to know that well within living memory the US had a genuine news media with genuine working journalists. There has always been an element of bias in the media (how can there not be, in a human endeavor?), and the bias has been mostly leftward for at least a century, but there has also been a sincere effort toward objectivity in reporting. At least there was.

The articles of this section discuss the media that exists today and map the history of how it came to be as it is. The purpose of the first of these chapters, *Pravda West*, is to demonstrate that most of the mass, or "mainstream" media is no longer a news institution at all, at least in the traditional meaning, but rather a propaganda organ for a political party. This is, as its title implies, the functional analog to the *Pravda* newspaper of Soviet Russia during the decades of the rule of the Communist Party. As the article points out, there is at least one important difference, but that difference exists only because the Democrat Party is not identical to the US government, as the Communist Party was to the government of Russia. In short, the party controls the mass media, but it does not control the government. Not yet, anyway.

The other articles amplify and elucidate that central premise. You may feel the sad sense of betrayal that runs through them all. There is one outlier in the section: *Objectivity and Other Lies; Rights and Other Wrongs* addresses a few other issues as well as the media and could accompany articles on religion and philosophy or science. However, the discussion of objectivity (and, sad to say, lying) seems to fit it among the media articles. Anyway, this isn't the happiest section of the book, but it is one of the more important.

Chapter Thirty

Pravda West

There is indecision these days as to what to call what used to be called the mainstream media. They still call themselves that but it's a tepid joke. Their content is mainstream in only a few quarters of some of our coastal cities (plus Chicago and maybe a few others), and even fans, while they may enjoy it, don't really believe it's news. In the other 99% of our nation's vastness these media outlets are so far out of the mainstream they may as well be reporting from Mars. We speak, of course, of ABC, NBC, CBS, CNN, MSNBC, PBS, the New York Times, the Washington Post and a plethora of their comrades. It is obviously far too tedious to type out all the initials and names every time we refer to them, and feelings would be hurt among those left out, so we need a collective label for the lot.

I've been calling them the alphabets, but that covers only the broadcast media. Many other names, such as the rather harsh "lamestream media," have been used, but they are insufficiently descriptive. We need a term that resounds with historical allusions and connotations, that summarizes the entire spectrum of meaning of what this piece of our culture is today. Upon careful reflection, I have selected "Pravda West" as my chosen cognomen for what was the mainstream media. I shall endeavor to explain the reasoning below.

The newspaper *Pravda* (which means "truth" in Russian) was founded by a Russian railroad magnate shortly after the turn of the 20th century. Its editorial function was soon taken over by social democrats (forerunners of what was to be the Communist Party), apparently somewhat to the dismay of the founder. Its fortunes varied for a while, including being banned after political uprisings against the government. Control of the paper became one of the bones of contention between intellectuals of the Mensheviks and Bolsheviks, the two main factions of the Russian Social Democratic Labor Party, with the latter mostly winning. With the Romanov abdication in early 1917, *Pravda* was revived and moved to Moscow. As is typical of the internecine fights of the Left, the least intellectual and most ruthless of the factions won out, and Lenin's Bolsheviks took control of both nation and newspaper in the aftermath of World War I. From 1918 until 1991, *Pravda* lived its glory days as the official organ of the Soviet Communist Party.

Other state-controlled newspapers thrived in the USSR during this period, including *Izvestia* ("news" in Russian), the organ of the Supreme Soviet, and *Trud* for the trade unions. None had the circulation and influence of *Pravda*, however, for the Party ruled Russia and one had to read it to know what the Party was going to do and what it wanted one to believe. *Izvestia* was primarily devoted to international affairs and played a distinct second fiddle to *Pravda* in a society as closed as Russia's. None of the other papers were nearly as important, and since the era of social media and cellphones had not yet begun *Pravda* was thus the primary source of information in one of the world's greatest countries. The editors of the newspaper were among the elite, but cause and effect should not be confused here. They held their positions because they were high in the Party, not the reverse.

This raises a point about the functions of state-controlled media. Unlike the free media, the purpose of a state organ like *Pravda* is not to inform but to convince, and if not to convince at least to control. It took its content directly from the Party bosses; indeed, as noted above, the editors were themselves among those bosses. *Pravda* worked by means of half-truths and agitprop with a clear objective: to help bend the populace to the will of the Party. There is a vast difference between information and coercion, with persuasion somewhere between. *Pravda*, in common with its various counterparts in socialist regimes everywhere and at all times, operated primarily in the persuasion bandwidth of that spectrum, but in the service of the coercive end. A free press, on the other hand, may display bias but it is still free of direct state control. In terms of the spectrum, it works on the information end, although it may stray too often into the persuasion mode.

This brings us to the media of our own time. There are several distinct and very important differences between *Pravda* and any media outlet in the US today. One is that none among the latter are directly controlled by the government. Another is that the audience is no longer captive -- there is an array of information sources outside the traditional media. This means that in theory, no matter how one-sided the media may be, it is still free. It can still change its ways without government pulling the plug or otherwise sanctioning it. It also means that it can be sanctioned by its public, simply by people tuning out. These are undeniably important points. On the other hand, freedom also means that the media can voluntarily continue in its biased ways without government sanctions, and that is what has happened.

It is difficult to pinpoint the beginning of a leftist slant in the US press, but it is safe to place it not long after the birth of the Progressive movement near the end of the 19th century. Certainly there was some sign of it by the time of Woodrow Wilson's presidency, and more during the presidency of Franklin D. Roosevelt, but the tradition of genuine objectivity in the media, in practice as well as theory, was still alive and well at a much later date. However, I would place the onset of the capture of the media by the Left with the Walter Duranty affair in the 1930s. That epoch, during which socialism became respectable outside a coterie of mainly academic intellectuals, coincided, more or less, with the Spanish Civil War. As described in other articles herein (see *The Russian Paradigm*), Duranty whitewashed Stalin's Ukrainian genocide and other crimes while serving as Moscow bureau chief for the New York Times and won a Pulitzer Prize for his transgressions. The Times sort of apologized years later but kept the Pulitzer. Sympathy for the Republican party in Spain, despite its darker side, added to the media support for leftist causes.

The real dominance of the Left in the media dates as far back as the 1950s, but it was largely undetected because a relatively few news sources had an effective monopoly of the broadcast industry. The press was far more diverse in numbers of outlets, but it too was overshadowed in national news by a handful of urban papers, led by the New York Times and Washington Post. Journalism schools of essentially all major universities were also taken over by the Left as the last half of the 20th century progressed. Most new reporters that emerged from these schools were infused with leftist ideas by the time they graduated, and the managements of the major media corporations were not disappointed by that fact. The final straw was the Vietnam War. Widespread public opposition to the war took on a distinctly leftist taint, in large part because of the media. The frenzied hysteria of the opposition both fueled and was fanned by media activism. By the '70s, the major media were largely an organ of the Left.

Through the fat decades for the major networks and printed media, which is to say from their capture by the Left until the rise of the use of the internet by the masses, there wasn't much opportunity to judge media bias. That is, there was little outside them with which to compare their news coverage. A consumer listened to Walter Cronkite (aptly named: his surname is an anglicized form of "sickness" in German) and accepted it at face value because every other news source was telling him pretty much the same thing. When Cronkite told us the Vietnam War was lost (just after the battle that destroyed the Viet Cong as a military force), it was lost. The influence of the major media on public perceptions was at its zenith.

The reaction of the major media to the first leaks in the dike of the news monopoly was interesting. There were two possible routes to take when it became evident that alternative news sources were becoming available. One, the rational route, was to shed the bias, at least in substantial part, undertake a reformation and return to the older tradition of genuine objectivity. The other was the route taken. Major media sources began by pooh-poohing the credibility of internet and other alternative sources, claiming that all the real reporting by trained professionals was being done by them alone. In this claim they were not entirely wrong: there was (and still is) a great deal of bogus information floating around outside the major media. Of course, there's a lot of it floating around within the major media as well, and enough truthful material came out to make that fact evident. To make matters worse for Pravda West (better for the cause of Truth), another major corporation came along to take advantage of the situation. Fox News quickly took the lead in audience numbers as the only outfit appearing to present balanced reporting.

The current stance of the older mass media could be described as cocooning. The various companies have retreated into a defensive shell, feeding off one another and still claiming to be the only game in town that has any news legitimacy. But one after another, false stories appear, are presented as straight news and passed around from one outfit to the rest, discussed intensely for a few days, then shrugged off and finally lost when their mendacious nature is revealed. The tendentiousness of every one of these leans the same, and they are designed specifically to embarrass the current president and his administration. This has long since passed the point of any possibility of coincidence. The major media has lost all pretense to objectivity, and most of its credibility along with it. It is therefore fair to think of it as an organ of the Left, and specifically of the Democrat Party. The citizens of the Soviet Union, with the mordant fatalism of the Russian sense of humor, said of their newspapers that there was no truth in *Pravda* and no news in *Izvestia*. Our proud major news sources of yesteryear have a striking resemblance to their old Soviet counterparts.

Pravda was, quite openly, the organ of a political party. The collective leftist news media has for at least two decades effectively been an organ of a political party. The differences are that *Pravda* was an organ of a ruling party and its editorial staff was also part of the government. The US media fronts for a party that is forced to share control of the government and its editors and reporters are only tangentially part of government. The collaboration of the media with the Democrat Party is not as open as that of *Pravda* with the Soviet Communist Party, but it is nevertheless obvious. The revelation of debate questions by a media "moderator" with the DNC's selected candidate in the nomination runup to the 2016 election was a rather laughable example, but less blatant ones are abundant. Memos from the DNC provide talking points for media spokespersons on a daily basis, as is evident from the exact wording of anti-conservative "news" stories from a dozen different sources. This is *Pravda* to a "T," a direct pipeline from party to media outlet.

Some may object to the identification of *Pravda* with our new Pravda West on the basis that the sundry media outlets of the latter aren't directly owned by the government. This argument is a technical one inasmuch as, first, *Pravda* was in theory also an independent entity and, more important, the privatization of agitprop doesn't change its nature. The DNC, one may say, has simply outsourced its propaganda, much as the US defense and intelligence establishments have been known to outsource their less savory operations to private organizations. The important feature is functional control, not legal ownership.

Speaking of government agencies, it might be added that the media also shills for our government bureaucracy with regularity. The use of it by Deep State officials to hammer President Trump recalls a similar, and so far more successful, scheme to overturn another election in the early 1970s. That's the stuff of another article, perhaps, but meanwhile I recommend an article by John Marini in the March, 2019, edition of Hillsdale College's Imprimis to those who can't wait. The main point here is that Pravda West has long operated as a sort of nongovernmental organization (NGO) on behalf of the permanent bureaucracy. I suppose we could also call it the Deep State News (DNS), but that would equate agitprop to real news. And calling it The Swamp Sheet is excessively snarky. I prefer Pravda West, which is far more accurate and descriptive.

And so much for the media's own hogwash about speaking truth to power. Pravda West's *modus operandi* is more like speaking lies to the ignorant on behalf of the powerful.

Actually, if pure geography is a factor, perhaps we should say Pravda East instead. At their closest point, the Bering Strait, the international borders of Russian and the US almost touch, and that is east of Moscow, *Pravda*'s home. But we traditionally think of the US as of the West and of Russia as well to the east of us, so the name of Pravda West for the US leftist media establishment feels better. And it fits well, from the *modus operandi* of misleading half-truths and outright falsehoods to the final product of thoroughly spun propaganda. It is appropriate to close this out with another quotation of the inimitable socialist George Orwell: "The very concept of objective truth is fading out of the world. Lies will pass into history."

8/27/19

Chapter Thirty-One
Debunked

It seems that I've heard the word "debunked" more often in the past few years than ever before. It's a relatively new word in the English language, derived from "bunk," meaning nonsense, which isn't much older. It's probably only coincidence that "bunk" originated near the beginning of the Progressive Movement, around the turn of the 20th century and "debunked" about at the end of Wilson's presidency, when the movement was in full flower. That is no doubt highly appropriate, since the two words and the movement have been closely linked throughout the history of the last century or so. The increase in usage is also consistent with a trend toward the coarsening of our national popular culture and the loss of civility in public discourse over the last few decades.

If you are reluctant to accept the above statement, consider that there are words in our language that do the same job as debunked and have been around much longer. "Confuted," for example, is an old and useful verb. But when a statement or argument is confuted, there is a sense that that which has been confuted was wrong, perhaps, but was respectable and put forth with honest intentions. When one debunks something, there's an implication that the debunked item was somehow ridiculous and presented maliciously by a thoroughly nasty person or a crackpot. Since leftists view themselves as paragons of Righteousness, it is clear why they prefer to debunk anything that offends them rather than merely to confute it. To oppose the obviously Righteous is to reveal oneself as evil or insane, or both, and so deserving of a good debunking.

Hillary Clinton and her supporters are great debunkers. Examples are legion, since reported scandals involving her are also legion, and some are quite recent. A good one occurred just this August, 2019, when she addressed a report by Robert Epstein (himself of leftist persuasion and a Hillary voter) that Google had swayed a significant number of voters in the 2016 election toward Hillary. She referred to it as debunked, while apparently seeing the Russian collusion theory, which swayed votes the other way, as entirely viable. Her viewpoint was verified by a reporter from *People Magazine*, who called Mr. Trump's quote of the report an "unsubstantiated assertion" about his "significant popular vote defeat" (I know, you thought he won that election). She (the reporter) also wrote that Trump "has long pushed nonsense allegations of voter fraud," including multiple ballots by some voters. All obvious bunk, of course.

In reference to the same report, a Google spokesperson stated, "This researcher's inaccurate claim has been debunked since it was made in 2016." Well, that should take care of it! Unfortunately, there was no indication of who debunked it or how, just a simple declaration. Apparently no backup was considered necessary for the *People* reporter's remarks about Trump's veracity, either. When good people debunk something, it's toast, and further argument is absurd. If someone objects, he's declaring himself to be a deplorable and a waste of protoplasm, and likely a racist to boot.

In October, 2017, Hillary declared in a C-Span interview that allegations of her *quid pro quo* involvement in the 2010 Uranium One deal with Russia were "debunked." She went on to mention "real Russian ties between Trump associates and real Russians." Again, she had her defenders. The scandal was debunked by Annenberg "fact checkers" that same month, and also by a Snopes "fact check." The latter noted that Hillary herself said she wasn't "personally involved," and that various revelations didn't "prove" a Clinton *quid pro quo* agreement. Pretty convincing stuff, that. As it happens, a new investigation of the matter has since been opened. Since it is being carried out by the House Intelligence Committee (the one headed by Adam Schiff), we may confidently expect to see more debunking of the scandal in the near future.

Fact-checking is a favorite device of debunkers on the Left, and most of the mass media outlets have reporters who are dedicated to that end. Much of the media fact-checking talent has for years been devoted to defending the rather colorful record of Bill and Hillary Clinton. Bill's activities related to women are especially notorious, but there has been plenty to defend beyond those. An especially enlightening article on that topic appeared in *The Fix* on April 17, 2015, under the title "Snopes.com has been debunking Clinton rumors since the Clinton years." The article is sympathetic to David Mikkelson, co-founder of Snopes, who in turn has made a good living in the amazingly fruitful field of defending the Clintons against all comers.

This post is not about Snopes, its methods or its politics, however, but rather about debunking, and it is one of Mikkelson's quotes in that article that is of interest here. He stated, "Generally, 90 to 95% of the political stuff we write about is anti-Democratic, anti-liberal. You really have to hunt to find anti-conservative things to debunk." This is one of those unintentional gems that reveal the mindset of the speaker in starkest glory.

It is probable that Mr. Mikkelson really believes what he said. His worldview is such that he sees nearly all facts putting the Left in a negative light as fallacious and those that do the same to the Right as simply true. No one of balanced mind could seriously believe that over nine-tenths of all BD (balderdash) is generated by right-wing zealots and that almost all left-wing-generated BD is pure as the driven snow. Reality just doesn't work that way; people of all political, religious, philosophical or other persuasions are capable of honesty, dishonesty and error in approximately equal proportions. One suspects that if "you really have to hunt to find anti-conservative things to debunk," you're not hunting with excessive zeal.

But I do not wish to pick on David Mikkelson or Snopes exclusively; in fact, the entirety of Pravda West is oriented similarly. It has been repeatedly documented that over 90% of the media coverage of Mr. Trump has been negative. Given the actual facts of his record on the economy alone, it is unlikely that this coverage could be considered remotely fair. Most of the American media spends most of its energies debunking all things conservative, and all people deplorable. Hillary Clinton had a full-time job as First Lady vigorously debunking her husband's sexual accusers (before she had to turn to debunking her own ethics accusers) and was staunchly supported by the press. Now the press is much occupied in debunking its own accusers. And so it goes.

The real fun starts when the Left starts debunking the debunkers of some of its own pet causes. Examples are abundant, since every time some poor soul attempts to confute one of leftism's holy icons he's gang-tackled by both Pravda West and most of academia, plus bureaucrats from a dozen agencies -- but an especially good one is the famous "hockey stick." This is a graph first published in 1999 by Penn State climate scientist Michael Mann that was presented to prove anthropogenic global warming by computer analysis using proxy indicators. Mann's results were widely accepted by almost all politically oriented environmentalists, most agency bureaucrats and a great many "mainstream" climate scientists. The hockey stick graph and its implications became the gold standard for mainstream climate research for the next couple of decades and Mann was riding high. Then he overreached. He filed what many felt were SLAPP suits (lawsuits intended to shut people up) for defamation, for millions of dollars against several of his critics.

Unfortunately for the hockey stick, the suits were filed in Canada, where plaintiffs can be required to demonstrate there is no substance to the critics' statements. To the shock of many in the scientific community, Mann refused to do so, claiming his methods were proprietary. All of this, the layman should know, is highly irregular in science. Discourse between scientists is traditionally robust (to put it euphemistically) but lawsuits are almost unheard of. Even worse, a scientist does not hide his methods: they are laid out clearly for all to see, examine -- and criticize. Mann's refusal to do so stunned many who had used his work uncritically, relying on his reputation. The Supreme Court of British Columbia dismissed Mann's defamation suit and moreover awarded the defendant scientist full legal costs. Pravda West promptly dropped the whole story as though it never existed, although all its outlets had been debunking the debunkers of global warming vigorously for nearly two decades. So it goes.

Whistleblowing is related to debunking in a number of ways. Mainly, it's a means to disparage particular ideas, persons or institutions in the cause of truth or justice. Also like debunking, whistleblowing can be a two-edged sword. Edward Snowden, for example, became a Deep State pariah by revealing unethical (and illegal) domestic spying by certain Intelligence Community agencies. He was widely condemned by the Establishment, not surprising since those agencies are firmly ensconced within said Deep State. Another example is the revelation that Planned Parenthood was routinely marketing baby body parts. Since abortion rights are popular on the Left, the undercover investigators who blew that whistle were thoroughly vilified in most Pravda West outlets, and, like the critics of Michael Mann, taken to court in retribution. They were convicted (in California, of course), since in US courts telling the truth is no defense.

Whistleblowing became very popular in the same outlets more recently, however, with the allegations against President Trump concerning the Ukrainian telephone call. Oddly, one of the same agencies that was busiest debunking whistleblower Snowden was the prime instigator of this case of whistleblowing (I won't mention the name, but the initials are CIA). Even stranger, the same news media that excoriated the whistleblowers of the Planned Parenthood scandal are most worshipful of this one, whoever he or she may be. It would appear that whom to debunk and whom to elevate among debunkers or whistleblowers depends not on the act itself but on whose ox is being gored.

It should be pointed out that debunking, as executed by the mass media, is not an especially rigorous art. More often than not, the journalist assigned to debunk a conservative organization or concept takes the passive approach, which is inexcusably lazy. Throughout almost every story one reads, every statement by the conservative or Republican subject is accompanied by the words "without evidence" or "unsupported by facts" or "baseless" or "unsubstantiated assertion." It can be entertaining to count how many of these phrases one finds in even a short article these days. Hardly ever does the reporter point out an alternative idea or explanation, itself buttressed by sound facts, that would tend to refute the other. In other words, the reporter attempts to shift the entire burden of proof to the other side.

Worse, the bar for that burden is generally raised impossibly high. An example is the current Joe/Hunter Biden Ukrainian/Chinese imbroglio. Any reference to possible wrongdoing by the pair becomes a "conspiracy theory" that is "without evidence." That is as though a $50M/month board seat occupied by the son of the high official responsible for doling out foreign aid to the country, a young man without a shred of credentialed qualifications or experience, whose father openly bragged about withholding cash to get the prosecutor looking into the company whose board the kid occupies, isn't evidence in itself. That's what our steely-eyed investigative reporters have come to: mere bald assertions of "no evidence" and end of story. It is notable that the bar for sufficient evidence is not so high for Pravda West's own efforts. The litany of stories with vague anonymous sources that prove fictional in the end is long and sad.

Without control of the mass media, the coalition of Left, Establishment and Deep State (each of which includes many of the same individuals) couldn't have such an easy time with debunking. It's the media that allows the lazy way out, the way of simply declaring whatever they don't like to be officially debunked. With the shreds of a credibility left over from better days, the media can still (sort of) get away with the casual "without evidence" or "unsubstantiated" without providing any evidence or substantiation of its own. Strangely enough, Trump, with all his faults, who stands accused of lying a "documented" several thousands of times (also unsubstantiated), tries harder to provide evidence for his sundry statements than any Pravda West outlet. Which is not to say he tries that hard; it's just such a low bar that the media sets for itself.

Even more striking than the media's casual pursuit of evidence is its new objective. The traditional role of press and broadcast was to expose scandal, to reveal to the public the underside of political life. Now the media has no interest in that; it exists to debunk such scandal, to actively hide it to protect the Left. It also delights in inventing scandal that doesn't exist, always in favor of the Left. The Russian Collusion fiasco, now the Ukrainian affair that has been turned on its head: these and more were inventions of the Deep State that were enabled by a media that doubles as an echo chamber of itself. How many times in the past few years have media outlets promulgated false narratives by quoting other outlets that have quoted .... and so on.

So the Left and its Pravda West debunk some stories and invent others, all in the service of leftist political goals. Debunking and invention are thus two sides of the same coin. The name of that coin is: Propaganda.

7/21/19

Chapter Thirty-Two

Faking Out Ty Cobb

A retired baseball player back in the late 1950s found himself in something of a quandary. He'd had great fame back in the day but discovered that, as the game moved on, the public was well on its way to forgetting about him. As is typical of older men, he fretted about his legacy. After all, a legacy is about all that older men have going for them. So he decided to write an autobiography that focused on his playing career, just for the record. His name was Tyrus Raymond ("Ty") Cobb, and he may have been the greatest ballplayer of all time.

A middle-aged sportswriter/journalist around the same time found himself a little short of work, and therefore funds. He had run into something of a roadblock in his career: he'd been blackballed by several of his best markets because of a bit of bad luck. He had fabricated a number of "facts" in various stories. That was apparently routine with him; the bad luck was that he'd been caught. Then some good luck struck: he was offered a chance to ghost-write an autobiography of a famous baseball star. He was determined to make the best of it. His name was Alvin ("Al") Stump, and as a journalist he was all too typical of his modern counterpart.

We'll probably never know exactly why these two men were brought together. Cobb apparently floated the idea of his autobiography to several publishers and Doubleday & Company took it up. In better times, Cobb might have penned it himself; he was highly literate and a life-long voracious reader, especially of history. However, he was by then old and infirm and obviously needed someone else to do the writing. What is not clear is why Al Stump was selected by the publisher to be that person. It wasn't an obvious choice: the sportswriter's reputation was, as pointed out above, none of the best. He was generally considered a hard-drinking hack, not the kind of writer to attempt a project that required a delicacy of touch, a certain sensitivity, as this one did.

Ty Cobb was a larger-than-life figure, a genuine American hero, but patently not a saint. He was generous with his time and money, intelligent, witty, honest and driven to succeed, but he was also prickly where his sense of honor was concerned, demanding of the best in others and, like so many successful people, not short on ego. His combination of intense competitiveness and thin skin could be explosive, and he was caught up in numerous fights, physical and otherwise. He wasn't well-liked, even by many of his own teammates, and he was feared by those against whom he played.

On the other hand, he was genuinely respected by his fellow players. Although even during his playing career there were rumors in the press about him cheating and intentionally spiking others, the men on the field uniformly attested that he played hard but fair. The fear of his opponents was that of being humiliated, not hurt. He was capable of feats on the base paths that today seem almost mythical: he stole home 54 times (a record that still stands) and once stole second, third and home on three successive pitches. He had perfected nine different slides, and one catcher testified that Cobb never had to spike anyone, his slide was "too pretty" for that. He was also an awesome hitter; his lifetime batting average is still the all-time highest and was over .300 every year of his long career except the first.

Ty Cobb's objective in wanting an autobiography was to officially set the record straight concerning his baseball legacy. He was apparently looking for a sort of combination biography and instruction manual for young men who wanted to learn to play well. A book of this sort had actually been published a few years earlier by a respected sportswriter named John McCallum and entitled *The Tiger Wore Spikes: An Informal Biography of Ty Cobb* (1956). Cobb seemed to be satisfied with that result but wanted something more complete and perhaps more personal. Certainly, given the complexity of the subject, he needed a skilled and sensitive writer to do the job. In retrospect, it is evident that Al Stump was not that writer, even had he been honest, and one might think editors at Doubleday would have known that.

Ty Cobb by that time was a very wealthy man. His fortune resulted less from his fame (ballplayers in those days were notoriously ill-paid and rarely could rely on their baseball popularity to carry over into their post-playing lives) than his business acumen. He owned houses in his hometown in Georgia and on Lake Tahoe in California, and Al Stump chose the latter location for his interviews. He spent a total of no more than three weeks over the period of nearly a year, starting in the spring of 1960, with the sick and aging star. That short time was later put to good use by Stump, as will be seen. The time the two passed together was apparently not much appreciated by Cobb, who distrusted his ghost writer. According to Stump, it was not congenial to him either, but who knows? As it turned out, little that Stump said concerning Cobb could be taken at face value.

Cobb repeatedly requested from the publisher a draft of the upcoming biography, without result until it was too late. He was profoundly disappointed with it when he finally saw it and threatened a lawsuit to prevent its publication, but went into the hospital for the last time before he could do anything. He died in July of 1961. The autobiography, which was entitled *My Life in Baseball: A True Record* (1961) came out a few months later. Stump was hardly through, however. He managed to sell an article to *True: A Magazine for Men* that same year, which bore the title "Ty Cobb's Wild 10-Month Fight to Live." It was based on the short time he'd spent with the old man during the previous year and a half, and it certainly lived up to its title. It was filled with anecdotes that were wild enough for a hormone-laced teenager, not especially convincing for a failing old man. It was sold to the magazine ("True"?) as a blockbuster, which it was. It is highly doubtful that any of it was factual.

Stump's book may have left a great deal to be desired from an artistic point of view, but the article that followed set off a firestorm. Actually, it wasn't especially credible even on the surface: Stump related a litany of violence and mayhem on the part of a dying man that simply did not jibe with either evidence or common sense. The blood was in the water, however, and any shark of a writer who needed a few bucks dove in. An influential example was Charles Alexander, a university professor who, in 1984, decided to augment his academic income by publishing a book that repeated all of Stump's calumnies and added a few of his own. Others piled on in the course of time, conforming to the best journalistic standards by culling all past accounts without doing any research to confirm them.

Among the more prominent of the pile-ons was Ron Shelton, who directed a film entitled *Cobb* in 1994. In order to help promote his film, he encouraged Al Stump to issue another supposed biography of Ty Cobb, which he did. The title, *Cobb: The Life and Times of the Meanest Man in Baseball* (1994) speaks for itself. The movie, fortunately, was a bust. The book, unfortunately, sold well. That was good for Stump, whose need for money was acute at that point. He profited further from his evanescent association with Ty Cobb by selling Cobb memorabilia, which he claimed had been given to him, to collectors. A few items he had apparently stolen in the course of one of his brief visits to Cobb's home in Tahoe; most were presented fraudulently as having been owned by the great man. Worst of all were voluminous writings that were attributed to Cobb but were later demonstrated by experts to be Stump forgeries. These diaries and other items were not only profitable in themselves but also used to support Stump's defamatory fiction. The gullible filmmaker Ken Burns used Stump's 1994 book for his depiction of Cobb in his documentary on baseball (2010).

Ty Cobb's reputation has been somewhat rehabilitated recently by several writers, mainly Charles Leerhsen with *Ty Cobb: A Terrible Beauty* (2015). The book is well worth reading, if only because it relied on what at one time was known as journalism; that is, actually looking up the facts in original documents and interviews with people who knew the subject. It shows the man as he was: imperfect but decent, hardly a monster, and a transcendently accomplished and exciting ballplayer. Unfortunately, the damage has been done. An unscrupulous and greedy sportswriter trashed the reputation of a good man after his death. No matter what may happen in the future, through mendacity, thievery, libel and forgery, and all for money, the legacy of one of history's greatest ballplayers has been tarnished beyond redemption.

What about today? The journalism profession has in recent years been assaulted with repeated claims of "fake news." In most cases, this has not involved deliberate fiction of the sort fabricated by Al Stump, but something almost as bad: running with a story that fits an ideological agenda without properly checking the facts. Worse, if credible accounts are to be believed, such fake news is rarely taken as seriously as it should be. It occupies headlines for days or weeks, and when it is revealed as false, it is acknowledged (if at all) below the fold on page 31, or the broadcast equivalent thereof. The perpetrators may make a snickering sort of apology but in most cases are never held properly accountable.

A case in point is that of Dan Rather, a long-time CBS anchor with a long-time (and well-earned) reputation for liberal bias. He was finally demoted from his anchor spot after airing a negative story about George W. Bush's Vietnam service in the Texas Air National Guard that was based on what is still referred to as "unauthenticated" documents. These were actually confirmed as outright forgeries almost from the outset, and not especially convincing ones, but they fit Rather's biases so well that he accepted them uncritically. So he was punished – or was he? In fact, the demotion followed a substantial slippage of his show in the ratings, and it is likely that CBS was happy to find an excuse to make a change that would otherwise have been awkward. As it is, he was kept on at CBS for another year and continues in his profession elsewere to this very day.

Since the rise of Donald Trump, first as the Republican nominee and then, against all expectations, as President of the U.S., the situation with the journalism profession has become exponentially worse. It seems there's hardly a week that goes by without another story that announces a serious crime, or at least misstep, on his part. The entire media establishment (with the occasional exception of Fox) explodes in paroxysms of joy: "We've got him now!" or "This is finally it!" The "I" word is repeated dozens, if not hundreds, of times: the brass ring of impeachment is within reach! But of course the "news" turns out to be wrong, just another unsubstantiated canard that was too good to bother to check out before airing. And whoever got the false scoop is so closely followed by the baying pack of newshounds, who quote each other uncritically, that it is hard to remember who that first gull was. Sometimes a dupe is reassigned, sometimes a retraction appears where no one will see it, more often the entire incident is conveniently forgotten. It is as though it never happened, except that (with luck, from a leftist point of view), it may leave a stain upon the subject of the false story. Enough such stains and said subject will be tarred for real.

When journalists bother to talk about this phenomenon at all, it is usually to dismiss it as collateral damage of the business. Mistakes happen in any human activity, and we shouldn't wonder that they happen in such a high-pressure business as news reporting. This might even be a partly credible explanation, except for one verity: the mistake is always, without exception, in the same direction. In the case of Trump, how many mistaken reports have been favorable to him? The opposite is true: anything favorable to our current president, authenticated or not, tends to be seriously underreported or not reported at all. Statistics fail to support the mistake theory.

In case you believe the above to be no more than amazing coincidence, you need do no more than listen to some (more honest if not more ethical) journalists themselves. One, whose name I have mercifully forgotten, stated outright that his colleagues were not only justified but obligated to report about Trump in a biased manner – they owed it to their readers and their society to do so. In other words, it was vital to lie to the poor, dumb deplorables out there in flyover country, and to present the lies as "news," because they (the journalists) were right and their readers were clueless. In other words yet, it was necessary to betray both their readers and their professional ethics to sell a mendacious bill of goods because the journalists are so much brighter and purer than their audience. Lying to a populace that is looking for news is virtuous when done in a good cause.

The results of this profound ideological dichotomy in American news reporting are obvious. President Trump is pounded daily by a media barrage that is reminiscent of the beginning of a WWI offensive on the Western Front. Any book, blog or news outlet that expresses opinions from the Right is mercilessly mocked. Any individual of a conservative political bent is held to the highest standards of behavior, and some are crushed even when they have maintained those standards. Meanwhile, on the Left, standards are, shall we say, more relaxed. Outright criminality on the part of leftist heroes and heroines is justified or simply ignored. Sloppy reporting may be rewarded with a Pulitzer Prize.

One major casualty of the collapse of journalistic ethics is the journalism profession itself. There has always been some tendency toward bias in news reporting, and inevitably so. People are human. But until relatively recently there was a professional obligation for a journalist to at least make an honest effort to attain objectivity. Some were more successful in that endeavor than others, but the standard was always there. Al Stump was the exception, not the rule. Now that the ideal itself has been largely abandoned, the credibility of the profession is bleeding out like a butchered pig. Polls are showing that the trust of the public in the reliability of the mass media is at an all-time low – matching the trust in the ethics of politicians. Tragically, modern journalists have sacrificed their ancient and noble profession on the altar of leftist political ideology.

But there is another element in this depressing situation. Looking again at the ruined legacy of Ty Cobb, we must ask the obvious question: *why* was a single sportswriter, already professionally disgraced, able to do the damage he did? Stump did it for money, not ideology, but his motivation is secondary; the question remains as to how he was so successful in savaging the reputation of a man who had been a foremost celebrity of his time and a hero to millions? And why is the output of a distrusted profession still absorbed with willing credence by so many who actually know better?

The answer, I am sorry to say, lies with the consumers of this avalanche of misinformation. We all have certain ideas of which we are very fond. When we hear one of these ideas expounded, no matter that we suspect its authenticity, no matter that we don't fully trust the source – we *want* to believe it. People were titillated by the lurid tales about the hero Ty Cobb, and they feel justified in their superior discernment when a favorite notion is borne out by apparent facts. In effect, we provide the market for "fake news," for it couldn't exist without one. In the end, we have no one to blame but ourselves. In the famous words of Pogo: "We have met the enemy, and he is us."

6/24/19

Chapter Thirty-Three
Conspiracy Theory

With Christmas coming on, I enjoy playing DVDs of old Christmas movies in idle moments, including the classic *Polar Express*. One scene especially comes to mind, when the protagonist first meets a ghostly railroad bum on the ice-coated roof of the rushing train. When it becomes evident that the boy doesn't believe in Santa Claus, the bum chides him for his fear of being played for the fool, using all the terms ("bamboozled," "led down the garden path," "taken for a ride,"etc.) associated with that ill fortune. The kid still doesn't believe in Santa Claus, of course; he'd rather be a cynic than a dupe. The point is that everyone is chary about being thought gullible and goes to great lengths not to be caught out in a scam or otherwise taken in by false information. No one likes to feel stupid or, worse, unsophisticated. For that reason, the epithet "conspiracy theory" has great weight in discouraging people of discernment and perspicacity from professing opinions that may in fact make good sense. It is for that reason that the Left, which collectively has never been a fan of free speech, uses the epithet to such good advantage. And that, in turn, is the reason that discussion of the activities of former VP Joe Biden and his family in Ukraine has become a political third rail.

Needless to say, there have been conspiracy theories that are perfectly ridiculous and with which no one with a sense of decency, or any sense at all, would wish to be associated. A classic example is Holocaust denial; another is the notion that the 9/11 crime was engineered by the U.S. government. Some are less atrocious and more comical, an example being the suggestion that Neil Armstrong's landing on the moon was the product of a Hollywood studio. That one could only have originated in a rural barber shop in Louisiana. Sinister accusations of government suppression of accounts of little green men and alien abductions are more extreme examples in the same category, which perhaps could be considered more whimsical flights of imagination than theories, conspiracy or otherwise. All these have something in common, and it is not that they are merely unsupported by facts. After all, the General Theory of Relativity was largely unsupported by facts until sometime after its proposal by Albert Einstein. The common denominator of those fables mentioned above, both wicked and whimsical, is that they are also inherently improbable to and beyond the point of incredibility.

The deluded souls who subscribe to conspiracy theories are given convenient labels. Those who doubt the reality of the Holocaust, for example, are "deniers," those who think the destruction of the twin towers was a government plot are "truthers," those who suspect Barack Obama may have been born outside the borders of the U.S. are "birthers." But wait: which of these is the outlier? The obvious answer is the birthers. The first two groups are adherents of ideas that are obviously crackpot, that fly in the face of facts the way the Flat Earth Society did for decades. But were the birthers truly crackpots? They may very well have been wrong in their conclusion, but their thesis was not genuinely bizarre. Surely Barack Obama's rather mysterious past history and the factual basis of a childhood spent in Indonesia, his extended and coquettish refusal to present his birth certificate for public scrutiny, his continued refusal to allow his academic record to come to light -- all these provide some basis for the birther idea. Which is to say, the conspiracy theory of the birthers is of an entirely different species than those of the other two examples.

So there are conspiracy theories and conspiracy theories, or more accurately, classic conspiracy theories of a crackpot nature and controversial theories that have a rational basis, however off-target they may be. Actually, the former are not theories at all, in the real sense of the word, and the latter range from mere hypotheses to something more closely approximating actual theories, depending on the credibility of their factual underpinnings. For a first-level evaluation, most of us have what is commonly called a "smell test" for any such narrative we hear. This is a common-sense sort of approach that probes the surficial credibility of the tale with reference to known facts and our experience. For some, that initial test is the whole story; they rarely change their minds regardless of what further data and analyses come to light. The more open-minded and analytical among us use the smell test not definitively but as a sort of filter to decide if further research and thought might be worthwhile. Needless to say, the factor of bias comes into play. Purely political reasons, for example, may cause us to tend to give credence to some narratives over others at the smell test level and continue to sway our analysis even after more facts are revealed.

Which brings us back to the Bidens and their little frolics around the world. Looking first at the Ukraine, the core facts are that while VP Joe Biden was in charge of doling out US funds to that nation, his son Hunter was made a board member of a Ukrainian natural gas company with the princely income of (in round numbers) a million dollars or so a year. Hunter had a resume that included no international energy background and little relevant business experience. Not long after his appointment, Hunter's father, in his official capacities, held up substantial payments to the country in order to force the firing of a Ukrainian prosecutor who was threatening to investigate the company on the board of which Hunter held his lucrative seat. Joe later bragged in public about his feat, so that fact, at least, can hardly be challenged. Does this pass your smell test? To be sure, it was argued that the prosecutor was himself corrupt and his removal was widely applauded as a favor to the world. As to Hunter's good luck -- well, it was just good luck, nothing more. Nothing to see here, folks, please move on. This is no more than a conspiracy theory, easily debunked.

Oh yes, then there's China. Hunter accompanied his father on the vice presidential plane when the latter went there on an official mission. When they came back, also together, Hunter had a cool billion and a half dollar contract to deliver to his stateside company. I haven't heard what Hunter's commission was, but it couldn't have been trivial. More good luck because, as it was explained, Joe and his son never discussed anything about business on their long plane trips there and back. They must have talked about golf and grandkids, like Bill Clinton and Attorney General Loretta Lynch in a plane on an isolated tarmac in California while his wife was under FBI investigation (I know, also a conspiracy theory). There are a few other coincidences, such as the enrichment of a Biden brother, but I have limited space. The point is that, taken together, for most of us this makes it over the highest smell test bar. Yet it is widely passed off as a conspiracy theory and therefore many otherwise level-headed people are afraid to touch it.

For those who have managed to convince themselves the Left is correct and whose smell test filters have let the Biden excuses pass, let us try a little mind experiment. In the Ukraine story, substitute the name "Donald Trump, Jr." for "Hunter Biden" throughout and see if it makes a difference in your thinking. Then do the same thing for the China trip, keeping the facts identical, with President Trump in place of Joe Biden, of course. Is your smell tester acting up yet? Do you think the story would get the same pass in Pravda West, aka the mass media? If you are honest with yourself, you will realize that Mr. Trump would have been long out of office by now, and probably inhabiting a small cell in a maximum security federal penitentiary (if not hanged, drawn and quartered). The level of hypocrisy is astounding.

Before the Ukrainian impeachment inquiry, the country was put through well over two years of turmoil with the Russian collusion caper. As it happened, the Russian collusion was a true conspiracy theory, in its old crackpot sense. In fact, there actually was collusion involving Russia, but not involving Russians in more than the usual meddling way. It turns out that the collusion was between the DNC and the Hillary campaign, on one side, and federal agencies on the other, namely the Justice Department and FBI. And that is *not* a conspiracy theory. But in the end, the perpetrators were let off without consequences and Trump was persecuted and his administration hobbled for more than half his first term. To this day, Hillary proclaims that the story of her own misdeeds is "debunked," and Pravda West still sees any reference to abuses on the part of government agencies as conspiracy theorizing. And people who should know better are still afraid to touch that third rail and look goofy in the eyes of the Left.

This is all straight out of the leftist playbook: projection and attack. As in the old Southwest Conference, the motto is "a good offense is the best defense." Projection is endemic on the Left; if leftists are guilty of something they are certain their opponents must be up to the same tricks. The Democrats are vulnerable on both issues -- the Russian fiasco and corruption in Ukraine, so they project their misconduct onto Trump, his family and his associates and attack with all the weapons at their disposal. These weapons aren't insignificant: they have Pravda West, for what that's still worth, and they have the embedded bureaucrats of the Deep State. With their supreme self-unawareness, many of them seem to believe they are protecting the Constitution (which otherwise they hate) and the traditional values of the nation (which otherwise they're not so fond of). Many others, of course, are simply cynical, which at least is more self-aware, if not especially honest.

And they get away with it, by and large, even though everyone knows better. As in Andersen's fable, *The Emperor's New Clothes*, no one wants to be first to speak up. Everyone is afraid to call the Left out. All the culpability of all the Democrats involved in these affairs has been debunked; all the accounts of their transgressions have been labeled conspiracy theories. Once the conspiracy theory accusation has been invoked, the subject is *verboten* to polite discussion. One must pretend to possess no sense of smell to avoid looking like a surly dupe, maybe even a deplorable, and surely a crackpot. It's conspiracy theory phobia and most people, even confident people, have a touch of it. But hey, "no guts, no glory," so I'll say it outright: Trump may not be a saint but he's still a victim, and Joe and Hillary are crooks. Does this make me a crackpot conspiracy theorist? If facts don't count, and in the annals of the Left, it doubtless does. Make of it what you will: these would-be emperors have no clothes.

12/8/19

Chapter Thirty-Four
Easy Courage

American journalism has a stirring history to look back upon and admirable traditions to sustain it. Valiant colonial presses were instrumental in initiating the American Revolution and had a great deal to do with its success. During the centuries since, journalists have, like all others, had their ups and downs, but overall their profession established itself as a fundamental cornerstone of the republic. It has been noted by many statesmen that without a free and active media, democracy itself cannot function as it should and the constitutional republic we enjoy cannot thrive. Indeed, the media considers itself the virtual fourth leg of constitutional democracy and few would argue against that claim.

Given the above, it isn't surprising that the self-image of journalists of all stripes is rather flattering. One of the proudest elements of that image is courage. Every reporter would like to be thought of as a person who will "speak truth to power," as the popular phrase has it. Certainly, it requires fortitude to tell a potent individual or institution something that he or it doesn't want to hear, and to say it publicly so everyone else hears it also. It is to deliver facts in the face of intense displeasure of the highly placed and the retribution that is almost certain to follow that separates the lions from the sheep of the world. Journalists think of themselves as among the most lion-like of professionals.

Another important element of journalistic self-image is the idea of bringing light to the world, especially the world of democratic self-government. As noted above, people cannot exercise their native wisdom in a fruitful way without accurate information, and providing that information is what the ideal media does. The core of this idea is contained in the excellent corporate motto of the E.W. Scripps Company: "Give light and the people will find their own way." This elegant little sentence sums up the entire purpose of journalism, at least in its intended form. Of course, as we shall see, the definition of "light" can vary, depending on circumstances.

Vital to any journalist's view of the profession is the image of a driven seeker of truth who turns over every stone in the unrelenting search for the next key fact that will make the story. The reputation for reportorial diligence, even carried to an extreme, is the stuff of many a fiction story and movie plot, and historically it has some basis in fact. Journalists have traditionally been willing to take risks to get the story, and not just in wartime, and many have paid the ultimate price over the years. Beyond the risks, however, the day-to-day work of determined investigative reporters can be exceedingly arduous. The best continue to dig for the real facts despite hardship and discouragement. It's a great tradition.

Finally, there is an ethical standard on which the media prides itself, and it is based largely on the principle of objectivity. It follows from the E.W. Scripps motto mentioned above, which basically means that consumers of the journalists' products should be justified in their confidence that they are getting the real facts, and all the facts that are relevant to the story, without excessive coloration. Objectivity is the subject of much of what follows, because it is central to those other elements of the journalistic self-image already described. Objectivity is also not very popular among journalists at this time, except as an abstraction, and has not always been a realized journalistic standard. A very brief history of the profession in America may illuminate this issue.

The pre-Revolutionary War press was unabashedly and openly partisan. The principle of objectivity wasn't a factor in colonial journalism, and as it happened, the press was on the right side of history. Without its efforts and the real sacrifices made by the operators of colonial presses it is questionable whether the people of the American colonies could have been mobilized behind the cause and success achieved. After liberty was won and up until the time of the Civil War, the partisanship of the press continued, but took a rather different form. This was the era of the so-called "party press," when a large majority of newspapers were partisans of one political party or another. The partisanship was entirely open, with no pretense of any sort of objectivity, and the content could be scathing and even scurrilous. No holds were barred in the service of political partisanship, and much of the writing was downright libelous.

The term "objectivity" has been used only for the last century or so, but the principle is older. Perhaps the first clear statement of its definition was made by Lawrence Gobright, AP Washington chief, in 1856. By the 1890s the principle was well established, if not always followed. The rather gross anti-German propaganda campaigns of World War I emphasized to both public and profession the desirability of objectivity in reporting, and this was for both economic and ethical reasons. The economic incentives for the press were obvious: an objective news organ could draw readers from the whole spectrum of political opinion rather than a narrow corner of it. Ethical virtues of the principle are more subtle but also obvious.

World War II and its aftermath saw some reorganization of the news media that coincided with a sort of national consensus as to what the country was all about. The result was that objectivity as a journalistic principle was at its strongest. This lasted until the social unrest of the '60s and '70s, much of it fueled by the Vietnam War. Increasingly bitter social division thereafter strained objectivity but it remained a guiding light for most journalists. The strain increased as time passed, partly because the economic incentive diminished. Newspapers declined as alternative media became more widely available and profits were driven more by intense consumer loyalties to partisan outlets. Perhaps more important, there was a rise in its own sense of moral and intellectual superiority by the Left that seemed to make objectivity not only outmoded but actually dereliction of duty. Also, some critics noted that complete objectivity was not only immoral but impossible to attain with human reporters. If it couldn't be done perfectly, the argument seemed to be, why try at all?

The election of 2016 led to the greatest challenge of all to the objectivity principle in journalism. Given the political proclivities of a huge proportion of those in the mass media – namely progressive – a feeling of profound disappointment with the ascension of Trump to the presidency was evident almost everywhere in the industry. Added to this was the shock of missing the story so completely. These factors led to a pervasive miasma of groupthink that combined with that sense of self-righteousness that afflicts so many on the Left to shatter the foundation of media professional ethics: objectivity. Trump Derangement Syndrome affected the mass media even more intensely than most institutions (academia excepted).

At this point, the abandonment of objectivity – in the service of the Greater Good, of course – is essentially complete. It was even formalized in a New York Times article by Jim Rutenberg that was published in August, 2016, well before the election. Rutenberg asked what a reporter was supposed to do if he believed the nominee of a major party, namely Mr. Trump, was bad for the country. The traditional answer, of course, is that the reporter should stick to facts and not let his opinions run away with him. But that wasn't the answer in Rutenberg's article. His answer was that duty to the readers demanded actively biased reporting. That answer could only be acceptable to one who believed his opinions were somehow sacrosanct, passed down from a cloud on graven tablets. It was the answer of one anointed, of one whose communication with ultimate Truth places him above the masses. And it was an answer acceptable to a substantial proportion of leftist media figures.

The cult of political groupthink that made a casualty of the objectivity principle led to the loss of much else that was noble about journalism. Primary among the losses was the mission defined by the Scripps motto. When true journalism is replaced by propagandizing, the idea of giving light is turned on its head. Much of the effort of newsrooms these days is given not to revealing facts but to hiding them. In its new incarnation as Pravda West, mouthpiece of the Left (in general) and Democrat Party (in particular), the mass media systematically manages to miss any story that cannot be manipulated to fit the ideological agenda. Facts must be subordinated to the higher truth, which is always defined by leftist standards.

The upshot of this upside-down vision is that the ideal of courage is similarly reversed. A recent example is the New York Times story by Kenneth Vogel (lead writer) of May 1, 2019, concerning the adventures of the Bidens, father and son, in Ukraine. Vogel is himself an anti-Trump leftist, but apparently retains some vestigial instinct for actual journalism, and a story as big and obvious as Biden/Ukraine was too much for him to ignore. His reward was scathing condemnation from his own tribe, which was directed at the Times as well for allowing such heresy to be printed. Vogel and his editors should have realized that speaking real truth to real power is out of fashion these days. One can attack President Trump, who stands exposed, alone and naked to the combined power of the Establishment, with any vicious canard one can invent, but to speak facts about fellow socialists, who hold actual power, is a no-no. It takes some courage to do that.

The NYT also caught recent flack from the Biden campaign directly for allowing into its otherwise pristine pages an op-ed by investigative journalist Peter Schweizer, on October 9, 2019. This also concerned some of the Bidens' international (and highly lucrative) shenanigans. It is hardly surprising that the campaign would like the whole story to go away, and in that interest to declare it "debunked." The interesting feature about the episode is that Democrats can be so candid and open when ordering the mass media about, as though it belonged to them, and to confidently expect that the media will perform. As, of course, it does. After the chiding by the Party, it is unlikely that the Times will print Mr. Schweizer's stuff again any time soon, especially if it's convincing.

There is an effect of all this on the media's bottom line. Its most precious asset, credibility, has been severely and perhaps irremediably damaged by its transition from independence to a partisan mouthpiece. Worse, the partisanship isn't clearly declared, as in the old partisan press days prior to the Civil War, and it isn't spread around the parties. We now have a "party press" that includes nearly all the older mass media but belongs entirely to one political party. Predictably, its market is correspondingly diminished. Fox News, the one big outlet that still attempts to be reasonably objective, has eaten the lunch of the others. Fox, of course, is relentlessly vilified by the rest and no doubt cries all the way to the bank. That's the price to be paid for the surrender of all the old journalistic ideals to groupthink, and that in the service of a mostly unpopular political cause.

Of all the losses, the one most painful to us romantics is that of the traditional courage of individual reporters. There really is something about speaking truth to power that makes the adrenaline flow. But when the truth is distorted and speech is directed at the vulnerable rather than its proper, and truly powerful, targets, the courage is false. It is easy courage, for all courage that is genuine is hard and has a cost. Furthermore, most of those who still cling to the words of Pravda West in these fallen times are brainwashed by a cynical educational establishment or otherwise willfully uninformed. Most of the media are, unfortunately, not primarily interested in either speaking the truth, piquing the powerful or informing the wise. As observed previously in these pages, journalists now speak lies to ignorance.

11/3/19

Chapter Thirty-Five

Objectivity and Other Lies; Rights and Other Wrongs

There is an unfortunate tendency to try to apply the concepts of scientific theories to phenomena far outside the proper purviews of those theories. In the process, the meaning and significance of the theory itself is distorted out of recognition for anyone not versed in the science. A classic example is Charles Darwin's famous theory, published in 1859 under the title "On the Origin of Species." The idea of evolution of life forms through time wasn't original with Darwin, but his publication led to its general acceptance by scientists and popularity among the public. In only a few decades it also led to some bizarre offshoots, both within and without the scientific community.

Within science, speculation arose concerning the origin not just of species but of life itself, which is another subject entirely and hypotheses on which, unlike evolution of existing life forms, are unsupported by evidence. Outside science, Darwin's purely scientific conclusions led to an unfortunate family of hypotheses known as social Darwinism. Among them is eugenics, which led in turn to justifications for the practice of forced sterilization, abortion and outright genocide, all based on race or congenital problems. Closely related to social Darwinism is cultural Darwinism, which, among other things, served as a theoretical basis for aggressive militarism. None of these aberrations of the original scientific work are in any way part the theory, and Darwin himself, despite sharing some of the racial views of the age, would have been shocked at what paraded under his name.

The most celebrated scientific theory of the 20th century is what has come down to us as the Theory of Relativity. Its first publication by Albert Einstein, in 1905, was entitled "On the Electrodynamics of Moving Bodies" and is now called Special Relativity; the second part is known as General Relativity and came out ten years later. It was first called the Theory of Relativity in 1906 by the physicist Alfred Bucherer in notes to a critical review of the paper; he had in turn followed the use of the term "relative theory" by Max Planck in the same critique. It was perhaps unfortunate that the title coined by Bucherer came into common usage, because the meaning of "relativity" in the context of the theory -- referring to the relation of time and space – can be confused with its general meaning. Einstein himself reportedly disfavored that title for his theory, preferring Theory of Invariance, but went along with the popularly accepted title by the time his Theory of General Relativity was published in 1915.

The "invariance" preferred by Einstein referred to his two foundational postulates for the whole theory: (a) the speed of light is constant no matter the point of view of an observer, and (b) the laws of physics never change. The irony of all this is that the title finally assigned to his theory was soon twisted to justify a point of view that was virtually the antithesis of invariance. It didn't take long for certain people who hadn't the first clue about the actual theory to misuse its title to justify their own predilection for anarchy. "Relativity" was confused with "relativism" and the prestige of Einstein's elegant theory was transferred to the proposition that everything is rootless and dependent entirely on the point of view of the observer. This notion had become firmly established in leftist gospel by the end of the first surge of the Progressive Movement in the 1920s and became the foundation stone of what is known as postmodernism, beginning in the 1980s.

It isn't difficult to understand why relativism is compatible with progressivism. The whole leftist mindset favors maximum fluidity in matters of principles and morals. Human nature itself is, in the progressive worldview, infinitely plastic and amenable to whatever metamorphoses are required to attain the left's version of earthly paradise. Relativism allows the leftist to project his own views upon reality, so that reality becomes whatever he perceives it to be. It isn't much of a jump for the postmodernist philosopher to reject the concepts of objective truth and universal ethical standards, or to reject objective reality itself. If one reads, without actual scientific understanding, Einstein's accounts of his "mind experiments," wherein, for example, he imagines what a light wave looks like when one is traveling on an adjacent light wave, the theory seems to a postmodernist to be the scientific counterpart of his own philosophy. In reality, relativity theory is nothing of the sort, and in fact, as pointed out above, is founded on objective reality, a constant speed of light and the invariability of physical laws. But the damage is done: the Left is confident that Science supports its own strange vision of the universe.

A general rejection of the existence of objective truth is entirely consistent with atheism also, but profoundly antithetical to the principles of the U.S. Constitution. The beginning of the Declaration of Independence, issued on July 4, 1776, sets out in clear terms principles the Constitution was designed to actualize. The first paragraph references "the Laws of Nature and of Nature's God." The second begins with: "We hold these Truths to be self-evident, that all Men are created equal, that they are endowed by their Creator with certain inalienable Rights...." These words are obviously anathema to postmodernists and progressives of every stripe. In the leftist universe there are no natural laws or self-evident (i.e., objective) truths, and rights are doled out only by government. Besides, there is no Creator: the leftist cosmos is the result of an accidental explosion and life started with a bunch of chemicals that were activated by lightning, or whatever. That, presumably, is Science in action. Trendy current views of both truth and rights are firmly opposed to those of the Founders. But, since the Founders are no more than dead white guys, let us examine some practical aspects of the rejection of objective Truth and Natural Rights in our society.

As stated in previous chapters, there will always be journalistic bias. News people are people, and it is only human to hold certain opinions. It is unfortunate that in our age the political opinions of journalists are not notably diverse; in fact, a conservative reporter or editor on the staff of a major news outlet is a rare anomaly. From journalism school onward, news people are marinated in leftist opinion, and few escape that mindset, or wish to. Journalists are aware of this situation and, for the most part, freely admit it. To counter its effect on reporting, they invoke the principle of objectivity. That is, whatever the personal viewpoint of reporter or editor, the individual has the professional training to maintain an objective state of mind toward facts that permits them to be reported free of bias. That is a wonderful concept, except that in practice it all too obviously doesn't work. The news from all major outlets (yes, even Fox, albeit to a lesser degree) is tainted by a leftist bias. Some outlets don't even bother to reign it in or hide it, while still rather half-heartedly claiming objectivity. In fact, objectivity cannot work on the Left even in theory, and a little thought reveals why this should be so, despite leftists' best efforts.

Relativism has so permeated leftist thinking, progressive as well as postmodernist, as to erase acceptance of objective truth altogether. The Declaration of Independence may as well be written in Sanskrit for a progressive as far as "self-evident," which is to say objective, "Truths" are concerned. And journalists are almost uniformly progressive. How can they follow the principle of objectivity when they reject the existence of objective truth? To a reporter or editor, as to any progressive, each person has his own truth --

it's all relative. Therefore, what a neutral observer (if there were any) sees as a biased presentation of facts appears to the progressive journalist as truth. And it is, in a sense. It is that individual's truth, which will do, since for them no Truth, in the objective sense, exists. As a result, journalism as a profession is capable of collectively believing that the highly biased material it offers as news is simple truth. In fact, it is objectively propaganda, since it corresponds not to Truth but to the opinions of the individuals reporting it. In short, there can be no objectivity where there is no objective truth.

Moving on to the question of rights, we encounter a similar problem. The notion of natural rights is even less congenial to the leftist mind than that of Truth. A good progressive cannot imagine a right that originates anywhere other than government, preferably the federal government. Rights are conceived by wise and benevolent techno-experts, whether they labor in Washington think tanks, the staffs of politicians or within bureaucratic departments. They are then issued by said politicians as laws, whereupon the same bureaucratic experts polish them to bureaucratic specifications and release them upon the public for enforcement. There is none of this messy "natural" nonsense; the idea that the masses have Rights independent of any governmental authority is repugnant to the progressive mentality. Among other faults, such notions may give deplorables illusions of self-worth and make them restive under the benign yoke of governmental experts. It also encourages thoughts about a God that are not only atavistic but may foment undue independence of thought in more general ways.

The Declaration of Independence directs attention to the existence of natural rights; the Constitution then enumerates and elaborates upon some of them, specifically in the Amendments. It is notable that several of the Founders hesitated to include the original Amendments with the Constitution, not because they disagreed with their content but because they felt them to be unnecessary. In other words, everyone knew that the rights of the Amendments existed: they were "endowed" by God and need not be iterated by men. But wisdom (as it turned out) prevailed, and progressives have been trying to get rid of constitutional rights ever since. As we look through them, it becomes evident that most of the more important rights listed in the Amendments have been and are now under attack by the Left. Rights of speech and religion (1st Amendment) and of self defense (2nd Amendment) are under furious and constant assault by progressives; the right of freedom from search except with probable cause (4th Amendment) and others relating to criminal process are being more subtly eroded. The right of peaceable assemblage (also 1st Amendment)) has effectively been eliminated already, apparently replaced by a "right" to violent riot, provided it is in a cause approved by the Left. Finally, the 9th Amendment clarifies that other unenumerated natural rights exist and are not to be abridged by government. It would seem that progressives consider the 9th Amendment to be no more than evidence that the Founders had a sense of humor.

To make up for their rejection of natural rights in general and those of the Constitution in particular, the Left has unleashed a plethora of other rights (should we call them "unnatural rights"?). These have proliferated beyond measure and range from major (e.g., abortion rights) to petty. In fact, the very idea of rights has been eroded to the point of meaninglessness. The vital difference between rights and privileges has been essentially erased, and the whole concept of a right has been expanded out of recognition. A politician recently defended voting by email by saying the right to vote shouldn't have to conflict with the right to good health (*re* coronavirus). A "right" to good health? Someone else referred to the "right" to clean drinking water. Really? We can all agree that good health and clean water are great benefits, but what happened to the meaning of "rights"?

It has come to the point where anything that a progressive believes might be a good idea is now a right. Sad to say, where everything is a pseudo-right, there are no real rights. Where every right is granted by government, every right can be extinguished by government. Since real rights -- natural rights -- not only exist independently of government but were regarded by the Constitution as protection of the citizens from the government, the threatened extinction of the concept of natural rights by the Left effectively removes the shield that has heretofore protected Americans from the behemoth that is centered in Washington, D.C.

The effacement of objective truth and confusion of rights by postmodernists and progressives have real-world effects beyond the obvious. The loss of real standards in our society means no rule of predictable, Constitution-based law, no dependable journalism, no religion or firmly-based ethics -- indeed, no basis for a stable society other than the application of raw power. In its postmodernist extreme, there is a loss of recognition of reality itself. The alternative to a stable society is one wherein chaos reigns, which is to say one of misery for the vast majority of the society's people. Chaos benefits only the powerful, by removing the shields that protect the productive and the innocent and so making them vulnerable to unrestrained might. This means the man with the strongest sword arm or the person who is wealthy enough to hire such men wins: say, Genghis Khan then, George Soros now. Of course, in time it will be swords only, as the wealthy are consumed by their own greed-motivated destruction of fragile civilization.

The very concept of objective truth is fading out of the world. Lies will pass into history.
George Orwell

Chapter Thirty-Six

Catch-2020

A celebrated dark humor antiwar novel, *Catch-22* by Joseph Heller, describes the misadventures of a fictional group of World War II bomber crews in the Italian campaign. In it, the protagonist, a B-17 pilot, wishes to avail himself of a provision in the regulations that bars an insane pilot from flying missions. However, there's a catch, catch-22: one has to make an application based on his insanity. Since no sane person would want to fly highly dangerous missions, the act of application means the pilot isn't insane. He must therefore continue to fly. Various other forms of the nefarious catch-22 are found throughout the book. In addition to whatever value it may have to its genre, the novel contributed its bit to the English language. The expression "catch-22" is now widely used to refer to a paradox, the internal logic of which prohibits anyone trapped within it from escaping.

Two other chapters herein deal with the Democrat Party and the establishment media as they approach the 2020 election: *Pravda West*, which examines the role of the media, and *Under the Lamp Post*, which focuses on the situation of the party. This post combines their conclusions to examine the methods to which the Democrats might resort to have a decent chance for success in the upcoming election, given the fact that they appear to be at a distinct disadvantage as to the substantive issues that are of most concern to the voting public. In fact, Democrats are at such an extreme disadvantage in that regard that one should expect them to largely avoid debate on the issues and rely instead on their considerable nonpolitical assets. Of course, everything is political in a sense, but I refer to assets that are not always directly associated with politics, including (without limitation) the judiciary, the educational system, trade unions, racial blocks, immigrants and the media.

Progressives, and therefore the Democrat Party, have indeed amassed an enviable treasure of nonpolitical assets during their Long March of the past century through American institutions. The question is: which of these assets, some of which are listed above, can be employed to best advantage by the party in the current campaign to compensate for its weakness as to actual issues? Upon examination, the answer seems to be: fewer than one might think.

Control of the educational system, for example, is a tremendous resource for Democrats in the long run but can't help them much in this particular election cycle. As a long-term asset, it has marshalled large and influential chunks of entire generations behind leftist causes, but its value in the short term, for a specific election, is limited to the money and energy of education establishment employees. The judiciary, which is a mixed bag for the Left anyway, is another longer term asset. Trade unions have been stalwart supporters of the Democrats for nearly a century, but they grow weaker with time and it is difficult to see how they can do more than they already are. Illegal voters have huge potential for future elections, but it is doubtful if enough can vote in this one to make enough of a difference, especially in the states that can swing the result. As to the black vote, it is difficult to see how Democrats can garner more than the 90%-plus they have been getting all along. Much the same can be said about the Hispanic vote. In fact, legal voters of Hispanic ethnicity tend to be less happy about illegal immigration on the southern border even than other Americans. Jewish voters have long trended Democrat but are unlikely to swing further in that direction in 2020, especially given the situation with Israel and current leftist flirtation with anti-Semitism.

This leaves Pravda West, the asset that has been left-biased for many decades and is now rabidly anti-Trump to boot. The Democrats' tame media has, in the absence of issues and the incapacity of other assets to generate enough additional votes in the right places, become their last hope for the 2020 contest. Pravda West is a sadly diminished asset, so overused for so long that its primary strength, credibility, is at a record low level and still sinking. Nevertheless, the old horse is being whipped to make one last try, one more great surge to heave the sclerotic old party over the finish line. The daily rumor mongering, innuendo and spin generation that has long been the hallmark of Pravda West has, since President Trump's entry into the White House, been supplemented by a series of desperate outright lies. Many of these have been in support of political schemes by both Democratic politicians and the Deep State bureaucracy, but some have been revealed that are Pravda West originals.

The lies were mistakes. They were the result of overenthusiasm in the white heat of Trump hatred, and they backfired. It was all too obvious, and when mendacity becomes obvious it becomes a liability. It allowed Trump to be a victim and badly eroded the scant credibility left to Pravda. And it *was* revealed in each case, because it was clumsily done and, mostly, because there are now other avenues of information available. Pravda West -- the offending outlets and their associates in crime -- was able to damp down the full force of consequences by hiding retractions or simply forgetting about the whole affair. Still, much damage was done to a structure that was already a bit rickety. Pravda West began to see the error of its ways and took another course. Not by giving up the blatant bias, of course; they just got sneakier. As it happens, there is one technique that, used with a degree of skill, gains some real traction without much risk. We may call it catch-2020.

Catch-2020, as used by Pravda West, takes several forms, all with a common denominator: pick up trivial items, blow them up, and spin them so as to embarrass the president or his family and associates. The "news" items to be employed have to be trivial because there aren't any big ones. As noted above, the big stories have all proven to be bogus and backfired badly, further eroding media credibility. But small items can be found everywhere, taken out of context or distorted, and spun to make the victim(s) look incompetent, corrupt or ridiculous. Hardly a day goes by that at least one of these stories is not produced, and subsequently picked up and disseminated by all the other members of Pravda West. The catch is that the victim must either react or do nothing. If the latter, he appears to accept the reality of the story; if the former, he can be made to look small, petty and defensive -- and altogether unpresidential. Either way, he loses. He is caught in an awkward situation with no way out -- catch-2020.

On top of the usual catch-2020 techniques is the daily barrage of *ad hominem* attacks by Democrat politicians and operatives that is amplified by Pravda West outlets and added to by its own personalities. It can be freely confessed that President Trump's New York attitude indeed grates against the sensibilities of us flyover country denizens and many other deplorables everywhere, but we don't call anyone a criminal or a racist without clear evidence. Being more tolerant and easygoing than our urbane coastal compatriots, we are willing to shrug off certain eccentricities and look for the actual accomplishments behind them. These, by the way, are not difficult to detect. To objective view, Trump doesn't appear to be more criminally inclined than any other high-rolling businessman, and of racism there is no sign outside the fevered imaginations of militant #NeverTrumpers. If he "throws children of color into cages" (which is somewhat hyperbolic), it might be pointed out that the children weren't invited, there isn't much else to do with them on a temporary basis, they are fed and cared for at public expense, and the cages were built and used by his predecessor anyway. If he bites back at critics on Twitter, how else can he reply when the same critics control the media? And so on. Trump is far from perfect but he is an effective president and he's not Hitler reincarnated. Unjust demonization on the scale he endures only makes him act worse, which is of course the point of catch-2020.

Speaking of the *ad hominem* assault which Pravda West amplifies and augments, the most vicious aspect of catch-2020 is the constant drumbeat of innuendo that Trump is mentally unstable. This hearkens back to the foulest methods of the Soviet era in Russia, when dissidents were summarily dispatched to mental hospitals on the pretense that they were schizophrenic. The now-debunked theories of a rogue psychologist, Andrei Snezhnevsky, provided a pseudo-scientific foundation for this disreputable practice. Pravda West and its contributors don't have even that fig leaf for their slanders against Trump. The trick is beneath contempt, but it is catch-2020 to the core. When Trump ignores this baseless charge he invites further slander. When he fights back, he "proves" it. Catch-2020.

The trivialities used in the catch-2020 scheme have the additional function of helping to hide the genuine big stories, which in the current administration's case have been mostly good news. Since the Democrat Party is already stuck in a hole where all that is good news for the country is bad for the party, hiding big stories like the buoyant economy is a great bonus for the Democrats from the catch-2020 process. The daily assault of trivial embarrassments is like a smokescreen. The mission of Pravda West is, like that of its original Pravda paradigm, not to disseminate real news but to mask it. At its most effective, propaganda is a defensive as well as an offensive weapon.

A corollary of the above is that spin at its best isn't recognizable as spin at all. The unwary recipient simply won't see it; it will appear to him as a straightforward presentation of facts. Again, this technique is more difficult to bring off in an internet environment than it was before. There are always people out there who are more acute and have more sensitive BD (balderdash) meters, and many of these people have computers. They will point out the more misleading elements of Pravda West stories to less perceptive souls, and the internet being what it is, the word tends to get around pretty quickly. There are plenty of low-information people around who are comfortable with the BD version of Pravda West "news" and don't particularly want to hear the truth, but that can hardly be helped. Of course, there is always the question of how many of each category are going to end up voting. If the Democrats can inspire enough of the less acute people to go to the polls in 2020, they may have a chance.

As stated in Chapter 22, *The Key*, good news for the country is bad news for the Democrat Party, and (short term) *vice versa*. For this reason, the Pravda West spin is relentlessly negative these days. Just a few years ago, during the Obama administration, the spin was amazingly upbeat no matter what the substance of actual news. I suppose the positive spin could be a touch odd at times: calling stagnant economic growth and dead industry "the new normal" might not be considered optimistic by everyone. Still, Pravda West was far more lighthearted than hysterical during the Obama years. Now, demonization of the president and cries of "woe is us" fill the airwaves and the diminishing volume of printed pages. In accordance with the observation that good news is bad for Democrats, Pravda West is working hard to convince us that we are all miserable and the nation is sunk in unprecedented depths of oppression and despair. If you are not in anguish, in fact, you are probably a racist.

So here we are, with the crucial 2020 elections fast approaching, one party clueless as usual and letting a viciously maligned president do the heavy lifting, the other having lost its moorings and gone adrift in a socialist sea. The Republicans have found themselves, through little fault of their own, in possession of nearly all the keys, if one is old-fashioned enough to think that actual issues are still the keys, to winning an election. The Democrats now rely on the sheer rabid energy of their rather small leftist base and their control of Pravda West, what used to be the mainstream media. The former is frightening even to traditional Democrats; the latter is quickly running out of steam, if by steam one means its stock of credibility. The issue of the election, at this point, seems to rest on whether enough low-information citizens (or non-) can be herded out to the voting booths, and whether the old media can summon enough residual influence to push the party of the New Left over the finish line. I wish us all good luck.

11/17/19

PART VI

The Law

The stability and prosperity of any nation, but especially a republic and democracy, are based upon the rule of law. It is necessary that the body of law be sound, clear and universal. Law by its nature has gray areas, since the complexity of reality cannot be predicted or encompassed by any pre-written prescriptions, no matter how wise and prescient the authors. Nevertheless, the written law must be reasonably unambiguous and sufficiently to the point so that a competent judge can explain it to a jury of average citizens and be assured of the understanding of its members.

By and large, we have that body of law to serve the English-speaking world, mostly as a legacy of the old British legal system. When historians think about the roots of the British legal tradition they typically go back to the Magna Carta of 1215, but in fact the tradition was founded long before that. The Low German tribesmen who invaded the Roman province that became England brought a primitive but strong legal tradition with them that evolved into the British system we know now. That system, unique to Great Britain and its former colonies, is resilient, responsive to changing conditions and enduring. When they broke from the mother country, Americans didn't have to invent a new legal system the way they formed a new kind of governmental structure. They already had one, functional and excellent. The Constitution, which is the basis for American law, accepts the British tradition in its entirety and enshrines it in elegant phrases.

Having a superior legal system derived from a robust tradition is highly advantageous, but as with any system staffed and operated by humans, it must be constantly and rigorously maintained. The cornerstone of the American legal system is the concept of equality under the law. The law is fine, but care must be taken that it is applied the same way to every citizen, and that no individual, regardless of wealth or status, may rise above the law. No one may realistically expect perfection in that effort; we are only human, after all, and the rich and powerful among us will always be treated differently. But we can work toward the ideal and do our best to bring accountability to those who would abuse a good system to their narrow advantage. Unfortunately, these days we have become lax in that regard. One has only to look at the Clintons and a handful of rogue billionaires to understand that equality under the law in the US is fast becoming a bad joke. Finally, there is the problem of politicization of the legal system, as there has been with so much else.

The articles below make the case that the reverse Midas touch of the Left has begun to corrupt the legal system as it has all US institutions. *The Deep Law* discusses fundamental reasons for that corruption, reasons that are deeply imbedded in the leftist psyche. The series on *Killing the Constitution* is the core of this section, explaining why the Left cannot tolerate a document that restricts its reach into the lives of all citizens and how it has gone about the chore of dismantling it. The final two articles deal with specifics of the Left's attack on the American legal system. In a nation based on the rule of law, an ideology that controls the law will control the nation. The law may seem arcane to laymen, but it crucially affects us all. It is vital to our freedom that every citizen should appreciate that fact.

Chapter Thirty-Seven

The Deep Law

There is a passage in the C.S. Lewis fantasy novel, *The Lion, the Witch and the Wardrobe*, in which the witch refers to "the deep magic." This is a level of magic beyond normal (is that an appropriate word?) magic, a dark magic that is at the foundations of the very concept of magic and out of the reach of the everyday magician. It's an interesting idea, and perhaps one that's applicable to other arcane (but nonfictional) bodies of knowledge as well. Bodies of knowledge such as, for example, the law.

Any lawyer will tell you that you're not quite a lawyer the day you walk out of law school, or even the day you pass the bar exam and receive your license to practice. What they try to teach the young scholar in the three years of law school is to think like a lawyer. They also present some of the rudiments of the law of the jurisdiction in which the school resides, as well as those of the United States as a whole. But as to the cut-and-thrust of daily professional practice, only experience can teach a young lawyer and experience is always a rough road to tread. There is yet another aspect of law that both the schools and experience barely touch at all, and that is the elusive nature of the foundations of law. One might refer to those foundations as the Deep Law.

Let us consider a question: can a law be effective if it does not reflect custom? More specifically, if a law, written down, duly passed by proper authority and on the books, does not conform to the customary usages and traditions of its society will it be obeyed with good spirit? Or will it be resisted and obeyed only through coercion by the state? If you responded that only coercion will keep that law in effect you may congratulate yourself. Laws -- genuinely good laws -- merely codify customs and traditions. Those that don't do so are unpopular in direct proportion to the degree they vary from a society's customs. Sooner or later, no matter how rigorously they are forced down the people's throats, they will either be repealed or fall into disuse. The more rigorously they are enforced, the more unpopular they will become, and with them the regime that supports them.

There are some people who will insist that the unpopularity of and resistance to a law passed by proper authority, if that resistance is a result of its nonconformance with tradition and custom, are signs of that stubborn peasant streak in unenlightened elements of the population. Those individuals -- in our current society we may call them elitists -- ignore the fact that the best and most entrenched traditions are, however unknowingly, based on sound science. Prohibitions against incest, for example, are based on applied genetics. Those who never heard the word "genetics" knew, based on observation, the ill effects of incest on the progeny, and so on the human race as well as the individuals. Ask the Hapsburgs about that, and any number of other royal and noble clans. Similarly, homosexuality, for all that those with homosexual proclivities have equal rights to security with the rest of society, does little to promote human survival. Laws against it may have been unduly harsh and unfair, but the traditions against it are founded in reality. Murder is another example of an activity that is counterproductive to the prosperity and increase of the race. No wonder that tradition and custom condemn it, or any random killing not in self-defense.

This leads to the concept that has been known since Enlightenment days as natural law, and dates from ancient Greece. It was mentioned by Cicero and there are references to it in the New Testament. Probably the first powerful statement of natural law under that name is found in the late 17th century writings of John Locke, and Locke was specifically cited by the American Founders as an inspiration for the Constitution. The basic idea is that natural law is independent of government and derives from the fundamental rights possessed by each individual human being. Other laws, of course, are instituted by governments and deal with all sorts of complexities of life as it is lived in complex societies. But those laws do not supersede or replace natural laws. Governments cannot, without consequences, attempt to void the latter as they apply to individual citizens. They belong, in a profound sense, to the Deep Law.

The idea that there is an entire body of law that lies outside the capacity of government to give or take away is anathema to the progressive way of thinking. To a good progressive (or socialist, or whatever of the Left), government is the be-all and end-all, and any limitation to its power and reach is not to be countenanced. To speak of ancient customs or established tradition is distinctly heretical and even vaguely pornographic to a leftist. It is witchcraft to the Left (witchcraft itself, as currently mimicked, being entirely acceptable). But the serious thinker must approach tradition with caution and reverence, because it is the distilled wisdom of a thousand generations of those who have preceded us. It is the essence of the human experience.

In the course of the tens of billions of human lives that have taken place on this planet, there have been at least that number of ideas generated, some brilliant and some mundane. One may think of each one, perhaps too romantically, as a scintilla of bright light. They are born in men and women, people in all walks of life: a subsistence farmer in Roman Gaul, a scribe sitting on a ziggurat in Hammurabi's Assyria, a woman holding a baby in a hut on the south Russian plain, a Cro-Magnon cave painter contemplating the coming hunt. Many are lost to humanity, like sparks from a campfire that rise into a dark sky and fade away. Others survive, one way and another. The farmer tells a tale to his grandson; the scholar inscribes a clay tablet that is later baked in the flaming doom of his city; the woman sings a lullaby to her child; the artist forms a masterpiece. Each of these sparks of the human brain becomes a tiny facet in the vast and wonderful jewel that is the tradition of a culture. Each scintilla contributes its small bit to the Deep Law.

The concept of natural law is inextricably linked with that of natural rights, and the most casual mention of natural rights will produce froth on the lips of a true leftist. If there is one fundamental principle on the Left that rises above any other it is that all good things flow from government, and especially a long litany of rights. The right to all manner of "free" stuff, from medical services, food and higher education to protest banners and condoms, is sacrosanct to the socialist. And of course, what the government giveth the government taketh away from those who are politically incorrect or offensive to protected groups, or who are just generally deplorable or whatever else the Left finds distasteful. The idea of a core of just a few natural rights that is independent of and sheltered from the government is even more alien to leftism than the existence of the related body of natural law.

Central to the mindset of the Left is the principle of the essentially infinite plasticity of human nature. It could even be fairly stated that true socialists don't believe there is such a phenomenon as human nature. What few natural tendencies may exist in humans are, in the leftist view, formed by the society in which a person was nurtured from birth. It is therefore the duty of those higher beings in that society (themselves, as it happens) to erase such traits and mold the individual psyches of its citizens to conform to the best interests of the whole. In so doing, they will also be raising the individuals to the level of their highest potential. That, by the way, encapsulates in a nutshell the political philosophy of Hegel and, to a large extent, Rousseau, and thus of their successors in the Progressive movement of a century ago. The socialists, democratic socialists, communists, liberals and other leftists of our time are the intellectual heirs of all the above.

It is abundantly evident that the traditions of a culture, as described above, will not be much respected by the Left. In fact, the very idea of tradition is the active enemy of any committed activist of a leftist persuasion. That jewel that sparkles with the scintillas of millennia of our forebears resists the efforts of progressive thinkers to mold us in whatever manner they see fit. It is the primary roadblock to the entire progressive agenda, to all that will make us more modern, more efficient, more useful and more submissive to government and its programs. It is, if not the basis of then at least highly compatible with, the repulsive (to leftists) concepts of natural rights and natural law. Most proximately, it is what has given us the oppressive U.S. Constitution, which insofar as it still exists does so much to keep the Left from running our lives for us. It is, in the end, what makes us deplorables.

So who is right? Is it those antediluvians who cling to a traditional view of the individual in society or the enlightened progressives who work toward a utopian vision brought to reality by their own perfection? My personal choice is the former, partly because of the evident hubris of the latter. It is hubris for a single individual to place his own ideas above the brightest flashes of inspiration of the millions who have lived before him. It is even greater hubris to attempt to mold mankind into one's own image, which is no less than an attempt to take to place of God. That is certainly the ultimate hubris. In their defense, the leftists may declare that God is within each of us, and therefore we are all gods and may take our immanence into our own hands. How can anyone argue with that? We can all be gods! Indeed, that would appear to be the highest form of democracy.

Hubris on that scale is bad enough, but there is, unfortunately, a problem with the last argument that goes beyond hubris alone. The arrangement somehow never turns out to be very democratic at all. All men may be gods, according to the old leftist dream, but to paraphrase the famous line of George Orwell in *Animal Farm*, some men are godlier than others. Socialist societies are invariably rigidly stratified. All their people tend to be poorer than citizens of free market societies, but the gap between richer and poorer is even greater. What is more, the gap is not just one of wealth: there is a gap of power that is yet more significant. Money is power in any human society, but in a socialist paradise the elite have power over the basic rights and freedoms of those beneath them that is far stronger than its analog in a free country. That is only logical: when natural rights and natural law are rejected, both rights and law are controlled by government alone, and government is controlled by the god-like elites.

One concession must be made to the Left: their concept is in this case integrated, which is to say internally consistent. If Man is indeed God, then there can be no denying the warrant of government to determine both rights and laws. Without a higher power than mankind, there can be no such things as natural rights or natural law. If men are gods, some may indeed be godlier than others and be reasonably expected to both mold lesser men to their specifications and to retain the usufructs of their positions. In this situation if there is no utopia here and now (or soon), no paradise on earth, there cannot be one at all. What you see is what you get.

The internal consistency of the Left's position extends to their notion of the plasticity of human nature. If human nature is hard-wired into our DNA, how is a good progressive going to make us perfect? Worse, if whatever molding of the psyche that can be done is done by a society that is itself directed by traditions and customs that were formed by hundreds, perhaps thousands, of generations of human brilliance, how much room remains for the Left to operate upon our minds? Obviously, if men are gods, they are also masters of their own destiny. There can be no innate human nature, and therefore natural law must be ignored. The Left has devised a new twist on *The Lion, the Witch and the Wardrobe*, and discovered its own Deep Law. The New Deep Law, decreed by man-gods and enforced by all-powerful governments, trumps the old laws of the U.S. Constitution, which are based on natural rights and ancient tradition.

But *The Lion, the Witch and the Wardrobe* does not end with the invocation by the witch of a Deep Magic known only to her and a few other masters. There exists in the novel a yet deeper magic, which the lion invokes to trump her Deep Magic. This has its counterpart in the narrative portrayed above. The Left's dismissal of human nature is simply erroneous: no matter how diligent the effort to efface it or ignore it, human nature is a fact of life, and is constituted by the deeper law upon which natural law is founded. The New Deep Law cannot prevail against this Deeper Law, no matter how brutally it may be enforced. In the long run, laws that run counter to human nature will fail, as will the governments that promulgate them and coerce their citizenry to obey them. Even the soft coercion of political correctness cannot succeed forever.

Finally, it is evident that although individual would-be progressives may believe in a real God who is not man himself, atheism is a requirement for a true believer in the religion of the Left. The integrated view of the universe of leftist ideology demands that there be no gods other than mankind. The New Deep Law is conceptually empty without atheism. If God does exist, a fundamental premise of the New Deep Law is false. If human nature is real, yet another premise fails. No matter how well-integrated and conceptually beautiful an ideology may be, it collapses if based upon false premises. Perhaps that is why socialism has never worked over any length of time in practice. History points to the failures: the Argentina of the Perons and their successors, Soviet Russia, Venezuela and the various fascist states are a few among them. Let us close with meditation on another quote by George Orwell:

In our time political speech and writing are largely the defense of the indefensible.

Chapter Thirty-Eight

Killing the Constitution

Of the many documents that are considered milestones in the evolution of law and governance in Western civilization, the Magna Carta and the United States Constitution stand preeminent. There are many differences between the two, but one central theme for both: they are designed to protect citizens from the tyranny of a central authority.

The Magna Carta dates from 1215 A.D. and went through a mixed history before being confirmed by Edward I ("Longshanks") as part of English statute law in 1297. Basically, its terms shielded the baronage of England from overbearing royal authority. The Constitution, on the other hand, protects the rights of all citizens of the U.S. from their own governments (primarily federal but also state and local). Although the Magna Carta had a limited immediate effect, and none at all for all of England's population other than the nobility, it is considered a cornerstone of English liberties -- and ultimately those of the entire English-speaking world -- because it was the first formal curb on the power of the king. It was, so to speak, the mother of the concept of basic human rights so precious to Western civilization ever since.

The Constitution was specifically designed by the Founding Fathers of the United States as a bulwark for individual freedom. The royal excesses of the British king in his treatment of the American colonies were fresh in their minds, and they wished to ensure that the government they were in the process of designing could never replicate that oppression. They also had to design the framework of that government, and the Constitution does that. However, even the very design of the government is such that its capacity for mischief against the people is limited, while still allowing it a defined space in which to govern.

A brief overview of the Constitution gives some idea of the brilliance of its design. The first three Articles establish the tripartite framework of the federal government, with its inbuilt separation of powers into the Legislative, Executive and Judicial branches. They deal also with the fundamental mechanics of the institutions, including the makeup of each branch, elections, their duties and powers and various other matters. Articles IV, V and VI establish the relationships of the states with each other and with the national government. The seventh Article gives the conditions for establishment of the Constitution by the states (nine of the thirteen had to ratify it) and contains the signatures of the representatives from each state. It is a work of brilliant simplicity.

The men (yes, they were all men, and worse, all of Caucasian ethnicity, and essentially all English to boot) of the Constitutional Convention were well educated and steeped in the political and philosophical ideas of such thinkers as Montesquieu and Locke. They were also familiar with the work of the English legal scholars William Blackstone and Edward Coke, who among other works extended the principles of the Magna Carta to apply to all the citizens. In short, they were not working in a vacuum, but had access to the best thinking of a highly productive era. The document was drafted in 1787 and ratified by the states after intense discussion in 1788.

Ratification was not a simple matter. Each state had its own convention for the purpose, and not all of the states were an easy sell. Rhode Island, for example, was largely despaired of. The Articles of Confederation that tied the former colonies together after their liberation from Great Britain were awkward and inefficient, and totally unsuited for national defense, but gave each state maximum autonomy. As the smallest state, Rhode Island along with several others felt threatened by incorporation into unity. In order to convince the people that mattered that the Constitution was a good thing, three of the Founders wrote a series of articles that became known as the Federalist Papers. More than any other source, these writings by James Madison, Alexander Hamilton and John Jay provide the most accurate insight into the thinking of those who gave us this magnificent document.

In the end, in order to placate the states that feared an overbearing federal government, the Founders acceded to ten amendments that addressed those concerns. Collectively, these became known as the Bill of Rights. Hamilton, in particular, opposed the adoption of these amendments, less because he wished to deny states and individual citizens their protection than because he considered that the protections were already embodied in the Constitution itself. Hamilton was in favor of a strong central government, but not at the expense of individual rights; Madison and Jay (along with Thomas Jefferson and most of the other Founders) esteemed individual rights above all.

It is useful to view the Bill of Rights in terms of functional groups, in a similar manner as done above with the main body of the Constitution. The first three amendments are safeguards of specified liberties -- freedom of religion, freedom of speech, the right for individual citizens to bear arms and prohibition of forced quartering of troops. Of these, the first three are hot topics today, and a thorn in the side of many progressives. Amendments IV through VIII have to do with judicial process and individual rights, including prohibitions of unlawful search and seizure and "cruel and unusual" punishments, the right to a jury trial and formal processes for criminal trials.

The last two amendments are especially interesting and were added to allay any fears that the enumeration of certain limitations on the power of the government in the Constitution (both main body and Bill of Rights) were not plenary. That is, because a specific limitation is not mentioned does not imply that it doesn't exist or is not valid. This was emphasized by the authors of the Federalist Papers, especially Madison, and by other Founders in their various writings. Thomas Jefferson, in particular, dwelt on this point at length, and Benjamin Franklin as well. The ninth amendment is so direct and succinct that it can be quoted in full here: "The enumeration in the Constitution of certain rights shall not be construed to deny or disparage others retained by the people." The language is direct and simple, and not much amenable to "interpretation." It is no wonder that this amendment should somehow slip from the memory of our contemporary progressives.

To summarize, the two objectives in the Founders' minds for the Constitution were to establish the form of the federal government and to limit the government's power and scope. As noted above, the first mission was designed to serve the second, by means of a tripartite separation of powers. During the first century of its existence, these missions were clearly understood and, despite contrary pressures, held largely inviolate. President Madison set the example, when presented with a proposal to use federal money to aid destitute French refugees from the slave rebellion in Haiti. His famous quotation was, "I cannot undertake to lay my finger on that article of the Constitution which granted a right to Congress of expending, on objects of benevolence, the money of their constituents." It's a statement, from the Father of the Constitution, that would raise gales of laughter among the congresspersons of today.

Even as late as near the end of the 19th century, President Grover Cleveland was vetoing spending bills for the same reason as that given by Madison: the Constitution did not specifically sanction such expenditures, so the government had no right to make them. This began to change soon after, with the accession of President Theodore Roosevelt, the first progressive president. The movement of which he was a driving force began in the U.S. around the turn of the 20th century, following after Britain's Fabian Society (founded in 1884). Whereas the Fabians were avowed socialists, the American progressives sought many of the same goals but goals cloaked in more pragmatic rhetoric. Roosevelt's charisma and personal popularity gave the movement its first big push.

The erosion of the Constitution began with the rise of the progressive movement. Early on, the progressives felt unnecessarily constrained by constitutional limitations on what government could do. They were ardent reformers, obsessed with the need for perfection in society in general and impatient to increase the power and efficiency of government in order to attain this perfection. The provisions for amendment of the Constitution were far too cumbersome and uncertain for them, so they sought alternative means to avoid the document's restraints. The best route proved to be what the Founders had feared was the weakest of the three branches of government: the Judicial.

Space does not permit a discussion of the shrinkage of the Legislative branch, the one most directly controlled by the people, in favor of both the Executive and Judicial. Suffice to say that under pressure from the progressives, judges at all levels began making law through the instrument of constitutional interpretation. All of this innovation ended up at the Supreme Court, of course, given the structure of the American court system. Several influential justices of the Court in the early 20th century, including Oliver Wendell Holmes and Louis Brandeis, were firmly progressive in their judicial outlook. Holmes was a prominent legal theorist as well as a judge, and formulated the idea of "legal realism" to justify the use of judges' personal experiences and opinions in reaching decisions. Soon the notion of the Constitution as a "living document" became popular, and even dominant, in judicial thinking.

There is something attractive about the living Constitution concept. Surely, with all the profound changes in the nation -- economically, demographically, culturally -- we must make adjustments in our constitutional thinking to keep up with the times. One small example (actually used by progressives) involved laws prohibiting the sale or use of contraceptives that were on the books in some states. Courts found that privacy rights discovered in the Bill of Rights invalidated such laws. Since, in 1920, the Supreme Court had decided that the Bill of Rights applied to the various state governments as well as the federal government (it had never been thought so before), state laws prohibiting contraceptives were therefore struck down. No one thought much about it (those laws had rarely been enforced anyway) until the same broad interpretation of privacy rights was applied to laws prohibiting abortion. And so on. Whatever one may think of the results in specific cases, everyone can agree that, over time, the Constitution was being altered substantially.

But, some observers asked, if the Constitution is as infinitely plastic as progressives needed it to be in order to carry out their wonderful reforms, why have a Constitution at all? And they did work toward that end. Wars and depressions impelled the biggest changes. When the Supreme Court blocked some of Franklin D. Roosevelt's proposals, he threatened to expand the Court with additional justices sympathetic to his program.

The sitting justices prevailed at the time, but to avoid future threats they went along with enough of the (obviously unconstitutional) programs to placate FDR. World War II placed additional pressures on the Constitution as it was written. By the time of the Great Society, the living document concept was well-established, in practice if not in theory. The Constitution, as written by the Founders, was a living document but had become a dead letter.

The problem is that the Constitution's interpreters are very selective in what they choose to interpret. An almost throw-away phrase in the brief introduction, "promote the general Welfare," is milked to build a monster welfare state and any number of other boondoggles. The longer phrase that immediately follows, "and secure the Blessings of Liberty to ourselves and our Posterity," is ignored. A simple commerce clause tucked away in Article I has been mined to yield amazing federal control over all the states, in ways obviously never envisioned by its authors, while the entirety of Amendments IX and X of the Bill of Rights is forgotten. In every case, the "interpretation" that maximizes federal power is accepted; any clear instruction that limits those powers is lost.

The point that many people, both liberal and conservative, fail to understand is that the Constitution, even in its eviscerated form, still serves its intended purpose to some degree. Progressives have been, and remain, frustrated by this fusty old document that was crafted by now-dead white men. And frustrating those who would usurp power unto themselves through government is precisely what the Constitution was intended to do. To make amendments slow and difficult is intended, to allow careful deliberation. The upshot is what one sees today: a bitter effort by Democrats to control the Supreme Court at any cost. No stratagem is too deceitful, no chicanery too low, to prevent their use to that end. Character assassination is a routine ploy, lying, cheating and pure obstruction are normal. The stakes are worth it to them: those who wish to preserve some semblance of a Constitution that protects the rights of the nation's citizens must not be permitted to do so.

Progressives were certain they were finally at the point of taking over America in the national elections of 2016. They feel that their well-earned victory, for which they had worked well over a century, was snatched from their grasp. Until they can rectify that sad failing, they must keep the Supreme Court of the land out of the hands of those who would stay them from fulfilling their vision of an earthly paradise. They must kill the Constitution, or whatever may remain of it.

Chapter Thirty-Nine

Killing the Constitution: An Addendum

The previous chapter, *Killing the Constitution*, calls for more explanation as to how the Supreme Court can change the Constitution of the United States and how they go about it. This is a reasonable demand, but one not easily met without introducing a sort of crash course in constitutional law. This chapter will be brief (considering the subject matter) and avoid all but the most basic legal jargon.

The first legal concept that one must be familiar with is *stare decisis*. That means, in Latin, "stand by your decision," and is a requirement for any court to follow the legal guidelines set by case law by a higher court in the same jurisdiction. To understand what that means, one must also understand something of the hierarchy of our court systems. Yes, that is plural, because not only does each state have its own constitution and law, but its own courts as well. And there is also an entirely separate federal court system in addition to the Supreme Court.

In any of the jurisdictions, state or federal, the lowest courts are those with which most people are probably most familiar. These are the courts in which formal trials are held, either jury or bench. In jury trials, the jury decides the facts of the case, under instruction of the presiding judge as to matters of law. In a bench trial, both the facts and the law are determined by the judge. A basic right in the U.S. is that one accused of a crime may choose a jury trial if he wishes. There are two types of trial: criminal and civil. In the former, the government takes the plaintiff role through a prosecutor; in the latter, both plaintiff and defendant have their own attorneys, unless one of the parties decides (unwisely) to represent himself.

In the state systems, the courts described above are called trial courts, and may be municipal, county or state. They may have various names in different jurisdictions (such as "Common Pleas" in Ohio). Magistrate courts are also trial courts. In the federal system, trial courts are called district courts, and there are 94 of them. They are not exactly the same, although the procedures are similar. State courts handle most general issues: criminal, probate contract, torts, family law and others. Federal courts are more restricted in the cases they can take, which include those to do with interstate disputes, those involving the constitutional validity of a state law, and matters of treaties, bankruptcy, habeas corpus and admiralty law.

Above the trial courts are appellate courts. In many states, the only court to which one can take an appeal of the decision of the trial court is the state supreme court; in others there is a separate layer of lower appellate courts. The federal system has an appellate layer between trial (i.e., district) courts and the U.S. Supreme Court, consisting of 13 courts around the country. A federal appeals court may take an appeal from the decision of a state court under certain circumstances, mainly where the courts of different states have come to differing decisions when the facts of the cases are very similar. The ultimate appellate court is of course the Supreme Court, which accepts appeals at its complete discretion. This means, in practice, that relatively few appeals are accepted, and those generally when distinct constitutional issues are involved.

With the hierarchical picture of the court systems in mind, the role of *stare decisis* becomes clear. In the British and American legal scheme, the law of any jurisdiction is established by both statutes and case law. Statutes, as drafted and passed by legislatures, are necessarily generalized. Actual cases are complex. It is therefore up to the courts to adapt the statutes to reality, so to speak. Although the facts (themselves difficult enough to determine more often than not) differ in detail from one case to another, courts can, in their wisdom, discern patterns that can usefully apply to a broad range of cases. Their decisions give form to the statutes in a practical sense; thus both statutes and cases make the law. *Stare decisis* organizes case law into a coherent body by delineating which cases define the law.

Since each court is bound by the decisions of the court above it in its application of law to its own cases, and since, at the end of the road, the Supreme Court is highest, ultimately a decision of the Supreme Court binds every court in the land, high and low. What is more, every court is so bound in perpetuity for all of its cases with a similar fact pattern. Unless an attorney can distinguish his specific case from the binding case by pointing out a significantly different set of facts, he's stuck with the higher court's decision, and that means the Supreme Court's decision whenever that court has handed one down. There is one exception to the "in perpetuity" part -- and that is the Supreme Court itself. Only the Supreme Court can revoke its own *stare decisis* and change one of its decisions.

One other element must be considered in this analysis, and that is the principle of judicial review of legislative law. This principle is actually not specifically mentioned in the Constitution. One may read all of Article III, which establishes the Supreme Court and lays out its duties, without seeing any mention of judicial review. It wasn't a factor in American government until 1803, when Chief Justice Marshall took advantage of a mundane case called Madison v. Marbury to enunciate it. Basically, it means that every law passed by Congress and signed by the President (and any state law) is subject to being evaluated for its constitutionality by the courts. Acceptance of judicial review by the government and the people of the United States, in conjunction with the court hierarchy and *stare decisis*, raises the Supreme Court to a position of power on a par with the Legislative and Executive branches.

How has the Court used this power? Its use of it has been variable throughout our history, but for the most part it has been decisive. With some notable exceptions, such as the infamous Dred Scott decision, the Court exercised considerable restraint until early in the 20th century and the rise of the Progressive Movement. Progressives were impatient to try out their favorite programs and unwilling to observe the constitutional restrictions imposed by the Court. The amendment process was far too cumbersome for them. They found it imperative to control the Court so as to change the Constitution in a timely (for them) manner. Progressive Presidents, notably Theodore Roosevelt and Woodrow Wilson, were happy to provide the justices who would accomplish this.

An early provision for the purposes of the Progressives was, as mentioned in the first post, the Commerce clause. It is found in Article I, Section 8, clause 3, and reads in full as follows: "The Congress shall have Power .... To regulate Commerce with foreign Nations, and among the several States, and with the Indian tribes..." That's it. It was included to allay the fears of some small states, Rhode Island in particular, that large states would shut them out of trade by tariffs and sundry other means. It was used by Progressive justices to permit the federal government to regulate about anything it wanted. The case of Wickard v. Filburn (1942) illustrates the extent to which this originally innocuous clause was stretched. In that decision, wheat grown on a Midwest farm for use only on that farm was declared to be in violation of the quotas of the time. Even though it was used locally, growing that wheat affected interstate commerce because it meant that an equivalent amount of wheat wouldn't be bought elsewhere. In practice, the Commerce clause, as interpreted, meant the federal government could regulate anything, anywhere.

The Welfare clause, also mentioned in the previous article, was expanded by interpretation to permit the entire welfare state that has devastated entire swathes of the population. Privacy rights have been found in the 4th Amendment from early days, but later from the language of the 14th Amendment as well. They were first used to protect parents and teachers from educational bureaucrats, but by the time of the Warren Court were being expanded out of recognition. Soon after, they were used to justify the porn industry and finally abortion.

A classic, and rather tragic, example is the career of Justice William O. Douglas. He was the youngest justice to be confirmed, at the age of forty, and showed promise of unusual brilliance. In the end, he was mostly a failure, both professionally and personally. As a justice he was sloppy and inattentive, distracted by political ambitions. His mission was to protect the individual citizen against government oppression, but he largely failed in that. He joined the leftist branch of the Court, perhaps unwittingly, and became an agent for the expansion of government power.

Douglas' best-known opinion is that of Griswold v. Connecticut (1965). Few people today would take issue with the decision -- it voided a law against having contraceptives in the home -- but it contained an unfortunate phrase. Douglas postulated the existence in the Constitution of provisions that gave out "emanations" that produced "penumbras" of meanings that couldn't be found in the plain language of the document. These phrases have often been mocked but, unfortunately, even more often followed when Progressive judges found constitutional restrictions too apt to crimp their style. One can always find a penumbra when he is trying to avoid the reality.

Thus, over the decades, the Constitution has been altered, in places beyond recognition, by activist judges. Tiny phrases can be picked out and expanded, penumbras discovered, and the larger meanings ignored. Government activities that would have been inconceivable by the drafters of the Constitution are taken for granted today. Given the combination of court hierarchy, *stare decisis* and judicial review, the Supreme Court has morphed from the inoffensive branch of government that the Founders feared into the prime mechanism for Progressive power.

Is there any wonder there is widespread concern over the selection of new justices to the Supreme Court? Note especially the comment above that the Supreme Court can void the effect of its own prior decisions. The Court has not only the power to change the Constitution but to restore it. It is this possibility that leads to the reckless, even violent, desperation of the Left at the nomination and confirmation of Justice Kavanaugh. As I began this post, the Senate was voting on the confirmation. As I end it, the deed is done. But are *we* done? The Left will not give up so easily, and unlike the Right, it is not morally bound by civility or democratic processes. I think of the words of the poet Yeats: "And what rough beast, its hour come round at last, slouches toward Bethlehem to be born."

1/3/20

Chapter Forty

Killing the Constitution: The Bail's in Your Court

In this, the third article of its series, we examine the plight of the American Constitution and the situation of the Supreme Court to which that document has been entrusted. The first two dealt with the Constitution itself, its authors and its sad history at the hands of the Progressive movement. The second, in particular, covered some legal aspects of constitutional law and the bases for the power of the Supreme Court. In this post, the Court, its structure and workings, and the possibilities for its future are studied.

It will come as news to few that nine justices, with their clerks and staff, comprise the Supreme Court. These consist of one Chief Justice (of the United States, mind you, not of merely the Supreme Court) and eight associate justices. It should be noted that there is less magic in being Chief Justice than one might think. All the justices have an equal vote, and leadership roles in the Court have less to do with titles than with judicial intellect and force of character. The late Justice Scalia, for instance, had more influence with decisions, in general, than the Chief Justices of his time. The primary duty of the Chief Justice, and the source of any influence he may have other than his own personality, is to assign the drafting of opinions among the justices. Even this power is somewhat limited, in that dissenting opinions are also published, as well as opinions of justices that may agree with the prevailing opinion but with different reasoning.

There are profound differences in the judicial philosophies and worldviews among the justices, to which some observers attribute the many split decisions that issue from the Court. Of course, it must be acknowledged that split decisions are inevitable regardless of such differences, given the nature of the Court's work. First, it is a court of appeals, so by far most of the cases that are presented involve valid differences of opinion by skilled lawyers concerning matters of law. Second, remember that only a small percentage of cases presented are accepted by the Court, and those accepted necessarily tend to be more ambiguous from a legal perspective.

That said, it has long been a matter of concern to legal scholars that an outsized percentage of the Court's decisions end up with a 5-4 split, and the justices on each side tend to be in the same group. This reveals a fundamental division among them, a division based on politics and philosophy as to what judges are supposed to do. On one side are the political progressives, four in number. On the other are four who are considered to be conservative. In the middle, until recently, was a single "swing" justice, Anthony Kennedy, whose vote swayed many a decision. It was Justice Kennedy's retirement in July of this year that set off the fireworks of the last Senate confirmation process.

Let us review briefly the pillars that support the power of the Supreme Court in our body politic. There is the hierarchy of the court systems, at the top of which is the U.S. Supreme Court. This, combined with the principle of *stare decisis*, which is discussed in the second post of this series, means that all the courts of the nation must allow themselves to be guided by the decisions and opinions of the Supreme Court. Finally, there is the principle of judicial review, which gives the Court the last word as to the constitutionality of laws passed by any legislature. Everyone, including every justice of the Court, accepts these three tenets. But everyone does not agree on precisely what each of them involves or what the idea of "interpretation," as applied to the Constitution, entails.

Differences of opinion about the scope of constitutional interpretation result from disagreements as to its plasticity in the hands of judges, plus the opposing ideals of sticking to the intent of the document's authors, on the one hand, or changing it freely with the times, on the other. This, along with emanations and penumbras, was discussed in the previous posts and need not be rehashed here. *Stare decisis* is firmly entrenched in American jurisprudence, but there can be plenty of wiggle room with the concept. Lawyers are always trying to distinguish the facts of their cases from those of a guiding case, also as previously mentioned, and judges have been known to skirt around the guidelines. The Court itself has overturned previous decisions numerous times. As to judicial review, although the principle is inviolate, the practice allows for variability. There can be a considerable degree of deference to legislative prerogatives and the intent of lawmakers, or there can be rigid standards for constitutionality. Chief Justice Roberts' opinion in the recent "Obamacare" case is a striking example of the former.

This brings us to the current makeup of the Court. In the traditional view, up until this July the four progressive justices were Steven Breyer and the three women: Associate Justices Ruth Bader Ginsburg, Elena Kagan and Sonia Sotomayor. The four conservatives were Associate Justices Samuel Alito, Clarence Thomas, Neil Gorsuch and Chief Justice John Roberts. The wild card, so to speak, was Associate Justice Kennedy. He was notoriously unpredictable, his vote apparently swayed by whim rather than ideology. The result was an uncomfortable standoff, a legal balance of power. This high wire act pleased no one, but neither side was in a position to gain the upper hand. Until the great upset of the 2016 presidential election, that is.

The above is, as I said, the traditional view. Under that analysis, the appointment of Associate Justice Brett Kavanaugh to replace Kennedy shifts the Court distinctly to the Right. Instead of a 4-4 standoff with a swing vote in the middle, the count is now 5-4 in favor of the conservatives. The generation-old balance is no more; the fury of the Left is unlimited. Talk on the Left, including their house propaganda organs of the media, is of impeachment and even revolution. Their determination to take back the Supreme Court, and more, is adamant. Strangely enough, the Right agrees with this view of the situation. They are both wrong.

My own analysis is rather different, being founded on the judicial philosophies of the justices and their views of the Constitution rather than simple political loyalties. In particular, I am concerned with the dedication of each justice to the principle of *stare decisis* and his or her willingness to limit judicial review to allow for legislative deference, as well as the degree to which each is willing to change the Constitution in favor of personal preferences. Instead of liberal, conservative and swing, I view the justices as falling into these categories: activist, passivist and reformist. The resulting picture is, I think, more realistic for the prediction of future performance.

An activist justice, by this model, has less than average respect for *stare decisis* in general. More accurately, an activist views *stare decisis* as a ratchet, to be strictly observed when considering a case (such as Roe v. Wade) that favored a progressive cause, but unimportant when a case that went the other way comes up. He or she is not especially impressed by a need for legislative deference (again, unless such deference helps support a progressive argument). Most of all, an activist thinks of the Constitution as a "living" document, to be bent to the justice's will.

A passivist justice places a great deal of value on stare decisis, more than any of the others. He is also highly cognizant of legislative deference and writes regularly about the intent of the drafters of any law. He tends also to resist changing the current body of constitutional law, whether to move it further in progressive directions or to return to original meanings. The primary emphases of the passivist are stability and predictability.

A reformist justice believes primarily in the Constitution as written. He (there is no she in this category) writes often of the "original intent" of the Founders and deplores the distortions of the document that have entered the body of constitutional law in the last century or so. In this regard, he will reject *stare decisis* in the interest of overturning what he views as an unconstitutional decision of past Courts. He tends to be as alert to legislative intent as the passivist, but is as likely to use that intent to strike down a law as to uphold it, depending on its compatibility with the Constitution.

Using the above analysis, the current Court stands as follows: four justices are clearly activists, three are (or probably will prove to be) reformists and two are (although less clearly) passivists. One of the passivists, as we will see, is definitely a political conservative but respects *stare decisis,* is less likely to support abrupt change and is fully on board with legislative deference. The activists are the same individuals as the liberals under the traditional analysis; the reformists are Thomas, Gorsuch (probably) and Kavanaugh (also probably). It is significant that both of the octogenarians on the Court are activists and the two youngest justices are probable reformists.

The most unabashedly activist justices are Ginsburg and Sotomayor. Both rely on their personal opinions as central to their decision-making. As an example, at her confirmation hearings Sotomayor stated that the Court needed "the wisdom of a Hispanic woman." Leaving aside the question of whether gender and ethnicity are the wellsprings of wisdom, a reformist would insist that a judge rely on the Constitution and case law as guidelines for decision-making, not one's own "wisdom." Breyer and Kagan, on the other hand, are more careful to cite constitutional law to justify their decisions and the content of their opinions, although the result may in the end be hardly more palatable to political conservatives.

The classic reformist is Thomas, who will not hesitate to ignore *stare decisis* in his efforts to restore the Constitution to something closer to the original. Indications are that the two newcomers, Gorsuch and Kavanaugh, will fall closer to this model than otherwise. A student of the Court will be surprised that I do not include Alito in this group as well, but under my analysis, he is more the passivist, although a right-leaning one. Alito has a great deal of respect for *stare decisis* as a principle and he also tends toward giving a great deal of deference to the legislature, within constitutional bounds. More of a pure passivist is Chief Justice Roberts, who, as was seen in the recent Affordable Healthcare Act case, gives maximum legislative deference and will bend the Constitution and case law into a pretzel to do it. Above all, it appears that Roberts does not want his Court to rock the political boat.

The actual structure of the Supreme Court today is, therefore, not a simple 5-4 division favoring conservatives, but a far more complex 4-2-3 mix of activists, passivists and reformists, respectively. Looking at it this way, the Left need not panic so violently: they still have the largest bloc of justices who are likely to vote their way, and either of two swing justices can give them the decision in any given politically charged case. But is this good enough for the Left? If one knows the Left, the answer must be a resounding No. Progressives were impatient enough with the relatively even balance that marked the Court for the last decade or more. They don't want stasis, they want action! And they thought they finally had it.

Antonin Scalia's untimely death appeared to the Left as manna from Heaven (if they believed in Heaven). It was a golden opportunity to replace the intellectual conservative leader of the Court with a liberal, even if it was a rather mild liberal like Judge Merrick Garland. They were frustrated by their minority position in Congress, and not happily so. Not to worry, however: they were certain to win the upcoming presidential election, and Hillary would reward them with either Garland again or, more likely, a nominee who was far more fire-breathing leftist. Uh-oh....

Yes, the unthinkable happened. Hillary lost, Trump won and Scalia was to be replaced by another conservative. The Court was still balanced, but progressives would have to wait again, and they were profoundly disappointed. But at least they were no worse off, despite having lost too many elections, and they could make it all up by taking over Congress in the mid-terms. All was far from lost. The Left would yet control the Supreme Court, the last American institution to have thus far eluded their grasp.

Then lightning struck again. The swing voter, Justice Kennedy, unexpectedly retired, and well before the midterms put the Democrats back in the congressional driver's seat. The President's nominee was a disaster for the Left, a full-blown political conservative, and quite young to boot. The Left saw the Court slipping out of the fingers that they'd thought to be firmly around it. As we see from the analysis above, that is not the case, but even if the Left sees it the same way, it wouldn't matter. They no longer will settle for parity -- they lust for control. Thus, the sheer deceit and ugliness of the confirmation proceedings; thus the unhinged screaming and threats; thus the demands for impeachment (and, sadly, worse).

Actually, it really could get much worse for the Left than what we see today. Until late last June, and for the best part of a year, the Supreme Court had not a single septuagenarian. Justice Breyer had turned 80 and Justice Thomas did not reach 70 for months thereafter. I don't know, but that may have been the first time in modern history that no one on the Court was in the 70s. The significance, of course, is that not only are the two oldest justices in their 80s, but that there's a ten-year gap between them and the next oldest. And both of the oldest are activists.

Two events must occur if the Left is to take control of the Court, or even maintain some element of parity. First, Democrats must take over the Senate next month in the midterm election. That would enable them to block any nomination the President might make in the second half of his first term. Second, they must win the presidential election in

2020, while maintaining their control of the Senate. It is unlikely that both octogenarians now on the Court will still be there six years from now. The current President, backed by a Republican Senate, will have at least one more reformist, or at least a right-leaning passivist, on the Court by the end of his second term. That will make, according to my reckoning, a 3-3-3 makeup at its leftist best; more likely it will be 3-2-4 or even, at worst (for the Left) 2-2-5. It is facing this disaster to their dreams that fuels vicious acts on the Left.

In the light of the history of socialism, communism and fascism in the last century, we cannot expect that the Left will eschew violence in its quest for dominance over this nation. Their Brown Shirts (aka Antifa) are already on the ground and active. Further defeats at the polls, if they occur, will only make them uglier. At the end of the previous chapter I appended a rather pessimistic quotation from Yeats. I will add another from Ray Bradbury, the title of one of his less joyful short stories: *Something Wicked This Way Comes.*

1/10/20

Chapter Forty-One

Hate Crime and Punishment

Dostoyevsky's classic novel *Crime and Punishment* is great on many levels, but in today's political climate it's good reading for yet another reason. Its protagonist (is that a good term for a cold-blooded murderer?) is able to justify his commission of the crime because he is (in his own mind) above the normal human herd and its morals. He's an elitist in a sense that would do the current Deep State denizens proud – a superman, an intellectual, a Napoleon. He is not bound by the ordinary mortal chains of societal ethical norms because he is just, well, too *cool* for that sort of nonsense. Violence, lethal or otherwise, is fine when exercised by a really super guy against lesser creatures.

He spends most of the rest of the novel agonizing over his bloody deed (the murders of a disreputable old pawn broker and her female friend) and is finally, mostly through love, able to recognize his own lowly humanity and confess the crime. His punishment, it is clear, is less the eight-year prison sentence he receives than his own inner torment. It's not the most cheerful read around, but I highly recommend it to anyone who has never experienced it. I would especially recommend it to young leftist radicals, but realize that, sadly, they are the least likely readers.

It may be useful to examine the crime and the punishment of *Crime and Punishment* in the light of modern Western jurisprudence. As to the crime, there isn't much to say. A double axe murder is a dramatically brutal act, now or a century and a half ago, and it would garner the same sort of attention in the modern media as in Dostoyevsky's fictional society. The main difference is in the investigative phase and reflects advances in forensics rather than principles of law enforcement. In 1866, even fingerprinting was not yet available to detectives. Other than that, murder is murder and it's still a crime. There were even similar distinctions in the kind of murder then and now.

The mental state of the killer of another human has been a factor for centuries. In the 19th century, as now, it was important to determine, first, whether the killing was intentional or accidental. If the latter, was it a pure accident or could it have been avoided with normal caution? If it might have been avoided, what degree of carelessness was involved? The difference between murder (intentional) and involuntary manslaughter (not) has always been critical. Within the framework of manslaughter, the primary concern is the level of negligence on the part of the perpetrator.

If it is found that the killing was intentional, there is still a level of murder that must be determined, also based on what was going on in the mind of the murderer. The highest level of the crime is reserved for a person who kills in cold blood, with advanced planning and for a particular purpose. This is the "Murder One" of legal thrillers and other pulp fiction. Other murders may be done in an inflamed state of mind, in the heat of passion and with no prior planning. The classic case here is the cuckold who discovers his wife in bed with another man, but it can apply to a wide range of actions. The important point is that the differences between murder and manslaughter, and the different levels of murder, are important to the assignment of punishment. There is a vast gap between the sentence for manslaughter and that for first-degree murder.

As one may imagine, the borders between the various categories of manslaughter and murder can be fuzzy and it is not always a simple thing to determine a person's mental state in a crisis. Difficulties aside, however, the basics of crime and punishment have been recognized for centuries, and although punishments have varied drastically through the years there has generally been an accommodation for the mental state of the killer. So it was in 19th century Russia, although only eight years of imprisonment for deliberate murder for profit seems a little weak today. On the other hand, eight years in Siberia may have been a bit tougher than eight years in the local state or fed lockup. Besides, now we have an entire class of crime, for purposes of determining punishment, that would have amazed and bewildered Dostoyevsky. Welcome to the world of the hate crime.

It is reasonable to suspect that one who visits violence upon another, whether it be mere assault or murder, is to some degree ill-disposed toward the victim. In fact, it was the very crimes during which the criminal felt the least hatred toward his victim that were considered most heinous. Those were the cold-blooded crimes, done for material gain alone, that sent chills up the backs of civilized souls. It is easier for normal minds to understand a violent crime perpetrated for reasons of hatred. But this is not exactly what we are talking about when we speak of the present-day hate crime.

Hate crimes, in today's usage, were officially born with the Hate Crimes Prevention Act of 2009. This legislation expanded the role of the Federal Bureau of Investigation to enable the agency to investigate crimes committed against certain "protected" categories of people. It is important to recognize that, at present, there is generally no hate crime unless there has been an underlying crime of a traditional nature. To put it another way, a person must be convicted of a physical act – assault, battery, murder or some sort of illegal intimidation – to be charged with the additional tag of a hate crime. Given a real crime, to be convicted of hate crime the action must have been not only illegal but committed against someone who is a member of a protected group, and not only that, but must have been committed *because* the victim was in such a group. That is, the criminal must have done the deed because of his mental state of hatred against a protected group.

To repeat, to be convicted of a hate crime one must first have been found guilty of a crime in the ordinary way. If a hate crime is then found to have occurred, the enhanced penalty is applied in the punishment phase. The theory is that a greater punishment will tend to deter criminal activity against certain groups of people. Anyone reading this will know which groups are protected: racial minorities, LGBTQ persons, women, the disabled and members of about any religion except Christianity. Others are added from time to time, according to the shifting sands of politics.

It is my opinion that, although there is something to be said for striving to deter criminal actions against people simply because they are who they are, hate crimes legislation is the first step along a dangerous path. In support of this contention, I would refer you to another classic novel, George Orwell's *1984*. This is a profound work that only increases in relevance with every passing year and should be required reading for every American citizen. It is not, of course, and the Establishment will ensure that it never is, at least in schools under its control.

Among the many images from *1984* that survive in popular culture is that of "thought police" (Thinkpol in the Newspeak of the novel). In the general usage of today there is no such organized agency, but rather that ubiquitous and amorphous "They." It nevertheless exists, as you will quickly discover should you venture onto almost any university campus in the country and utter an unorthodox thought. There is little doubt in my mind that the official body – the real Thinkpol – will become a reality if the Left takes control of the nation. The next step will be the criminalization of political speech that is unpalatable to the Left. We are, in fact, in mid-step for that even now.

Speech codes are the norm in academia. There may not yet be a criminal code in any jurisdiction that makes unwelcome speech a crime, other than that which constitutes a public danger (shouting "Fire!" in a crowded theater) or an imminent and defined hazard to an individual ("Get that f----r and string him up!"), but the effect on many campuses is much as if there were. A student may be expelled for saying something that makes persons with "protected characteristics" feel uncomfortable. This punishment has been carried out with few if any of the usual constitutional protections for the offender, those generally lumped under the term "due process."

Actually, in certain aggravated cases the transmutation of speech into a crime has already been recognized by courts, including the Supreme Court, in this nation. So far, the 1st Amendment has limited this trend more or less severely in the U.S.; in many of the countries of western Europe that are unbound by such restraint the process is far more advanced. Convictions and prison time have been the fate of some there who have criticized Islam, for example, or promoted causes that could somehow be connected to Nazism. Insofar as the Left is successful in taking over, the same will inevitably happen in America. In this scenario, any speech not approved by progressives will be defined as hate, and hate will constitute crime. When speech becomes a criminal act, the 1st Amendment of the Constitution will effectively be overturned.

You will note that all of the jargon mentioned above – hate, protected groups, protected characteristics – is defined by the Left. Only progressives are virtuous enough to tell us which humans must be winners and which losers. The Left divides to conquer, and by virtue of its exclusive occupation of the moral high ground can decide unilaterally how to divide us. Nor will they be finished with control of speech. Nothing but the control of thought itself will satiate the Progressive Movement. Orwell saw that clearly seventy years ago and described its results in unappetizing detail.

If this seems somewhat over the top to you, please contemplate the American campus of today. There are "safe spaces" for its innocent students. But safe from what? The answer is chillingly simple: from thought. The students must be protected from exposure to thoughts not approved by their masters. Such thought is, to academicians, criminal, and the students must be protected from crime. The concept of thought crime has already permeated much of contemporary society and moved firmly into the political realm. Hate crime is already being generalized; that is, no criminal act other than hate itself is required for prosecution. As unorthodox thought becomes hate, and therefore crime, and therefore is punished accordingly, any freedom left to ordinary Americans will be illusory. One day, the mere accusation of a bad thought will be enough for prosecutors, and that will immanentize *1984*.

We have a rather narrow window of opportunity to escape the fate that seems to be pursuing us. The Constitution may be sick, but it is not yet dead. If we protect what is left of it, and perhaps even regain some that has been lost, we may still be a free people.

Let us leave this discussion with a final quotation from the immortal George Orwell: "If you want a vision of the future, imagine a boot stamping on a human face – forever." We may still avoid Orwell's vision of our future.

11/12/19

Chapter Forty-Two

Bad Intentions

In her efforts to prod me to quit thinking about doing something and instead doing it, my mother used to quote an old proverb: "The road to hell is paved with good intentions." That may be an unpleasant thing to say, but intentions are nevertheless important, and in the field of criminal law it isn't the good intentions that are important but rather the bad ones. Evidence of ill intent regarding a committed crime is critical to determining the charge that a prosecutor will bring for the offense. This, in turn, is highly influential in determining the sentence for the perpetrator if a conviction is secured. It may therefore be stated, and as more than just an adage, that whether the road to hell is paved with good intentions or not, the road to the penitentiary is definitely paved with bad ones.

That said, the question of intent does not always have a simple answer. An example is an old argument for drunks who had committed an offense while under the influence, that they hadn't all their faculties about them and therefore were not responsible for their acts. That defense fails because, even though the drunk might not have been capable of good decisions at the time of malfeasance, he had previously made the conscious decision to overindulge in the first place. On the other hand, a similar defense is commonly successful for those who are declared insane, on the basis that they never made a conscious choice to become insane (as the drunk did for drinking). There is also a *degree* of intent that becomes a factor. Therefore, the person who carefully plans a murder for a specific reason may be charged for first-degree murder (or its equivalent in the relevant jurisdiction), whereas someone who murders his wife's seducer in that moment of rage when he catches them in the act will usually be charged with some lesser offense. Both committed the act of murder with intent to kill, but in the latter case that intent is blurred by emotional stress. When analyzing the human frame of mind, subtlety is required.

Intent is also a factor in sorting things out between criminal and civil law. Let us take a random example of someone who has sold a car with defective brakes to a buyer who later has an accident. The buyer (or his estate) sues for damages and a punitive amount in civil court. Assuming the court finds that the seller did in fact sell the buyer the car and the accident was in fact caused by bad brakes, an early question will be that of scienter. Scienter is a term of art in the law that refers to the seller's knowledge. Did the seller know the brakes were bad? If not, if the seller himself took the car from a previous owner without knowledge about the brakes, the question then goes to whether the seller *should* have known. That is, should he have been responsible for checking before re-selling the car? If so, he will probably be guilty of negligence. If it was a very basic responsibility that he blew off, he might be guilty of gross negligence. In either case, the matter remains in civil law and becomes a question of how much money he owes. Normally, even without scienter or negligence, the seller will be liable to the buyer for some amount to be determined. He may, in turn, then sue the person who previously sold him the car for compensation.

If, however, there was scienter on the part of the seller -- if he knew of the faulty brakes before the sale -- the case takes a darker turn. At that point, we may enter the realm of criminal law. The next question will again turn to intent: why did the seller make the sale even though he knew about the brakes? If he sort of knew but just didn't get around to telling the buyer, it may only be a case of gross negligence, depending on other facts. In that situation there could be some uncertainty about whether to bring criminal charges. If they should be brought, it might be for no more than manslaughter (in the case of a fatal accident). If, on the other hand, evidence arises that the seller also knew that the buyer was about to take a joy ride on Route 1 along the Big Sur coast in his newly purchased vehicle (more scienter), the charge may be elevated to murder. And if it can be shown that the seller had also discovered that the buyer was having an affair with his wife (more scienter yet), it could come to first degree murder. So the whole concept of intent in the law is highly complex, nuanced and fact-dependent. Bad intentions, if provable, can take a bad actor to bad places.

Are you confused yet? If not, perhaps you haven't been reading too closely (or else you're sharper than many lawyers). It may as well be admitted that the subject of criminal intent is neither simple nor unambiguous; as with many aspects of the law there is a lot of gray area within its bounds. In fact, even experienced lawyer-politicians may get it wrong, as the recent presidential impeachment charade demonstrated (in a cart-before-horse, House Democrats focused heavily on bad intentions and never got around to proving a crime). But however complex the law already was, it recently became worse. With the advent of the concept of "hate crime" (see the prior chapter, *Hate Crime and Punishment*) a whole additional layer of complexity has been added to this already complex and highly nuanced body of law.

With the new category of hate crime, the issue of intent is taken to another level. Once a criminal trial results in conviction, punishment is determined not only by intent, as addressed above, but also with reference to whether the victim belonged to a protected class, as established by government authority. If so, the perpetrator's mind is examined to see if he was impelled to criminal action by animus against the victim because of the protected status, apart from any more traditional motivations. If that is proved, enhanced punishment will be meted out as with an "aggravated" offense, which is to say one with especially nasty features. An example of an aggravated offense in traditional criminal law is felony murder (the name differs in different jurisdictions), which is murder committed in the course of an independent felony. An example of that is an armed robbery, a felony in itself, during which murder is incidentally committed. But the acute reader will note a significant distinction: in the case of a hate crime, the "independent felony" is not an act but a frame of mind. In essence, having in one's mind animus against a protected group is now, in law, equivalent to a felonious act.

Thus, with hate crime legislation, a giant step has already been taken toward enshrining fiction-style "thought crime" into law. As hate crime is currently defined in the U.S., it is still a requirement that a traditional crime be committed and conviction for it be obtained before the hate crime law of the jurisdiction becomes a factor. In other words, hate crime law applies only to the punishment phase of a trial. Elsewhere in the world, the next big step has already been taken in some countries, where hate crime can be prosecuted as a felony in itself. Even here, steps have been taken in that direction, and some jurisdictions can prosecute hate speech as an independent crime, even though there has been no criminal action other than speech. "Speech," of course, has long been extended to non-vocal expressions, so perhaps we are already at the point where showing a Confederate flag might somewhere be considered a crime. It's only a baby step from there to the classic thought crime of lurid fiction.

Can one commit a state of mind? If you harbor bad feelings toward your neighbor who is Muslim, or a POC, or transgendered, are you already a criminal, even if you have never acted upon your feelings? George Orwell addressed that very topic nearly three-quarters of a century ago in his novel *1984*. Ray Bradbury touched upon aspects of it in the novel *Fahrenheit 451*. These were based on observations of actual socialist regimes of the time. Writers other than Orwell, mainly in the science fiction genre, have written of "thought police" in their work, so the idea isn't so eccentric as it might appear. With hate crime legislation now firmly ensconced in our legal system, we are already halfway there, and there are numerous voices calling for us to travel the rest of the way. Resistance to criminalizing speech considered offensive to certain individuals and groups, said resistance based on the 1st Amendment of the Constitution, has slowed progress in that direction, but the pressure is there. Calls for increased censorship of "disinformation" on the internet are coming from candidates for the Democrat presidential nomination. Who gets to determine what information is false and what is correct? When the constitutional rights of free speech are proscribed, what barriers remain to the criminalization of thought?

The extension of the definition of crime from doing to being has ramifications beyond hate crimes. At the moment (in the U.S., at least), a person still has to perform a criminal action before his bad intentions are taken into consideration. If he should carry out a criminal act but can, as is in essence the case, be charged with an independent felony for being a racist or homophobe or whatever, in order to enhance punishment, we have crossed into new territory. We have opened the door to charging the person with the crime of racism or homophobia even in lieu of a traditional base crime. That is where we are now. At a minimum, it muddies the waters of an already complex body of law and creates an element of judicial confusion. But it can lead to far worse.

As a final word, it is good advice for anyone to avoid committing a crime; nothing new in that. In the service of that noble goal, cut off any tendency toward criminal involvement by reigning in all bad intentions you may harbor. And as for committing a thought crime -- don't even think about it.

The mind should develop a blind spot whenever a dangerous thought presented itself. The process should be automatic, instinctive. Crimestop, they called it in Newspeak.

George Orwell, 1984

2/3/20

PART VII

2020 Hindsight

It is useful to look back once in a while, if only because we cannot know where we are if we don't know where we have been. Hindsight is always 20/20, it is said, which means that it's easier to predict the past than the future. This is all the more truthful when a historical black swan event intervenes, which was the case in 2020. The articles in this section were selected on the basis that all pertain to the election in one way or another, and they all illuminate where we were in a way that tends to explain where we find ourselves today, and how and why it happened.

It should be noted that these articles, with one exception, were written before the election of 2020 took place. Most of them, all but the last two, were written before the coming of the coronavirus and the complete upsetting of the electoral chessboard. Please read them with that in mind. I expect it is already obvious to the reader that the world changed radically with the arrival of that virus. All the certainties we knew became uncertain. The basic facts about the political parties remained the same but all conclusions based upon those facts were turned on their heads.

The facts concerning the Left were laid out in Part III; this section looks at the situation from a more purely political point of view. *Under the Lamp Post* examines the Democrats before a national election, and the next three chapters dissect the party in more detail, with an emphasis on the competence (or lack thereof) of its leaders and officials to govern. *Bottoms Up* takes another look at the recent foibles of the party with a more humorous twist. *The Third Bite* reviews some of the actions the Democrat Party has taken in its attempt to compensate for its own deficiencies and speculates about its future options. The viewpoint is expanded to include the Establishment as well as the party in *A Tale of Two Presidents*, which discusses the *bete noir* of both party and Establishment (Mr.

Trump), in the context of presidential history. Taken together, these chapters provide a vivid picture of the all-too-brief Trump era that is almost eerie in retrospect. There is no wonder that Establishment, Deep State and Democrat Party could not afford to let things continue the way they were headed.

This leads us to the final chapter, *Cui Bono?* No further explication could add much to the article itself, which is more speculative than the others in this section. Of course, it had to be – it was written just after the election and looked to the future rather than the present. Now, several months later and more than two weeks into the term of the unlikely Joseph Biden, that future appears murkier than ever. One point is clear: the Left, including the Democrat Party, is determined to grab the brass ring of power with total disregard of consequences. Those consequences are likely to be dire. We are at this moment on the edge of one of the turning points in history.

Charles Dickens, in his scene with the Ghost of Christmas Past, painted a vision of what uncertain and foreboding future scenarios look like: dark, moody and threatening. That is the feeling most Americans now have. *Cui Bono?* lists those who benefited from the disasters of 2020, at least for now. We don't yet know who will suffer in the end, or how much. But at least we can see how we got here: that is the value of 2020 hindsight.

Chapter Forty-Three

Under the Lamp Post

A drunk was crawling around under a lamp post in front of a bar at closing time. He stated to a passerby who questioned him that he'd dropped his car keys and was looking for them. After helping him look for a few minutes without result, the passerby asked if he was sure that was where he'd dropped his keys. "Oh no," the drunk replied. "I dropped them over by that alley, but it's so dark over there you can't see a thing."

It's an old joke, but worth retelling because it says something about the human condition. Under stress there's a tendency to do what we can rather than what's actually needed. Applied to human nature in general, it's humorous. Applied specifically to politics, maybe it's not so funny. As of now, both political parties in the US are seeking to take possession of the keys to the 2020 national elections. Which is to say: to win, a party must seize the high ground on those issues most important to the electorate. At this point, one can say that those Democrats who have a clear view of the political landscape (possibly a minority of them) must fear that their party has lost its keys. Worse, it may be looking for them in all the wrong places.

All the polls, plus common sense, point to a handful of issues that are of paramount importance to most of us at present. At the head of the list, as always, is the economy. This is a given in essentially any national election, as pointed out decades ago by Bill Clinton. Up there with it this time around is immigration. Health care -- more accurately how to pay for health care -- and international threats, both economic and military, are not far behind. Various social issues, including education, abortion and First and Second Amendment rights, follow. These are the substantive issues, above all, that will decide the winners and losers in the 2020 elections. The Democrats are clearly drawing the short stick for nearly all of them.

Do the Democrats genuinely expect to go toe-to-toe with Donald Trump and the Republicans on the American economy? All indications are that they do not. Even the current generation of oddly self-unaware Democrats is realistic enough to dodge that one. Check out all sources within Pravda West to search for references to the economy and you will come up with little to show for your effort. The party of the Left is dealing with this leading issue by not dealing with it at all. It is studiously avoiding the entire subject in any substantive way; the only tactic used is throwing up a smokescreen of negativity. Mutterings about all the working people who have been left behind and how tax cuts have only helped corporations and the wealthy are the only references to a buoyant economy that can be found in Pravda West. The only offensive gambit is an extraordinarily weak one: tepid suggestions that the growth of the last two and a half years can be attributed to Obama's policies. All the advice given out by the former administration about stagnant growth, stagnant wages and permanently lost industry being the "new normal" is long forgotten.

The open borders cheerleaders on the Left are playing to an empty stadium. The support for strong border control is both widespread and intense, and extends to immigration law enforcement across the board. Even support for DACA has diminished in the face of Democratic overreach and been replaced by increased support for outright deportation of illegal immigrants (especially violent criminals). This puts Democrats at a distinct disadvantage on both of the current leading issues. On other important issues, they aren't doing much better. The old Democrat advantage on health care has narrowed because of greater understanding of the flaws of Obamacare and, again, overreach on dilution of Medicare and promotion of a single payer system. As for the international scene, most Americans are happy that, unlike his predecessors, Trump is trying to do something and is putting the nation's interests first in the process. Abortion has always been contentious and the issue isn't particularly helpful to either party at this point. Education is a longer-term problem and far from a Democrat advantage even over time. Gun control isn't very popular in most of the country outside firm leftist enclaves.

The bottom line is that the Democrats have indeed lost their keys. The recent debates of candidates who wish to be the party's presidential nominee highlighted that fact starkly. Every generally unpopular cause, particularly regarding the most important issues, was trumpeted by the debaters. As an example, most of the rest of us see the enthusiastic support of nearly all the candidates for "free" unlimited health care for all illegal immigrants as an invitation to disaster. It would be little more than a magnet for more illegal immigration from the entire Third World, it would overwhelm an already burdened system and its costs would be crushing. Most of the candidates' nostrums for other perceived problems were no better, and there's no way to pay for any of them. I suspect anyone who paid attention was struck by how far left the Democrat Party had drifted. In short, not only has the party lost the keys to the next election, it is looking for them under the lamp post.

Socialism, the key that Democrats seem to hope will open the door to electoral victory in 2020, is wildly popular. Unfortunately for the party, it is wildly popular, or popular at all, only among about 22% of the population by my calculation, which is based on dozens of polls about various subjects over recent years. Worse, that 22% is concentrated in relatively few districts in states that are deepest blue, and disproportionately includes people who tend not to vote. This is not favorable in terms of the Electoral College. Outside those few districts, socialism is about as wildly unpopular as it is popular within them, or perhaps more so. The current round of debates, as noted above, reveals a party that is flailing about in search of approval by a high-energy ideological minority. The individual candidates hope they can capture a large enough chunk of socialist support to seize the nomination. The party then appears to rely on the energy and commitment of those socialists to boost it to success in the general election an electoral force.

it will suffice to say that the Republicans hold nearly all the issue-related cards. Their domination of the issues may be inadvertent -- the GOP is not known for political genius -- but they would have to be extraordinarily bumbling, or the Dems amazingly brilliant, for them to lose this hand. It remains to be seen, but to date the Dems haven't shown much real brilliance. They've lost their keys and are now crawling around under the alluring but treacherous lamp post of extreme leftist ideology. Their left wing has dragged them so far in that direction that it is unlikely they can get back to where the keys lay by election time.

The burden of this article is that overt socialism is unlikely to be a winning formula at election time in the current political climate in America. Yet this is the hope we find in the modern Democrat Party. Bernie Sanders and most of the others in the socialist camp call themselves "democratic socialists," which may ring a bell for those who have read the *Pravda West* chapter. You may recall that at the turn of the 20th century, the organization that became the Soviet Communist Party called itself the Russian Social Democratic Labor Party. This is hardly a coincidence; the speed of the leftward lurch of the Democrat Party since the turn of this century has been startling. They left a vacuum in the center, of which even the feckless Republicans have been able to take advantage. Not all Democrat politicians have taken on the socialist label, or even most of them, but they may as well. That has become the hallmark of their party.

It's an unpleasant fact that the Democrats have managed to get themselves into an electorally awkward position. Now it appears that anything that is good for the Democrat Party is bad for the country and anything good for the country is bad for the party. This may titillate college professors but it isn't likely to play well in Peoria. Thinking back to the drunk under the lamp post, the joke ends before we find out if he ever finds his car keys. I expect most of us would hope he didn't. For the same reason, most of us wouldn't be too disappointed if the Democrats don't find theirs any time soon. Who wants a drunk to be driving the car?

11/3/19

Chapter Forty-Four

Get Serious

As November approaches, two major political parties (plus maybe Kanye West) are whetting their blades for an electoral contest that will determine the fundamental nature of our country for decades to come. One of them now holds the White House and Senate and is campaigning on the basis of economic and social policies that are well known, having been in place for three and a half years. These policies are, in fact, underlain by fundamental principles that are based on the Constitution and have guided the nation for over two centuries (with some major variations during that period). The other party, the Democrats, brings to the table a set of ideas that is entirely novel, even alien, as far as the U.S. is concerned. These ideas have been tried elsewhere around the world, invariably with unfortunate results, but the Democrats, who have by now become one with the Left, assure us that they will work under their wise administration. Let us examine the party and its platform with an eye to deciding whether we should take those assurances seriously. To do so, of course, we must agree to take the party itself seriously.

Some recent efforts of the party have not, in truth, been especially encouraging. Some have been downright comical. A hilarious example is the party's own primary in Iowa, which took the form of a caucus. Keeping in mind the need to maintain our usual grace toward others, we need not dwell on the results of that exercise in detail. It shall suffice to mention a few words that are most descriptive of the occasion: incompetence and lack of professionalism come immediately to mind. I haven't heard that the final results are in yet. Did Pete Buttigieg (remember him?) take the prize in the end?

Actually, the above example, however typical, is relatively trivial in the long run. A much more significant one is the grand attempt, at full charge with bugles blaring, to take over on behalf of the federal government the nation's healthcare system, initiated at the outset of President Obama's reign. A power grab for a huge percentage of the national net worth by the federal government is a very serious matter, but how it was done shows why the party that made the attempt is difficult to take seriously. First, the project was sold (or the sales pitch was made) by means of the most brazen lies ever uttered by a presidential tongue. Obama's promises that we could keep our current doctors and plans if we liked them, made at a time when he knew perfectly well that we couldn't once the program was implemented, go into history as classic whoppers. How could we ever take his word seriously again? Second, implementation of Obamacare, as it came to be called, was a nightmare of high comedy that wasn't at all funny when the price tag became known. Months (and billions) were spent developing the website to allow those seeking the "affordable" insurance to sign up. When the scheme was finally rolled out with fanfare and celebration, it fell flat. The site crashed and burned. Just over $2 billion in tax money had been paid out for federal website development alone, for what should have cost about $100 thousand. The total tab counting state websites came to over $5B. Plus, the program itself is wasteful, cumbersome and unworkable to begin with. Mostly, it was an embarrassment.

Speaking of embarrassment, one thing Democrats have on their side is a total lack of the capacity for shame. This has sustained them through many a rough patch, and it was never more useful to them than during these last three years. The Russian collusion fiasco would have shut down anyone who is capable of embarrassment for at least the balance of President Trump's first term, but it didn't seem to faze the Dems. Never before in the history of American politics did an outgoing administration actively attempt to sabotage its successors, using a weaponized bureaucracy and Deep State intelligence agencies to do it. Never before was the internal judicial process, including a special prosecutor with a stacked-deck team, so profoundly abused. That was bad enough, from an embarrassment standpoint, but it got worse. Malice is one thing, blundering another. They messed up the attempt, totally and inexcusably. With every advantage, they lacked competence even in malfeasance. So surely they would draw in their horns, hide in a corner and try to make everyone forget it as quickly as possible, right? Wrong. They slipped almost seamlessly into another sabotage attempt against the same target that was not only feckless but entirely unserious.

One Democrat member of the House of Representatives (from California, of course) gained a reputation for screaming "Impeach! Impeach!" even before Trump had been inaugurated. An adult from the party should have taken her aside and explained that impeachment requires a crime in office, a "high crime" at that, and that she should wait at least until Mr. Trump takes office to speak of impeachment. But there were no adults, and her screams were echoed, a little more quietly, by many others of her party. Thus it should have been no surprise that, as soon as the Russian collusion "investigation" collapsed, the party, by then empowered by control of the House, found a pretext to begin an impeachment inquiry. Trump threw a wrench into the process at the outset by releasing the transcript of the phone call upon which impeachment was intended to be based before the rumor mill could get cranked up. Nevertheless, committed as they were and backed as always by their pet media, the Democrats forged ahead. There was not even a pretense of due process, or even simple fairness, and the inevitable impeachment vote was followed by even more clownishness on the part of the Speaker of the House. The whole thing promptly fizzled in the Senate, of course, and is now, mercifully for the Democrats, largely forgotten. Another fiasco, another shrug of the collective shoulders of the party, and again no apology, no embarrassment, no problem.

It has been pointed out (in *Under the Lamp Post*) that Democrats have no issues that could win more than a handful of votes in a national election. They are therefore relying on their control of Pravda West, on infantile capers like those mentioned above and on the occasional crisis to sustain them through the current election campaign. Fortunately for them, a wonderful crisis arrived in a timely manner, imported from China. They have hyped the coronavirus invasion to the maximum and are still working diligently to prod us into completing the destruction of the American economy. Other than that, their plan for fighting the spread of the virus seems to include open borders, no criticism of China, massive riots, no travel bans and no church attendance. Of course, blaming all the misery, medical and economic, on Trump is part of the restoration process. But, also as mentioned above, there is an exception for going to a church. It's quite alright as long as the purpose of the trip is not to attend the church but to burn it down.

After Democrats spent two years completely in the political wilderness, the American public in its wisdom did give them control of at least a piece of the federal government: the House of Representatives. It's difficult to understand why they would do such a thing; perhaps it was just to see how the party would govern when given a chance. The public saw. There was the show trial impeachment, of course: the absurd abuse of a most solemn and ultimate measure to be resorted to when all else fails, all to score a few political points. But even in trivial ways the Democrats managed to convey their lack of seriousness. Speaker Pelosi's puerile little act of tearing up her copy of the State of the Union address, with a lemon-sucking expression on her stretched face, was typical. Hey, is that statesmanship or what? Otherwise, you can judge how well the party has handled its opportunity to govern. Production of a $3T coronavirus relief bill that was little but a socialist wish list and had nothing much to do with the virus or the economic ills that accompany it was about the only major legislative effort (besides harassing and tormenting Trump) of which the House has been capable.

In other arenas where Democrats have been given a chance to show their stuff in governance, the results have been predictable. They've been running most of the big city governments in the country since Giuliani left the NYC mayor's office, and we can look there to judge their management expertise. Or perhaps it's best not to look. At the moment, rioting in the streets is running unchecked, and the Democrats' solution to the problem is to call it not a problem at all but a peaceful exercise of First Amendment rights, and that in a good cause. The rioting is complemented by a huge rise in violent crime of a more individual nature, with the death toll shooting (so to speak) to record highs. The solution to that is to denigrate, defund and even disband the police. So far, and perhaps not unsurprisingly, the various Democrat solutions to these and other problems don't seem to be working out so well. At least they're predictable, if not especially serious.

But perhaps I've been too hasty in dismissing the party's concern for serious policy innovations. After all, there is the Green New Deal, which is as serious as it gets. Or at least, as serious as the Democrats have gotten. The Green New Deal is expected to work even better than the original New Deal, which extended the Great Depression by a decade and was ended only by the onset of World War II. In fairness, similar efforts by the Republican administration that preceded FDR contributed to the longevity of the depression, but the heaviest damage was Democrat work. As for the Green New Deal, we are to spend trillions of dollars (the projected amount appears to be quite flexible) to accomplish the following: ban most energy production and put America back into dependency on foreign producers; put an end to air travel and severely restrict all travel; raise the cost of living to levels that will impoverish the average family; globalize our economy for the benefit of international elites; and...well, you get the idea. You have to admit, this is pretty serious stuff. Give them credit for thinking outside the box. After all, windmills and other medieval technologies may not be original but are at least out of the ordinary. Poverty maybe not so much.

The party may have forgotten how to govern, but their mass media servants have forgotten even more about news. Pravda West is just not serious anymore about real journalism, no more serious than their Democrat masters are about governance. Even its propaganda is weak because, with a few exceptions, reporters and commentators can't so much as lie competently. When they stick to the tried-and-true techniques of their Soviet era model, telling half-truths, spinning with subtlety, ignoring certain key facts and refusing to cover stories that don't advance the agenda, they do fine. But too often, in their zeal to break the big one they come right out with a whopper, made up whole cloth and buttressed by fictitious anonymous sources. Alternatively, they plunge in to boost a hoax, usually with racial overtones, without bothering to check facts or even consider its plausibility. Then there are what they laughingly call "fact checkers," the most blatantly obvious liars of all. In short, many modern journalists (who are nearly all Democrats) are not serious about their profession as journalists, or even as propagandists.

These few examples don't begin to exhaust the supply. It is all too evident that the Democrat Party is simply not serious about governing, or even thinking about how to govern. There is one thing the party is all *too* serious about, however: gaining power. Democrats are willing to do essentially anything necessary to gain control of government at all levels, and tend not to worry much about the Constitution and rule of law in the gaining of it. Once in power, their focus will be on keeping power and enjoying its usufructs, not on what is good for the common people. Think about it: do you believe the Democrats will govern wisely and competently if they seize the presidency and both branches of the federal legislature in November? Do you expect good results for the nation as a whole if that should happen? Are you genuinely optimistic about the future of our country in Democrat hands? Are you thinking about voting the Democrat ticket in November?

Get serious.

6/19/20

Chapter Forty-Five

The Russian Paradigm

On May 26, 2012, in Seoul, South Korea, then-President Barack Obama of the United States said a few informal words to then-President Dmitri Medvedev of Russia. They were spoken with the understanding that the microphone between them was off. The mic was in fact hot, with the result that Obama's words and Medvedev's response were soon known throughout the world. Basically, Obama was asking for some "space" in the discussions between the two countries concerning U.S.-sponsored missile defenses in eastern Europe. He stated that he would have more flexibility to negotiate on that and other issues after the upcoming election, the last in which he would have to cater to public opinion. Medvedev said, "I understand. I will transmit this information to Vladimir [Putin]."

Four years later, during his campaigning for Hillary for the next presidential election, Obama criticized candidate Donald Trump for his "continued flattery of Mr. Putin and the degree to which he appears to model many of his [Putin's] policies and approaches" (quote from CBSNews.com). This is an example of the projection so well exemplified by the Left, inasmuch as it was precisely what Obama himself had applied himself to so diligently during his administration. But more to the point of our present subject is the reference to the Russian model. It can be demonstrated that through the decades since the Bolshevik revolution the Left has been fascinated by how the Russians do things. It is no wonder that leftists expect President Trump and others on the Right to do the same.

As we examine the history of this phenomenon it becomes apparent that although the leftist view of Russia has been generally quite positive it can also occasionally be a bit muddled. The positive attitude is understandable, given the fact that Russia was the first important nation to embrace communism as a way of life. Infatuation with the Russian communists started early. A year after the Bolsheviks gained power, in 1922, an English-born American reporter named Walter Duranty became the Moscow bureau chief for the New York Times. A decade later he had won a Pulitzer prize for his reporting about the country, mainly as a result of his friendly relationship with dictator Josef Stalin.

Coverage in the NYT of Soviet Russia in general was apologetic throughout Duranty's residency, and that of Stalin was uniformly favorable. But coverage of the genocidal famine in Ukraine was outright mendacious. Duranty denied that it happened at all for the most part and made no mention whatever that it had been deliberately engineered by Stalin. Years later, when the truth came out, there were demands that Duranty's Pulitzer prize be revoked. The NYT finally agreed that Duranty's work constituted "some of the worst reporting to appear in this newspaper," but punted the question of revocation of the prize back to the Pulitzer Prize Board, which weaseled out. The prize remains among the NYT's trophies. More important to the present discussion is the fact that the playbook for Duranty's reportage was copied directly from that of *Pravda*, the Russian communist party propaganda organ.

Similar propaganda techniques, mostly cruder and thus less effective than those of the Russian model, were employed by other socialists of the time, notably the Nazis in Germany and the Fascists in Italy. The Russians, however, were the masters of the art. The two sides of socialism squared off in the Spanish Civil War of 1936-'39, with the Russians supporting the internationalist Republicans and Germany and Italy supporting General Franco's Nationalists. The Nationalists may have won the shooting war but the Russians clearly prevailed in the propaganda war. Volunteers flooded into Spain from all over the western world, notably the U.S. and Great Britain, to join the ranks of the Republicans. Press coverage everywhere was openly sympathetic to the Republican cause, and books and movies perhaps even more so. Even now there is nostalgia for the Republicans and regret about the war's outcome.

Yet, on the ground, there was little about the Republicans and their cause to engender sympathy. They were ideologically hard Left and pathetically incompetent to govern. They failed even though they had every advantage at the outset. They fought among themselves almost as hard as against the Nationalists. Moreover, they were viciously anti-clerical and openly and joyfully engaged in the wholesale massacre of priests and other religious figures. It was mainly the whitewash of Russian-style propaganda that made them heroic to posterity. The same techniques are used now, on a daily basis, to promote the leftist agenda in the U.S. When they are employed to denigrate Donald Trump they are called out by him as "fake news," but they serve the larger purpose of advancing socialism and denouncing conservatism in general. The Russian paradigm lives on in our newsrooms.

In reality, propaganda is just one aspect of the Russian model for gaining influence and molding public opinion. More generally, the Soviets in their time employed an array of supposedly neutral front organizations to achieve their ends internationally. The objectives of these fronts were to spread good will for the Soviet Union and communism and to recruit vulnerable individuals to the cause. These recruits were known as "fellow travelers" to the controllers of the organizations in Moscow. The less well informed among them were called "useful idiots" by Vladimir Ilyich Lenin, a term that continued to be used by his successors. No doubt that odious phrase is still active in certain Russian circles.

Another important use of the front organizations was to help spread misinformation to the populations of target nations. That embraced propaganda, of course, but the objectives were broader than just politics. The misinformation distributed by the fronts could also sow confusion, foster divisions in a society and lead to general demoralization. Progressives in America have not been slow to adopt this aspect of the Russian paradigm. First among our own home-grown fronts are the "alphabets" of the mass media, plus most of the larger newspapers. It is impossible not to notice the uniformity of talking points disseminated across the media spectrum when "spin" becomes necessary for any news item, much of it identical in wording. It is also striking that errors in reporting are picked up and transmitted by many outlets so rapidly that it is sometimes difficult to determine where the error originated. Needless to say, the errors, which are increasingly common, all tend to be in favor of the leftist point of view. The claim of objectivity of most media organizations has become risible, as has been the case for all types of "neutral" front organizations of the Left from the beginning.

There are currently other front organizations than those of the media, most claiming neutrality and objectivity as a matter of course. One prominent example is the Southern Poverty Law Center, a throwback in its ruthlessness and methods to the glory days of the 1930s. The SPLC maintains a blacklist of organizations that they claim are racist, sexist, homophobic, Islamophobic, white supremacist and generally evil. A few of them no doubt are all of that, but most are perfectly respectable conservative outfits that simply decline to embrace socialism. This might not be especially important except for the fact that many other organizations, including some governmental and most social media entities, use the SPLC's veneer of respectability to actively discriminate against those on the list. The SPLC is only one of the most successful of many leftist fronts operating in the U.S. today. The Soviets, if they were still around, would be envious. Their model has been emulated and perfected by our own Left.

Specific examples of the Left's propensity for borrowing the Russian model are not difficult to find. One is the current debate over building a wall along the U.S. border with Mexico. There are few major media outlets that have not indulged in the sport of mocking the prospective wall while making a show of indignation over it. The motives of those who wish to build it are impugned. It is the butt of numerous rather unfunny jokes on late night comedy shows. Among the criticisms of it are that it is racist (but what isn't?) and would prove to be ineffective and wasteful of precious resources. Nancy Pelosi, Democrat Speaker of the House, called the idea of a wall "an immorality" (?), which must mean "racist," I suppose. She has a wall around her own abode, and many, if not most, of her colleagues also have walls or live in walled communities, so the charge of racism pales a bit and that of ineffectiveness loses some credibility. The call for frugality in opposing a wall, made by ardent leftists, is, shall we say, a tad specious. Nevertheless, criticisms of the wall as provocative, expensive and imperfectly effective must be taken seriously. Mustn't they? But where have we heard them before?

In 1983, President Ronald Reagan announced an ambitious program with the objective of ending the nuclear threat from strategic ballistic missiles. It was called the Strategic Defense Initiative, and involved lasers, particle beams, ground- and space-based counter-missiles and any number of other innovative ideas, plus control systems for the weapons. It called for a whole new way of looking at the threat of nuclear annihilation and for the resources of money and brains to make it real. It was aimed primarily at neutralizing the Soviet missile system, that was intercontinental and submarine-based. The Russians went ballistic.

The American Left opposed the entire concept, to put it mildly. They tried hard to laugh it into oblivion. Senator Ted Kennedy (you remember, the Chappa-something guy) coined the pejorative label "Star Wars" for SDI, to mock its science fictional nature. Soon that was all one heard it called by in the media, by commentators, everywhere. Learned academics and eminent scientists pronounced SDI to be totally unrealistic and unattainable. Leftist politicians claimed that it would be disastrous for our relations with Russia and would trigger an arms race (ignoring the fact that there already was an arms race and had been for years). Economists bemoaned the outrageous expense of even trying to do the impossible. Military experts pointed out that it would be ineffective even if it could ever become operational: it could never be perfect in the sense that every missile would be deterred. So SDI was roundly denounced as provocative, wastefully expensive and imperfectly effective. Kind of like a border wall, in fact.

One may well wonder why the peaceniks of the 1980s Left would so vehemently oppose a project that proposed to deter, or at least substantially diminish, the world-wide nuclear threat. The answer is simple: the Soviets were terrified of SDI. They were far less certain of its lack of potential effectiveness than Ted Kennedy. They had seen what American science and technology could do with that kind of project. They were aware of what the Manhattan Project had accomplished, even though Einstein himself had declared the unlikelihood of producing an atomic bomb. They had seen the strides in the space program, once President Kennedy had committed to it. They knew that SDI didn't have to be perfect to render ineffective their huge stockpile of nuclear warheads, on which they'd lavished so much treasure and resources (not to mention espionage efforts). It wouldn't have to be perfect to work: stopping just half their missiles would put Russia at a crippling disadvantage, and it might stop even more. They also knew they didn't have the money to match the American effort. What they did have was the Russian model for disinformation and manipulation, and they put the American Left to work on it.

Given all their experience with the model, the Left is now well equipped to use it on its own, as with the border wall and sundry other causes. One of those causes is gun control, although it must be conceded that, though certainly part of the Russian model, it is hardly exclusive to Russia. In fact, all oppressive governments of any political stripe, or governments that intend to become oppressive, take guns out of the hands of their citizenry. One can hardly have the oppressed masses running around waving firearms, can one? It's the whole reason that pesky Constitution has a Second Amendment. But it is also a basic element of the Russian model and followers of that model cannot be expected to neglect gun control as a routine element of the agenda.

Unintended consequences accompany almost all endeavors. Those undertaken pursuant to attaining the earthly paradise of socialism, as nearly all that employ the Russian paradigm tend to be, are no exceptions. An example, one among many, is the problem of income inequality. Soviet Russian society was remarkable for a gap in lifestyle between the Communist Party elite and ordinary Russian citizens that stuns the imagination. Caviar, champagne (sweet, of course) and villas on the Black Sea show a strong contrast to shabby little apartments and lines at understocked state stores to buy the essentials to sustain life. Those are, one charitably assumes, not the results our progressives have in mind when they employ elements of the Russian model to promote their agendas.

And the sad fact is that all socialist societies show extreme inequalities in wealth. In the early 1990s, Venezuela became the richest Western Hemisphere nation south of Texas. At the end of that decade, dissatisfaction with corruption and income inequality led to the election of an openly socialist president. The socialists, typically, tightened their grasp on the reins of power and increased it. The citizens of Venezuela now see quite clearly what inequality in earthly goods between the elite and the rest looks like. In America there is now some grumbling about the broadening gap between the "one-percenters" and everyone else. There has, essentially by definition, always been a sizable gap, but a little-recognized fact is that the gap increased substantially during eight years under the leftist economic policies of President Obama. Unfettered regulation, higher taxes and tightened government oversight in general were praised by a pliant media in true Russian paradigm style. The first big step toward socialism here went largely unrecognized but had predictable results. Since the reversal of policy under President Trump, jobs and wages have risen in the lower echelons of society. The middle class has some breathing room to grow and we can expect the gap in living standards between high and low to stabilize and, in all probability, diminish – no thanks to the Russian paradigm.

No discussion of the Russian model can be complete without mention of its effects on American education. It has been applied rigorously for a century, beginning with the efforts of uber-progressive John Dewey, and with obvious results. It would require a thick volume to do justice to this subject, however, so here it must suffice to mention that the corruption of our hideously expensive educational system would not have been remotely possible without skillful application of the Russian model.

As a final example of the Left's emulation of the Russian paradigm, we look to the repulsive use of psychology to crush opposition. This was practiced in Soviet Russian from early times but reached its apotheosis toward the end, under Brezhnev. A psychiatrist named Andrei Snezhnevsky perfected the theoretical basis for the political abuse of psychiatry as a weapon to crush dissidents, mainly the extension of the definition of schizophrenia to include many who showed no scientifically accepted symptoms of psychotic disorder. It was bogus, but it enabled the Soviet leadership to imprison those who had committed no crime in mental institutions, and to keep them there indefinitely without even a pretense of a trial. This phony diagnosis of mental illness, employed as a key part of the Russian model, was discredited even in Russia after the fall of the Soviet Union and condemned everywhere – until its apparent resurrection and revival by the American Left.

The failure of the Mueller investigation to find collusion after two years of diligent effort has traumatized the Left throughout the U.S. The questionable report that issued from the investigation left open the question of obstruction of justice, obviously as an invitation to continued political harassment of the Administration. Leftists eagerly leaped upon it, adding quixotic forays into the president's personal finances and those of his associates in their desperation to discredit him. Now we have, again in desperation, recourse to the old Russian ploy of the political abuse of psychiatry. Speaker Pelosi has made shrill appeals to the president's family and friends and any other interested authorities to call for "intervention" on his behalf. Other strident voices from the Left attempt daily to point out signs of mental instability. Actually, the goading the president endures daily from the Left would be enough to drive any normal human batty, and any sign of exasperation on his part is held up by politicians and press as proof positive of psychosis. Soviet Russia may be no more, but its model is alive and well on the American Left.

At present, infatuation with Russia itself among American leftists is at a low point. This does not reflect any diminution of the popularity of the Russian paradigm, which is at a peak. Disenchantment with Russia is a product of the aforementioned leftist tendency to project their own psychological aberrations onto their adversaries. The results of our 2016 presidential election were a profound shock to the Left. Little wonder that they account for the success of the Trump campaign by suspecting its use of the same methods they themselves have used with great success over the decades. And they intend to undo those unwelcome electoral results by more intensive use of those very methods. There are costs: the credibility of the leftist media in the U.S. is now at about the same level as that of *Pravda* among Russians during the Soviet era (for the same reasons). But the Russian paradigm has served the Left far too well for it to be abandoned by leftists now. As "investigation of the investigators" (to use the current phrase) goes forward, we will see the Left double down on its favored paradigm, even as it is revealed in all its bitter glory.

11/1/19

Chapter Forty-Six

Farewell, Fabius

Hannibal Barca was one of the greatest military geniuses in all history, right at the top of the list of generals of ancient times with Alexander himself. During the early years of the Second Punic War he was in his physical and mental prime. The Roman patrician Quintus Fabius Maximus Verrucosas was an old man during the same period, not physically impressive and rather timid despite his high position in the Roman hierarchy. He had abilities of his own, however, and was raised to the status of dictator and general after Hannibal inflicted severe defeats on Roman armies at the Battles of Trebia and Lake Trasimene. He feared the prospect of open battle with Hannibal's Carthaginian and mercenary force and resorted to harassment and delaying tactics instead -- what we would recognize today as guerilla warfare. The result was rather ugly for both the Romans, whose lands and those of their allies were devastated by the invaders, and for Hannibal, who was being frustrated and starved out. Fabius, for his efforts, received the nickname of Cunctator, which means one who hesitates or tarries. This ancient but critical episode of history occurred over 2200 years ago, but it resonates strikingly today.

Intellectuals have caused problems all through the human experience, or at least that part of it after the hunter-gatherers and the age of warrior kings. Actually, even during the latter, no doubt. It must be understood that the term intellectual need not involve intelligence. An intellectual is one whose ego requires that he be taken as an extraordinarily intelligent person by others, whether he is one or is a person of quite ordinary gifts. If an intellectual is combined in the same skin with an elitist, there is real danger. If a number of such people get together for a common cause, we have a potentially dire situation indeed. And that is precisely what happened in London on January 4, 1884, more than two millennia after the confrontation of Hannibal and Fabius.

Early members of the Fabian Society, as they came to call themselves, included such luminaries as George Bernard Shaw, H.G. Wells, Annie Besant, Emmeline Parkhurst, Ramsay MacDonald and Sidney and Beatrice Webb. Bertrand Russell was briefly a member, and more recently Clement Attlee, Tony Benn, Harold Wilson, Tony Blair and Gordon Brown have been members as well. The society was a founding organization of the London School of Economics and Political Science (1895) and a number of other well-known projects. Its avowed purpose was to make socialism the basis for the British economy and the nation's society. It took the name of Fabius the Cunctator because its founders (who were among the intellectuals who were actually intelligent) realized that their objective was profoundly unpopular among the general citizenry, and that a direct attack, as with the Romans versus Hannibal, invited total defeat. Patience was the key to their chosen methodology. Their original coat of arms (soon changed as a matter of discretion) was a wolf in sheep's clothing.

The early stages of the Progressive Movement in the United States trailed the Fabian movement by a little more than a decade and were substantially influenced by it. In the late 1890s the movement had a foothold in local politics, mostly in the western states, and it expanded nationally in the first decade of the 20th century. The Fabian tendency toward incrementalism and opacity as to underlying objectives was present in the early movement but had a distinctly American tint. Although it was socialistic from the outset and to the core, the movement originally painted itself as reformist in nature, opposing local bosses and monopolistic corporations and promoting labor, women's rights, world peace and other righteous causes. It successes were therefore striking, and progressives made strides in business, education and most other fields as well as in politics.

The initial enthusiasm for the movement dissipated somewhat after World War I for a number of reasons. The war itself caused division within the ranks between pure peace lovers and pragmatists, and some of the underlying objectives of progressives began to reveal themselves. The progressive contempt for the Constitution had become more apparent and such favorite causes as eugenics were repulsive to many people who had been entranced by the old reformist ideals. Perhaps more significant was the prosperity that marked most of the 1920s. Under good conditions, radical change is not as attractive. Then as now, what was good for the country wasn't especially favorable for the Left.

The reverse was also true. The next surge of socialism came with the economic disaster of the Great Depression. It has been demonstrated more recently that socialism went a long way toward producing the Depression, turning what would have been a sharp but short recession into a long period of economic misery -- see, for example, *The Forgotten Man: A New History of the Great Depression* by Amity Shlaes (2007) -- but at the time that fact went unrecognized. New Deal assaults on the Constitution and sweeping measures of a socialist nature were widely thought to have pulled the country out of an inevitable phenomenon of capitalism, rather than to have prevented normal capitalist processes from operating to cut the problem short. As it happened, World War II intervened to bail the economy out, while continuing to distort it. Hitler, a national socialist himself, may have been the best friend the socialists ever had.

The trend toward socialism crawled on after the war, albeit at a much slower pace, until another surge under Lyndon B. Johnson: the Great Society. In many ways, the socialist gains of that period exceeded even those of the New Deal. By 1980, progressives could look back on a legacy of unparalleled success in changing American society. That success was based on two related principles: patience and the ratchet effect. As to the latter, ratcheting was perfectly suited to the pulse-like nature of leftist progress. Gains made during spurts of socialist growth were locked in during intervening periods of stagnation. Periods of advance and stillstand and the Fabian habit of patience allowed the Left to consolidate gains made during the spurts in preparation for the next lunge toward power. Thus the ratchet effect: when there was movement it was always in the leftists' direction; when there was no leftward movement, socialists were content to preserve what they had already achieved. There was never a reversal.

Patience had in fact achieved a great deal. The Left's Long March through American institutions was little short of amazing. To achieve central government control over the educational system and then to radicalize the entire system, from kindergarten through graduate school, was no mean feat. It required constant effort over a period of generations, a sustained effort possible only with Fabian patience of a high order. Similar takeovers of other key institutions, including labor unions and American journalism, and even much of the religious establishment, were also only possible through steady work and patience, supported by the ratchet effect.

Radicalism engendered by the Vietnam War added, in the 1960s, a political dimension to the economic surge which continued and expanded as radicalized students entered their various professional fields. The socialists also looked over the political landscape of the rest of the world with a degree of satisfaction. Socialist regimes were in place in Russia and China, and smaller countries in Africa and Latin America, that seemed to certify the viability of their ideal society. The historical inevitability postulated by Karl Marx was a reality. The future was theirs.

But, as always with historical cycles, a counter-movement was building. First came the almost comical revolution of Barry Goldwater, easily slapped aside but worrisome as an indicator that some people were getting off the bus. It was quickly followed by a man named Ronald Reagan, who threw the entire Fabian strategy into chaos. After his landslide election, Reagan spearheaded the first real threat to the latter day Progressive

Movement and presented the first challenge to the ratchet effect. He not only stopped leftist momentum but actually succeeded in rolling back some of the programs. True, such was the effectiveness of Fabianism that the core strengths of the Left, mainly their hard-won control of the institutions, remained unaffected. But the sharp check to leftist progress was traumatic. The ratchet proved vulnerable after all. The assurance of historical inevitability was shaken, and shaken harder by the fall of the Soviet Union and failure of socialist regimes elsewhere. The Left was to win more battles, and soon, but the airy confidence of prior decades was lost forever.

Cautious recovery returned under the long reign of the Clinton-Bush dynasties. Several crises helped: as usual, what was bad for the nation was, in the short term, good for the Left. The 9/11 disaster led to major expansion of federal authority, and subsequent setbacks, such as Hurricane Katrina, also enabled leftist gains. Bill Clinton, in particular, was a great exemplar of the Fabian approach. He was perfect for the leftist recovery from Reagan: a committed liberal who made progress while avoiding overreach. The Bushes were also helpful to the Left, being conservative only in the sense of supporting the existing Establishment and weak enough to offer little real resistance to creeping socialism. But in was in 2008 that the Left finally saw the light at the end of the socialist tunnel. Barack Hussein Obama, an open socialist with an unambiguously radical background, was elected president with the wholehearted acclaim of much of the populace and at least hope on the part of the rest.

With the effective healthcare takeover by the federal government and numerous other leftist initiatives underway, the Left was able to relax a bit. The certainty of ultimate success began to return and socialists could look forward to the complete attainment of their long-yearned-for objectives. They were finally on the right road, the Fabian work of their forebears was bearing full fruit and there was every reason to expect a bright (for leftists) future. If Obama didn't quite finish the job, Hillary Clinton would have eight years to do it after he left office.

Disaster struck like a thunderbolt. The shock of the 2016 election totally upset the equilibrium of a Left that had not yet fully recovered from the Reagan reverse. And the first casualties of this unexpected and unprecedented calamity were patience and the time-tested tactics of Fabius.

Revealed to the general public for the first time was the existence of an elite Establishment with a Deep State that was willing to take extreme measures to preserve its existence and its daunting power. Also revealed was the extreme bias of the mass media, including social media, and the stunning fact that the media would sacrifice its precious credibility to protect not the people but the Establishment. The degeneration of a media that was once proud of its high professional standards into a simple propaganda organ for a political faction, a *Pravda* of the West, was the most obvious sign that Fabius had been abandoned. In its panic and hysteria the Left threw caution to the winds. No tactic was now too unprincipled, no lie too vile, to deter socialists from the goal of overturning a proper election and regaining power over the national government. The Left was through with Fabianism. It was ready for outright, pitched battle with Hannibal.

Why, after over a century of outstanding success with the strategy introduced by the Fabian Society, did the American Left abandon it so precipitously? There are a number of reasons besides simple unhingement and the disappointment of losing the brass ring that was within grasp. Perhaps the most likely is one that is never heard: the Left, as a whole, long since gave up religion. As was noted previously (*The Deep Law*), socialism and Christianity (or any monotheistic religion) are philosophically incompatible. Therefore, for a good socialist, there is no afterlife. Paradise must be achieved here on Earth or not at all. For the individual there is only his own lifespan, which is all too short. When one believes Paradise is at hand, right here in his own lifetime, and it is suddenly snatched away, it is little consolation that it may eventually return in some descendant's lifetime. Patience must be harder for someone for whom there is nothing more than what he holds here on earth.

With impatience to attain an objective comes the compulsion to coerce. Coercion is a central feature of socialism wherever it gains power. In fact, it is impossible to maintain a socialist regime without it. How many people will voluntarily and indefinitely submit to a socialist straightjacket, especially when they lived in a once-free society? When one attempts to impose socialism on such a people, one must expect resistance and be prepared to employ coercion without forbearance. The Left now appears to be in a mood for just that. Fabius is not the flavor of the season.

But let us return to ancient history. As it happened, and despite his relative success against the hardened troops and genius of Hannibal, Fabius Cunctator lost favor with the Romans. More accurately, the Romans lost patience with Fabian's slow methods and effectively fired him after his term as dictator expired. To replace him they called up the Consuls Varro and Paullus and raised a huge army of (it is estimated) over 80,000 Romans and allies. The army contained most of Rome's best and brightest, including a great number of its senators, and it marched with confidence to crush their brilliant tormentor at a place called Cannae.

The battle of Cannae was Hannibal's consummate victory. With a force only about two-thirds as numerous as that of his foe, he achieved the classic double envelopment that is studied by military scholars and generals to this day. The surrounded Roman army was annihilated in the most grievous defeat the Romans ever suffered, before or since. Most of their senate perished in the disaster, and if Hannibal had possessed a few siege engines he could have taken and destroyed the city of Rome itself. History might have been very different as a result of Cannae.

But the Romans, largely by luck, survived. They returned Fabius to command of what was left of their military, and he returned to his old strategy. Rome survived in the long campaigns that followed. What will happen to our modern day Fabians who have bid farewell to Fabius and taken to the battlefield? Rome got lucky; how lucky will be the American socialists?

12/22/19

Chapter Forty-Seven

Bottoms Up

The least respected of all the Olympic sports is probably synchronized swimming (now titled, by some, "art swimming"). There are plenty of jokes about it, and at least one widely shown television commercial that mocked it. Yet, it is undoubtedly elegant to watch and must require countless hours of patient and grueling practice to master. It's rather tragic, in fact – all that work and so little glory.

The most striking feature of the sport (that term used in the broadest sense) is the synchronization itself. How on earth do eight humans manage to perform all those complex evolutions at the same time, and in the water at that? I'm especially impressed by the part where they're upside down in the pool with their feet in the air, and sixteen feet are moving in elaborate patterns as though each foot knows what every other foot is doing. They can't see each others' feet when their heads are four feet under, can they? Well, they may not receive due appreciation for their efforts, but they surely deserve credit for doing what they do as though they are a single organism.

There is an obvious analogy between synchronized swimming and the Democrat Party of current times. What the Democrats do doesn't make a tremendous amount of sense when looked at piece by piece, but their cohesion while doing it must be considered impressive. They aren't particularly serious about the issues, and when one examines their positions it is obvious why they are not. As was pointed out in another article herein (*Under the Lamp Post*), they are on the wrong side of almost every one of them. The main issues, as always, are economic, and on these the current Democrats are hopeless to the point of humor. They are so far out in left field that they've wandered out of the ballpark, and they're still moving in the same direction. They do no better with their "solutions" for immigration and health care, and most other issues.

In fact, heading into the 2020 election campaign season, the Democrats have only one focus, and that is getting rid of Donald Trump by fair means or foul. Well, all foul, actually, since they haven't a single fair one available. Using their near-total control of Pravda West they pound Trump daily, his family and all his works with him. We are told relentlessly how everything he touches turns to fecal matter, including even an economy that has done exceedingly well under his ministrations. It's like the old line: "Who're you gonna believe, me or your lyin' eyes?" As to immigration, we are to ignore the damage it is has done to the nation and notice only that Trump eats babies. The words "racist," "fascist," "homophobic" and "Islamophobic" roll off Democrat tongues like sea waves on the beach. Hitler is reincarnated. Every rainstorm is the result of Trump's climate crimes. And so on.

The point is, hating Trump is not an issue and it's hard to believe that it can even be called a real strategy, but nevertheless all the Democrats do it in near-perfect synchronization. It's not politics as we have known it, even less than synchronized swimming is a sport, but like the latter it's kind of impressive in its own way. When CNN, MSNBC, the New York Times, the Washington Post, Yahoo News and all the others open fire in unison on a trivial non-story or fraudulent "bombshell" to humiliate or discredit Trump, it's like the heavy artillery of an entire infantry division erupting with blank ammunition. Spectacular, that is, and spectacularly futile. Kind of like synchronized swimming, in fact, but not nearly as pretty or as nice.

Speaking of issues, among all the out-and-out losers espoused by the Democrats, including socialized medicine, open borders and free everything for illegal immigrants, cancelling the First and Second Amendments and socialism in general, they have one issue that has been made semi-popular and almost respectable by years of relentless propaganda. That is anthropogenic climate change, or more accurately, global warming (since they are committed to the mechanism of the greenhouse effect). Unfortunately, they can't play even that hand right. What could be a winner for the party, or at least not a loser, has been swept up in the silly proposals of the socialist Green New Deal. All the GND has done is emphasize that the whole purpose of climate change has always been to advance socialism on a world-wide basis. The facts that climate change is based on shaky science (which is fast becoming more obviously shaky) and, despite the publicity, has always been a pretty low priority issue among the general electorate, don't help the increasingly desperate Democrat cause.

Aside from the idiocies of GND, Medicare for All, abolition of Constitutional rights and so on, what is left to the Party but pure negativity? Everything is painted in bleak colors by the party press, everything Trump does, says or thinks is evil incarnate, nothing is right about the economy or our rotten society, the end of the world is nigh. How does a political party win an election with this message? As though to prove the point, most

Democrat successes in this last off-year election were those members who strayed from the party line and talked like Republicans. Given the leading contenders for the Party nomination – socialists all – do they seriously expect to win?

Which begs the question: what is the Democrats' end game? The Democrat Party has always been considered the savviest of the two in terms of political machinations. Do they have a brilliant plan behind the apparent dunce-like performance? Are they actually trying to lose it all in 2020 in order to consolidate a greater victory in the long term? Is there a Machiavellian twist to all this that will only manifest itself when the plot has matured? One certainly would doubt it; odds are high that the party really has become as silly as it looks. Elections are fought to be won – now, this year, each election that is ever held. The Democrats, one can be confident (if confused), are playing this one to win.

The Party still has strengths, to be sure, all of them outside the issues. Many of its traditional voting blocs are still intact, especially among racial minorities; unions with their energy and money still support it; new imported voters have arrived, convicts are being turned out to vote and our institutions still brainwash the young. And of course, Pravda West still spreads spin and outright mendacity abroad in the land. But all these strengths are based on division and negativity, and are diminishing assets. Minorities are reassessing their options; unions are losing members; young people grow older and wiser; new media outlets are arising to challenge Pravda's leftist message. Surely the old traditional strengths of the Party aren't sufficient to counter the manifest weaknesses of its current substantive positions.

On the other hand, why not? We see, in bemusement, a world turned on its head. The recently played World Series proves that even the traditional old sport of baseball has gone upside down. Who could have believed that, in a seven game series, there wouldn't be a single home team victory? The old record was five wins by a visiting team; this year no home crowd of either city saw its boys succeed over the full seven games. Anything can happen in this strangely inverted world. It's almost Biblical: "In the last days .... your young men will see visions and your old men will dream dreams" (Acts 2:17). So why can't a political party win on a program of impeachment without a crime, and in a campaign without issues?

Whatever happens, the Democrats will stick together like an Olympic synchronized swimming team. They may sink or swim, but they'll do it *en masse*. They may have lost their senses, but they haven't lost their cohesion. It may be the remnants of their traditional political acumen or it may be the survival instinct of the herd, but they're all in it together. We can't know for sure if the last days are upon us, nor do most of us know a lot about the mysteries of visions and dreams. What we do know is that the Democrats are upside down in the water with their feet flapping in the air. One thing seems certain in this uncertain world: they are all upside down together and the feet are flapping in unison, so whatever happens to one will happen to all. Meanwhile, I find it entertaining to watch the show. Let's enjoy it and lift a glass, also in unison, with the most appropriate toast: Bottoms up!

7/11/19

Chapter Forty-Eight

The Third Bite

In another article, *Machiavelli and the Snowflakes*, it is pointed out that, in the West and for most of the last millennium, old centuries tend to hang on past their time. Most of them expire about a decade and a half late with a profound historical event that brings an era to a close. It also ushers in a new era, of course, but while contemporaries can see what is ending, that which is beginning is harder to discern at the time. The 20th century, in my view as previously expressed, conformed to the pattern. That statement is not intended to underrate the importance or impact of the events of 9/11/2001, but to recognize them as a continuation of something that has been going on for many centuries. What happened on November 9, 2016, marked a true historical termination. That was the day after the 2016 presidential election. It was the day that democracy died in America.

Once before in American history the losing side did not accept the result of a presidential election, and that led to what we call the Civil War. The situation then was fundamentally different from the present one, however. A distinct geographic region of the nation recognized the validity of the election but decided it couldn't live with the result and accordingly seceded from the union. In 2016, the losing side, or major elements thereof, did not accept the result of the election as legitimate and determined to take over the union. It simply didn't agree with those who voted for Mr. Trump and refused to recognize him as president, election or no election. It formed a self-styled "resistance" and proceeded to revile him and his supporters as racists, "phobes" of various sorts, deplorables and a plethora of other pejoratives. It worked hard to sabotage his administration and destroy his reputation and those of any who were related to him or spoke up for him. And it worked very hard to have him removed. In short, progressives, the Democrats and the institutions controlled by them had their bite at the apple, lost, and demanded a second bite.

The most important phenomenon about elections in this country over the last two and a quarter centuries is that they have, by and large, been carried out under specified rules and the results have been accepted, however grudgingly, by the losers. Without those conditions, there can be no democracy. We came close to losing our democracy when the younger Bush defeated Gore in 2000. The Democrats were, as in 2016, the losers, but in 2000 they had more of an excuse for their ill grace. That election was razor-close, both in the Electoral College and in the deciding state of Florida. The losers still grumble about that election, but, as it happened, they ended by acceding to the result. In 2016, the situation was very different. Trump's victory in the Electoral College, where it counted, wasn't close at all, nor was the result close enough in any single state that went to him to be questionable. The simple fact was that the progressives didn't like Trump. They didn't like his personality or his looks, his brashness or his style. Most of all, they didn't like his message: whereas Bush was clearly Establishment, Trump was an outsider who had pledged to break things in Washington. And, unforgivably, Trump had defeated Hillary, the darling of feminists, the heir apparent of Saint Obama and the anointed one of the Left and the Establishment.

So the Democrats/progressives decided to take their second bite at the apple. The bite had been prepared in advance for the slim chance that Trump would actually win, as was revealed by text messages exchanged by a pair of adulterous lovebirds high in the ranks of the Federal Bureau of Investigation (FBI). A plot had been hatched that involved a laughably incredible report that had been funded by the Clinton campaign and DNC through a private outfit called Fusion GPS and written by a British former intelligence agent who despised Trump. This document purported to show that candidate Trump had been involved with espionage for the Russians for years and was heavily compromised as a result. The "dossier" on Trump, as it became known, was a piece of fiction that was too crude and heavy-handed to have found a commercial publisher anywhere. Nevertheless, certain highly placed individuals at the FBI and Central Intelligence Agency (CIA) professed to believe it and took legally indefensible steps to investigate it. In reality, no trained intelligence person could have believed it; the dossier was no more than a flimsy excuse to spy on one political party's presidential campaign in the service of the other's.

Through leaks to a compliant media and other devices an attempt was made to discredit Trump and damage his chances (already thought to be small) of getting elected. When he won anyway, the dossier was used to initiate the backup plan prepared by the FBI (and encouraged by the CIA director) to set in motion a highly questionable special prosecutor investigation with the objective of taking down the president, or at the least fatally crippling his administration. That effort failed, but the failure was not from lack of trying. The special prosecutor, veteran FBI director Robert Mueller (retired), had put together a team of attorneys who were among the most virulently anti-Trump people in D.C. They were led by none other than one Andrew Weissmann, a highly partisan leftist and veteran of the notorious Enron witch hunt. The team knew for a fact that there was no "collusion" between the Trump campaign and Russia within a few weeks, if not days, of the investigation's outset, but labored on for another couple of years in the vain hope of generating some hint of obstruction of justice. When that, too, failed, they manufactured a 448-page manuscript that was designed to cover their lack of results. With no hope of coming up with any collusion, they managed to blow enough smoke through rumor and innuendo to claim they couldn't "exonerate" Trump from a charge of obstruction, although they had no way to charge him with it.

The whole second bite attempt ended in a crushing blow to the Left. First, a prosecutor does not exonerate anyone at the conclusion of his investigation. He either charges the subject with a crime or he does not; the subject is not responsible for proving himself innocent. Second, a president cannot be charged with a crime for doing something that is permitted to him by the Constitution, as was Trump. Third, Trump furnished the prosecutor with over a million pages of protected documents -- documents he could have legally withheld -- and didn't stop a single witness from testifying over the entire two-plus year ordeal. One recalls Hillary, who destroyed material with BleachBit and hammer *after* it had been subpoenaed -- and wasn't charged with obstruction or anything else. There was no collusion and no obstruction to be found. The second bite at the apple was an expensive and embarrassing flop.

And so on to the third bite. Yes, as might be expected a second bite at the apple wasn't enough for the Left, no matter how badly it failed. Nothing would satisfy the progressive appetite for vengeance and power except for their upstart nemesis to be, as several put it, "frog marched out of the White House in handcuffs." They don't want to see Trump merely removed from office, they want him to rot in a federal prison for the rest of his life. And they determined to make it happen, by any means at hand. Of course, with the time provided by the special prosecutor dragging the second bite out an extra year or so, there was plenty of opportunity to prepare some means. The Deep State went to work, using a different tool in its IC kit. Whereas the FBI did the heavy lifting for the second bite, the third would be initiated by the CIA. This was trickier, since the CIA is supposed to be restricted in its targets, with narrow exceptions, to non-American citizens, but no matter. A low-level CIA employee, rabidly anti-Trump in his political views, was selected to be the "whistleblower" in a plot to damage Trump and hopefully have him impeached.

Given what they had to work with, it must be said that the leftist operatives did their very best to make the proverbial silk purse out of a pig's ear. The raw material for the third bite was even flimsier than that for the second, a telephone conversation between

Trump and the new president of Ukraine that was, on the surface, pretty innocuous. The first step in the conversion of a vanilla call to an act of treason was to change the definition of "whistleblower" in CIA regulations to allow the blowing to be based on hearsay and rumor rather than, as previously, direct observation. This was accomplished by the CIA a few days before the designated whistleblower did his thing. There was careful coordination between the CIA, its whistleblower and the Democrats of the House Intelligence Committee in the weeks before the handoff of the operation to the latter, which would carry it forward to impeachment. The mass media was brought into the picture and fed sufficient information to carry out its part in the operation. The opening salvo was delivered by the chairman of the Intelligence Committee, a thus far unsuccessful screen writer, who gave a fictional account of the phone conversation based on Mafia legends. He later called it a parody, when criticized, but however ham-fisted it was as a piece of fiction, it became the official meme of the Democrat Party and its media servants.

The rest is familiar to everyone. The third bite at the apple is ongoing, as the House Democrats abandoned their best judgment and took the thin fiction to actual (100% partisan) impeachment. It now rests with the Senate to end the charade -- doubtless also on mostly partisan lines, given the current progressive obsession about anything to do with Trump. It is puzzling to an outside observer why the Democrats would pursue a course that holds so much obvious risk to so many of their elected representatives when it never had any remote chance of success. The third bite was doomed from the outset as a means of getting rid of Trump, so why would they go to so much trouble and take such chances? This is a more critical question when there is no time remaining for a fourth bite. In a few months there will be a whole new apple at stake and an opportunity for another first bite at it.

Which brings us to the only reasonable answer. Progressives have their eye on November, all right, but seek to damage not only Trump but the entire Republican brand before the upcoming election. They are, in effect, attempting to turn a first bite at the new apple in a new election cycle into a *de facto* fourth bite at the apple of the current cycle. If they were truly Machiavellian, it's possible that they might have given up the idea of defeating Trump (with their current stable of potential candidates that wouldn't be illogical) and are focused on extending their grip on the House and perhaps even taking the Senate. Given the derangement concerning Trump, of course, that sort of logic is out of the question. The strategy of progressives is no doubt to use the current shenanigans to somehow pull a rabbit out of the hat and defeat Trump, and maybe have gains in all other races, national and local, which would be a wonderful lagniappe. Or possibly there's no rational strategy at all: perhaps the Democrats simply gave in to emotion and

Trump-hatred and are at present hardly better than mad dogs. We will have to let the third bite play out to its bitter end and see what happens next. Do not expect a great deal of logic to drive events.

Chapter Forty-Nine

A Tale of Two Presidents

It is no secret that the U.S. Establishment reacts to populist movements much as a vampire reacts to the cross. This has been the case since the beginning of the Republic, and doubtless it always will be. The reason for this is obvious enough: populism threatens the very existence of the Establishment as it now flourishes. And its existence is precious to those who dwell within the Establishment's bubble. The word "privilege", so misused these days, is exemplified by their lives. They have both financial and physical security that the mass of the population outside the Beltway (in its figurative sense) can only dream about, and moreover they have, in varying measure, the aphrodisiac of power. Can there be any wonder that the Establishment will go to any extreme to protect itself from resurgent populism?

The situation might seem odd to an outsider, since the Constitution of the United States is itself populist at its core, designed specifically to protect the rights and privileges of the people at large against encroachment by the federal government. But it's inevitable, given the nature of the human beast. Whenever there rises a center of power, even power limited by fundamental law, there will be those who drift toward it and attach themselves to it like iron filings to a magnet. Thus have the layers of such people built up over the generations around Washington, D.C., and so has the encrustation developed that began as a handful of part-time politicians and officials and eventually became the crawling edifice of career bureaucrats, career politicians, lobbyists, lawyers and sundry hangers-on that we call the Establishment today. Back in the day there wasn't a word for what we now call the Establishment, but any of the Founders would have easily identified today's Establishment as part and parcel of the governmental forces the Constitution was set up to resist.

Periodically there has been a revival of the populist spirit, a movement to restore the power of "We the People" of the nation and reassert the Common Man's rights against the self-styled elites of the Establishment. The first of these that left its imprint upon history was led by Andrew Jackson back in the 1820s. He won the presidency in 1828 after being blocked by the Establishment of that long-ago day four years earlier, running on a platform of eliminating government corruption -- what we might term "draining the swamp" today. His focus was on returning power to the people, the basis for the founding of the Democratic Party. Another populist movement, this one of generally leftist character, arose in the 1890s but never succeeded in capturing a strong working class following. The modern resurgences of populism occurred in the 1970s and in the last few years. These were both of a strongly conservative nature, and it is about the leaders of these two movements that this chapter is concerned.

There are many similarities and many differences between Presidents Ronald Reagan and Donald Trump. The latter are obvious and result mainly from a distinct variance in personality between the two. The former are more subtle and, from a long view, more profound and important to history. Certainly, Reagan was the more personable and charming, more capable of generating bilateral action toward his objectives. Trump can be, and often is, abrasive and confrontational in his approach, unafraid to offend those who oppose him in a personal way. These differences in personality and mode of dealing with problems can in large measure be attributed to differences in background, geographically and professionally. Reagan was a genial Midwesterner from a working class background who succeeded through a pleasant combination of native tactfulness and firmness. Trump is far from that.

Trump is the quintessential New Yorker, brash and direct, who came to success in the rough and tumble game of high-stakes New York (and later world-wide) real estate. Unlike Reagan, he was born into wealth, although not the billionaire level of wealth that he now enjoys, and none of the glitz and notoriety. His father was a real estate mogul in New York City and therefore in a position to influence his son's career, although his business was of local scope only, and basically confined to renting to ordinary tenants. Still, Trump came up in an atmosphere of great business success, with the contacts and access that go with it. Even better, he had an example before him of how to get ahead in a tough game. He learned take-no-prisoners negotiation as a youngster, whereas Reagan learned persuasive diplomacy on his own. The glaring contrasts of their personalities and approaches are easily understood.

What is less obvious, but perhaps more important, are the similarities of the two men and their careers. Foremost among them is the fact that both can be seen as leaders of a successful populist uprising. In this regard, there is more in common in their backgrounds than first meets the eye. Both men became, in the course of difficult careers, tough as nails, despite their vastly different outward demeanors. In large part this is because both came up largely on their own. Reagan had no one but himself to start him toward success. Trump's father gave him no financial support or encouragement in his early efforts to expand beyond his rental business into big-time Manhattan real estate. Both future presidents had a dream and turned it into a reality.

A striking fact is that both future presidents had close and frequent contact with blue-collar workingmen over considerable time. Reagan, of course, was raised in a working class environment and held down regular jobs before achieving fame in Hollywood and then entering politics. Trump dealt personally and daily with construction workers, including union men in all trades concerned with building and renovating major hotels and office buildings. Both came to respect the people they worked with at all levels, both as workers and human beings. Career politicians and most Establishment figures, including government-related lawyers and other functionaries, do not, for the most part, share that experience. Reagan and Trump also developed, partly from appreciation for their own opportunities and partly from close contact with regular Americans, a genuine love of their country that not all their associates in D.C. shared, or share. It is evident to most observers that the populism of both Reagan and Trump came and comes from the heart.

It is interesting to compare the national and international context in which each of the two presidents worked. A major theme of both administrations was nationalism and the Common Man versus globalism and elitism, but the struggle now seems sharper and more starkly defined than it was in Reagan's time. There were billionaires during the Reagan administration, but there are many more now and most are far more militantly globalist. Even politicians are wealthier now, relative to the general population, than a half century ago, and their behavior tends to be distinctly more elitist, especially on the Left. The other big theme of both Reagan and Trump was that of the rule of law versus political corruption -- yes, once again draining the swamp. As to that, it must be admitted that Reagan's ambition far exceeded his grasp. He managed to slow the growth of federal government in size and power, but only marginally managed to reverse it, despite his best efforts. It's too early to come to a conclusion about Trump's success in swamp-draining, since so far he's had only one term. So far, given his almost single-handed progress in quelling excessive regulations and mobilizing the Senate to fill the federal judiciary with constitutionalists -- all in the face of desperate resistance by the Left and its media -- he has shown real promise.

Speaking of resistance, there are also notable similarities and differences in the treatment given the two presidents by their opponents. It would be difficult for a younger person to realize how roughly Reagan was handled by the mass media during his presidency, given the relative respect his memory is accorded by almost all parties now. He was routinely accused of senility, for one thing, and of falling asleep during meetings. Some of the accusations were a good deal more cutting, particularly after the Iran-Contra affair broke. But that is where the similarities end. For a populist, Reagan got off pretty easily in his dealings with a leftist press, thanks mainly to his genial personality and widespread popularity. There was certainly nothing in his treatment to reflect even remotely the pure hatred that Trump routinely engenders among his many critics -- and they include politicians as well as Pravda West. Few of the Democrat representatives and senators of Reagan's time criticized him in a highly personal way, and even the media exercised a modicum of restraint in their comments about him. In contrast, the vitriol poured upon Trump every day has no precedent in American history. Media figures wear out their thesauruses in a search for more novel and vile epithets to use against him; "literally Hitler" has become a joke from overuse and may in any case be the mildest of the insults he absorbs.

However, again in contrast with Reagan's experience, much of the abuse directed at Trump comes from what is presumed to be his own side of the political spectrum. Many Republicans are long-time Establishment figures, and their loyalty to the Establishment (and their own comfortable positions in it) takes priority over their loyalties to both party and nation. Mitt Romney, now a senator from Utah, is sadly typical of this contingent, as is neocon Bill Kristol; others are equally anti-Trump but have the sense to stay in the background, supporting the "Resistance" but keeping their hands clean. But perhaps the unkindest cut of all came from a person one would least expect. It might be thought that a prominent speech writer for Ronald Reagan himself would appreciate Trump's passion for the same causes as her boss, namely a government subject to constitutional restraints, the welfare of the Common Man and a foreign policy based on America's interests first. That is not the case. Peggy Noonan, normally a writer of vision and measured words, has proclaimed Trump to be "a bad man." Really?

A bad man? Think about that -- the condemnation in those simple words is plenary. There is no mercy in it. Its simplicity embraces all the ugliness and vituperation that the imagination of Pravda West could devise, from "literally Hitler" downward. He is nothing more than bad to the core, beyond any possibility of redemption. He is, in those three words, stripped of any positive quality whatever, of humanity itself. And this from someone who wrote much of what Reagan said, and about someone who did at least as much as Reagan to attain those ideals, in a shorter time and against even more desperate opposition. Surely life is not fair.

As a matter of disclosure, permit me to confess to a strong antipathy, on a personal level, to Donald Trump's New York persona. I am a product of East Virginia, from a family of meager means but long memories, and have not lost my preferences for what is accepted in the older South as gentlemanly reserve and mannerly comportment. On the other hand, I've lived in New York and other parts of the northeast and come (perhaps too reluctantly) to understand that despite their uncouth outward behavior, New Yorkers are as human and worthy as am I. They can be rough and pushy, but they can also be as kind and decent as southerners or Midwesterners or about anyone else. Under his New York exterior, and despite the abrasive edges developed in his tough business life, Trump is, I'm convinced, a decent man who performs many of his good deeds hidden from publicity (not that he'd receive any good publicity anyway). Perhaps I've matured somewhat over the decades. I'd hope others would as well.

In the end, the real plot of the tale of the two presidents concerns populism, specifically conservative populism. The end of the tale has not yet been reached. It may end in a couple of months or in four years or perhaps longer, depending on elections and events. But the effects of the tale may live on indefinitely. Or they may disappear into the mists of history, submerged by a seismic wave of socialism. One thinks of the Pharaoh Akhenaten, who ruled in Egypt in the 14th century B.C. He is traditionally thought to be the first monotheist; whether this is strictly true is debatable, but he certainly introduced major innovations in the Egyptian religion. This new way of thinking survived him only by a few years, however; within the short reign of his successor Tutankhamen the priests and people of Egypt had gone back to their old gods and practices. All that was left of Akhenaten's revolution was a new approach to architecture that accompanied his religion; of the religion itself nothing seemed to survive. Or maybe nothing: it has been speculated that a band of Israelite slaves who escaped from Egypt during the following dynasty may have taken a certain religious idea with them....

To date, after each surge of populism there has, as with Akhenaten's religion, been a retreat. Certainly that was true after Reagan left office: the long train of Bushes and Clinton was pure Establishment, and the socialism of Obama was a total rejection of conservative populism that led to the backlash that put Trump into the presidency. Will we see the same ebb of the populist tide after Trump, whether his departure occurs in a few weeks or a few years? Will the tale of the two presidents end as did Akhenaten's? Or will populism finally triumph and the true Constitution be restored as the basis of American law? Let us hope that populism will prevail. We have seen, over these last chaotic months, a hint of what the alternative would be.

9/14/20

Chapter Fifty
Cui Bono?

One of the few joys experienced in the practice of law is the opportunity to bandy Latin phrases about. It makes people think that us lawyers know something about what we're doing, or at least we think it does – which is almost as good. One of these magical little phrases, and one of the most useful, is *cui bono?* It means "who benefits?" and it is first found in history coming from the mouth of Lucius Cassius, a judge of ancient Rome who was revered for his integrity and wisdom. Cassius found it valuable as an analytical tool for determining who might be a perpetrator in some criminal scheme. Figuring out the identity of the beneficiaries of illegal or unethical activity is not a definitive means of finding a bad actor, but at a minimum it's a good start. In today's practice the method is used for white collar crimes and plots, financial and otherwise, rather than the street crime and other violent variety.

By no means must a *cui bono?* mode of reasoning be restricted to narrowly legal applications. It can be, and is, employed in a wide range of cases, and is especially useful, it would appear, in the resolution of the secretive and complex sort of manipulations we have observed in our political establishment the last few years. Nor should we be limited in its use to covert activity in Washington, D.C., and other political centers. Many strange and dangerous events are happening around the nation and the world about which a great deal might be inferred by their subjection to this sort of analysis. To choose a simple one – have you noticed that the news media, both nationally and worldwide, are making a lot of mistakes lately? Spokespersons for the various news sources invariably fall back on a standard excuse for their errors; to wit, the business is complex, there are deadline and competition pressures and we're only human. But this line doesn't explain the most blatant fact: the mistakes are invariably in the same direction. In every case, the errant "news" favors the Democrats and the Left. Have you ever noticed a false story that was in

President Trump's favor? We have only to note "who benefits" to infer a leftist bias in the media.

Another subject for *cui bono?* analysis, this one a little more complex, is the wave of rioting, looting, vandalism and arson that has recently swept across the country. Who could possibly have benefited from that phenomenon? Not the residents of the cities involved, and definitely not their small business owners. But someone must benefit – the riots are too well-organized, supplied and funded to be spontaneous acts of rage. And far too long-lasting: no one could stay so uncontrollably furious that they beat people up and throw Molotov cocktails for weeks on end. Some of these rioters have been living away from home for months, and without getting a wink of sleep at night to boot. The bill for supporting them must be running pretty high by now, so presumably someone thinks it's worth paying it. There's also a political bill to pay: the Democrat officials that control the cities involved are catching a lot of heat for their refusal to take measures against the perpetrators. So *in re* (wow – more Latin!) the current "mostly peaceful" rioting, we must look more closely to discover who benefits.

An examination of those directly involved may yield some clues. The simple looters may be dismissed as mere opportunists; they may benefit by having a new wide-screen TV, but they've only taken advantage of an existing situation. That's a case of *cui bono?* giving us a technically correct but irrelevant answer. Neither do the Antifa thugs fill our bill; they are just pawns, doing what they're told, having fun and doubtless being compensated for it. Their proximate enablers, the local Democrat authorities, are hardly beneficiaries, as pointed out above. Democrats at the national level may benefit marginally by the chaos, in that it's a distraction from the extreme weaknesses of both their presidential candidate and their platform. It also has a downside for them, however, by highlighting the general destructiveness of leftist policies, which probably more than balances out the benefit. I expect we must look elsewhere for the real beneficiaries of current urban unrest. A promising phenomenon to examine is the other major producer of social chaos over the last few months: an import from China called the coronavirus.

At this point I must interrupt myself to point out an important limitation to the *cui bono?* method. Many events occur in lieu of an active or deliberate perpetrator. A construction company may benefit from a tornado that neither the owner nor the employees caused or even wanted to happen. Naming a beneficiary from such an act of nature is useless and may even be misleading. Only an event caused by intent or negligence by a person or group of people is useful for the sort of analysis we are considering. It is therefore necessary to establish that premise before asking who benefits with an expectation of discovering anything meaningful. Let us keep that in mind while approaching the subject of who benefited from the most consequential calamity of the year 2020; to wit, the appearance on the international scene of the above-mentioned virus.

There are undoubtedly people who have benefited to a greater or lesser extent from the advent of the coronavirus. Some of these benefits are of a relatively trivial nature. The medico-bureaucrats who achieved brief fame, the media writers who found low-hanging fruit for their endeavors and similar beneficiaries may be dismissed from this discussion. Other benefits have been more substantial and even financial, such as those of companies working on a vaccine, making face masks or delivering goods to homes. Then there are those who have benefited monumentally although with no direct connection to the virus itself. Strange as it may seem, the most abundantly enriched among us have been the wealthiest. According to a CNN report of a study by The Institute for Policy Studies, the fortunes of the 643 richest Americans which corresponds rather closely with the nation's billionaires) increased by $845 billion from mid-March to September 18, 2020, a leap of a stunning 29%. Data from Business Insider and Forbes generally agree with this figure, although the amounts vary since the dates of the studies differ somewhat. This largesse accrued to the billionaires while the earnings of most Americans stalled or dropped.

For reasons that can be easily understood and are explained in the articles but are beyond the scope of this post, the superficially counter-intuitive data concerning billionaires is to be expected. The very wealthy thrive on social chaos, some more than others but nearly all to some extent. But they are not the only beneficiaries of the coronavirus epidemic – or, more realistically, to the panic it caused. The question *cui bono?* has two other important answers, both of which may have profound consequences for the country and the world. The first, and perhaps most obvious, is the Democrat Party. The results of the 2020 election are not in as of this writing, but whatever they may be, the coronavirus carried the party from certain and massive defeat into the apparent lead. As noted in several other articles *Under the Lamp Post, Bottoms Up* and *The Key, inter alia*), Democrats are on the wrong side of every policy issue that is significant to most voters. Moreover, as noted in the articles of *The Party of Poverty* series, their candidates for this election are extraordinarily weak. The lockdowns and other inconveniences related to the current epidemic gave the Democrats their only real issue a fake one, it's true, but an issue nonetheless) and put them back into the race. They brought about a severe disruption of the American economy and served as distractions from immigration and other serious matters, all of which had placed the Democrat Party at an impossible disadvantage. The epidemic saved them from electoral disaster.

The other major beneficiary of the epidemic and its accompaniments was, of course, the People's Republic of China. It's a fact that President Trump had the Chinese on the ropes in a budding trade war and a contentious series of talks that were designed to level a playing field that had long been tilting strongly in favor of China. The virus sidelined both, much to the relief of the Chinese leadership. Which brings up a further, and possibly related, question: who might benefit from a replacement of Trump by Biden in the White House? As more information slips through the Pravda West media barrier about the Bidens' financial relationships with mainland China, the answer is abundantly obvious. These two answers to *cui bono?* questions may not be related, at least in a cause-and-effect sense. In fact, there is no indisputable reason to believe deliberate malfeasance was involved at all. The official story is that, despite the testimony of a Chinese virologist and other indications, the virus was a natural phenomenon that appeared in central China and escaped into the world sort of by accident. Any other, darker, notion about what occurred is dismissed as a conspiracy theory. The *cui bono?* analysis is irrefutable, but, as noted above, it is not definitive as to the culpability of any player, or even the existence of a crime.

That said, however, it is manifest that *cui bono?* analysis must lead our thoughts in specific directions. The vital election year of 2020 is marked by events that have led to extraordinary chaos. This chaos is wide-ranging and had a large number of causes, but the two most prominent causes were coronavirus and rioting. Whether natural or synthetic, the virus undoubtedly originated in China. Whether by intention or incompetence, it was allowed to escape from the venue of its origin and spread around the world. It happens to be perfectly adapted for the purpose of creating havoc without necessarily being a *casus belli* (love that Latin!). That is, it's unusually contagious but not especially lethal except to those with severe comorbidities. And it so happens that the Bidens, candidate and son, have had certain relationships with the Chinese leadership that they aren't anxious to present to public scrutiny. And it also happens that Biden is a Democrat, and that both the Democrats and the Chinese have prospered greatly from the presence of the virus in the U.S. And so on....

But we're not finished: it also happens that another group that has benefited from the social and financial effects of the virus are our own beloved billionaires. And it happens that the billionaires have funded the Democrat Party overwhelmingly over the Republicans during this election cycle. It also happens that the other main source of chaos and angst this year, rioting spiced by racial tension, benefits billionaires and in some strange way Democrats as well, both of whom contributed to it in their own ways. Supporters of globalism of all stripes are, of course, happy with all of the above.

And that summary takes us to the limit of what *cui bono?* can do in these matters. If we tread further in the direction of blame for all that has occurred, we leave the realm of *cui bono?* and enter that of conspiracy theory. And we most certainly do not wish to enter that realm: we would become objects of derision to the Left and might even find ourselves the butts of a skit on *Saturday Night Live*. Actually, I personally wouldn't mind so much – you may glance at the article *Conspiracy Theory* to check my own attitude about the subject. But most people don't care to be thought conspiracy theorists or fruitcakes in general, and in all fairness it's inappropriate to make serious accusations without evidence firmer and more complete than that now available.

In the end, we may link the various beneficiaries of our current calamities – Chinese, Democrats, billionaires, thugs, journalists, globalists, etc. – to one another and even to causation, but we can't demonstrate criminality thereby. Let us be generous in spirit and avoid attribution of the chaos and destruction to some devilishly clever plot. Remember the words of Napoleon Bonaparte: "Never ascribe to malice that which is adequately explained by stupidity."

10/31/20